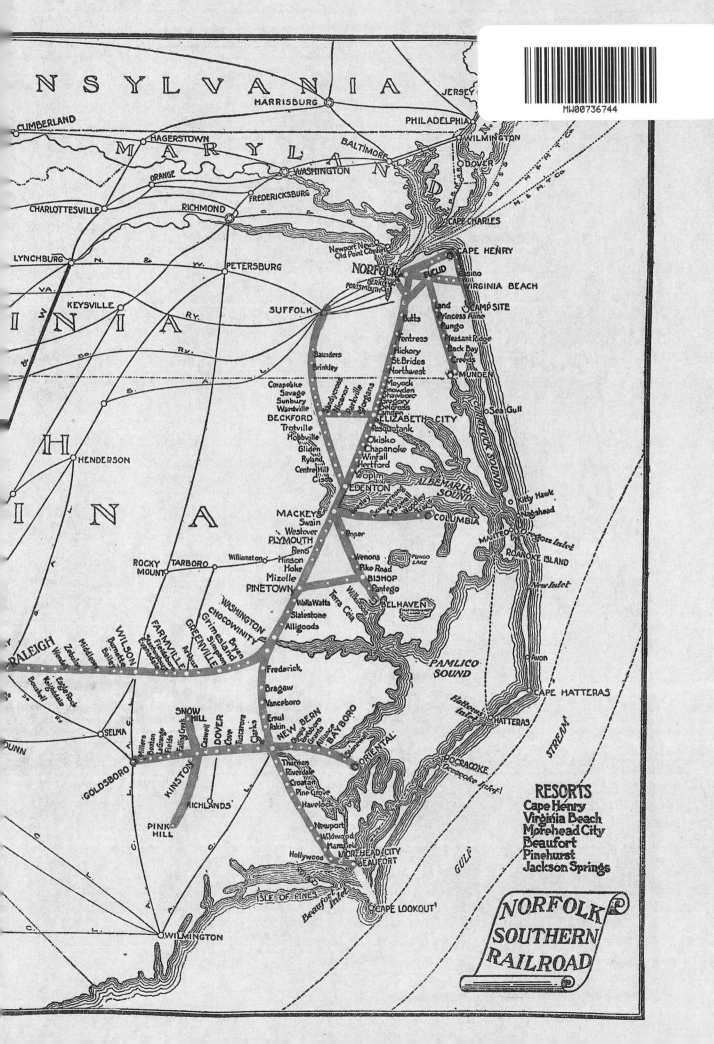

The Original Norfolk Southern Railway 1883 to 1974

by
Robert C. Reisweber
and
Dalton P. "Billy" McDonald

Garrigues House, Publishers

P. O. Box 400   **Laurys Station, PA 18059**

The Original Norfolk Southern Railway 1883-1974
copyright © 2007 by Robert C. Reisweber and Dalton P. McDonald

First Edition
First Printing

Published by:
Garrigues House, Publishers
P. O. Box 400
Laurys Station, PA 18059

Manufactured in the United States of America

Library of Congress Catalog-in-Publication Data

Reisweber, Robert C. 1930-2007
  The original Norfolk Southern Railway, 1883 to 1974 / by Robert C. Reisweber and Dalton P. "Billy" McDonald -- 1st ed.
        p. cm.
  ISBN 1-931014-05-1
  1. Norfolk Southern Railway Company--History. 2. Railroads--Uniteed States--History. I. McDonald, Dalton P. 1946- II. Title.
  TF25.N78R45 2007
  385.0975--dc22

                                        2007040664

Dedication

The authors wish to dedicate this book to the memories of their fathers, James D. McDonald, a locomotive engineer on the Norfolk Southern, and Alexander G. Reisweber, a civil engineer with Erie County (New York) Water Authority and earlier with the Erie and New York Central Railroads. It was they who inspired our affection for railroads.

Alexander G. Reisweber
Age 18, summer of 1912

James D. McDonald

Acknowledgments

It is customary to start this section of a book such as this with a statement that the book would not have been possible without the contributions of many people. Although this statement has been made so often that it has almost become a cliche, it is generally quite true, and in the case of this book, it is more true than for many other books. This is the case because many of the official records of the original Norfolk Southern Railroad have been lost in the years since the merger of the company into Southern Railway in 1974. We have therefore had to rely on the memories of many people who were familiar with the line and were willing to share their memories with us. We are also indebted to several people who took it upon themselves to preserve portions of the official records of the railroad which came into their possession, and allowed us to make use of the material.

We hesitate to single out anyone for special thanks, because there are so many people who have been very helpful that we do not have room to include a detailed description of all their contributions. However, a few people have made such large and frequent contributions that they deserve special mention, and we now do so.

Harry Bundy, a railfan before, during, and after his employment with the original Norfolk Southern, not only was one of the most prolific of photographers of the NS, but also knew the kinds of information of interest to railfans, and took the time to preserve much of that information, in the form of printed material, photographs, and in his own memories of the road. This book could not have been nearly as accurate and comprehensive without his help.

Fred Curling and Phil Coulter, Jr., also former employees of the NS, had much information and many good photographs of the railroad which they were willing to share with us. We appreciate their patience in honoring our numerous requests for material.

W. R. (Bob) Newton of Farmville, NC, a longtime acquaintance of both the coauthors of this book, inspired us with his enthusiasm for his hometown railroad, which convinced us there would be interest by people other than ourselves in seeing such a book published. Bob also made significant contributions to our photo collection and directed us to other contributors.

L. D. Jones, Jr., Richard Perry, and W. A. (Bill) Sellers also grew up along Norfolk Southern lines, developed an affection for the road at early ages, collected much information about it, and gladly shared it with us.

Coauthor Robert C. Reisweber also expresses special thanks to his son, Kurt R. Reisweber, first for the many pleasant days spent together photographing the Norfolk Southern and other railroads, second for his excellent book, *Virginian Rails 1953-1993*, which inspired him to attempt to produce a book of similar quality on the Norfolk Southern, and third for introducing him to the aforementioned Harry Bundy, a contributor to *Virginian Rails 1953-1993*, whose contributions are so important to this book.

We also thank Paul Kuehner, our publisher, for publishing this book. It required somewhat of a gamble on his part to agree to publish this one since the lack of general knowledge of the Norfolk Southern meant that there was no guarantee of a market for such a book.

In addition to the people we have just named, numerous people provided us with photographs they took or collected. Most of them also provided us with useful information about the road. Many thanks to all of them, including Mrs. Jane S. Adkins, Frank E. Ardrey, Jr., Bruce H. Baker, Jr., John Barnett, Allan H. Berner, Marvin Black, Bob's Photos, Ralph Bostian,

Edgar Brown, David Burnette, Scott Burns, Tal Carey, S. David Carriker, M. B. Connery, James D. Curtin, III, Dale W. Diacont, Frank M. Ellington, Paul Faulk, R. Edward Fielding, Felix Freeman, Steve Gibson, Larry Goolsby, Robert Graham, John Hahn, Jr., Edward Harris, J. David Ingles, D. Wallace Johnson, Willard E. Jones, Leon Jordan, Thomas King, Doug Koontz, Krambles-Peterson Archive, J. Parker Lamb, Curtis C. Lassiter, Jr., Charlie Long, C. K. Marsh, G. M. McDonald, Charles W. McIntyre, Philip McMullan, Jr., Jack Moore, William Nixon, Carl H. Overstreet, Bennie Pierce, Richard E. Prince, J. Raymond Pritchard, Jr., Raines and Cox Photography, James A. Ramsey, Anthony Reevy, Robert W. Richardson, William Robson, Louis Saillard, Bill Schafer, Wharton Separk III, Mrs. A. C. Shannonhouse, Tom L. Sink, Collon Snell, J. David Spanagel, Joe D. Steed, Hugh Sterling, John Sullivan, Dennis Terry, Curt Tillotson, Harold J. Vollrath, Jim Wade, Richard W. Walker, Tom Wicker, J. E. Winstead, and David W. Younts. In addition, a special thank you to Mrs. Wiley Bryan, Mrs. Robert Drake, Mrs. John H. Kelly, Jr., and Mrs. H. Reid for giving us permission to use their late husbands' photos.

In addition to the preceding individuals, the following organizations provided us with photographs, for which we offer our sincere thanks: DeGolyer Library of Southern Methodist University, Perkins Library of Duke University, Library of Virginia, Museum of the Albemarle, New Bern-Craven County Public Library, Norfolk Public Library, North Carolina Division of Archives and History, Old Dominion Chapter National Railway Historical Society, Railroad Museum of Pennsylvania, Pennsylvania Historical and Museum Commission, Randolph County, NC Historical Society, St. Louis Mercantile Library, Smithsonian Institution NMAH/Transportation, Southern Railway Historical Association, Suffolk, VA News Herald, U. S. Army Transportation Museum, Virginia Department of Agriculture and Consumer Affairs, Wayne County, NC Library, and Yale University College of Forestry.

We also wish to thank the following people who provided us with information on the railroad. Many of these people also offered us the use of photographs which we were unable to include because of space limitations: Matthew J. Ahearn, Ronald F. Amberger, Roger D. Bell, Ralph Bobbitt, William Bobbitt, George Bradley, Doremus Bright, James Correll, Bob Coltrane, Al Daughtry, Rodell Dickens, Robert Edenfield, Albert Everson, Fred Fearing, Major I. Ferrell, Mallory Hope Ferrell, Al Gerard, William R. Gibson, John Grabarek, John Hackney, Walter B. Hall III, Carl Hollowell, James B. Harward, T. V. Harris, Bill Hayman, Don Heimburger, Marshall C. Jennette, Allen Johnson, Danny Jones, Harvey Jones, James M. Jordan IV, William Kincheloe, Charles F. Latham, Thomas Lawson, Jr., Stephen S. Mansfield, Vernon C. Martell, Louis G. May, George Phillips, Bobby W. Poe, Robert Reardon, Paul Reed, Derrick Rolle, Ed Sawyer, W. Thomas Sawyer, Dennis Schmidt, Bruce L. Seaburg, George Smerk, Leslie E. Smith, Jr., Allen Stanley, Jack Stith, Thomas T. Taber III, Madge Van Horne, Forrest Van Schwartz, E. V. Wilkins, and Jim Wrinn.

Also worthy of special note are people connected with various museums, libraries, and other organizations who have been particularly helpful. These include Mark Cedeck and Gregory Ames of the St. Louis Mercantile Library, Kurt Bell, Robert Emerson, Ken Riegel, and Earl Compton of the Railroad Museum of Pennsylvania, Peggy Haile McPhillips of the Norfolk Public Library, Victor Jones of the New Bern-Craven County Library, Stephen E. Massengill and Sion H. Harrington III of the North Carolina Division of Archives and History, Linda P. Muir of the Pamlico County, NC, Library, Brenda O'Neal of the Museum of the Albemarle, Carolyn Parsons and Petey Bogen-Garrett of the Library of Virginia, Loretta Powell of the Norfolk Southern Credit Union, Paulette Biedenbender of Trains Magazine, Cliff Rhodes of the Wayne County, NC, Public Library, and Gail Spiewak of the Washington County, NC Library. Other museums and libraries from which we have obtained information, all of whose personnel have been very helpful, include the Beaufort County, NC Arts Council, Beaufort, Hyde, and Martin County Regional Library, Washington, NC, Belhaven Community Chamber of Commerce, Belhaven Public Library, Carteret County, NC Historical Society, Charlotte-Mecklenburg Public Library, Colonial Williamsburg Foundation Library, Joyner Library of East Carolina University, Kinston-Lenoir County, NC Public Library, Morgan Memorial Library of Suffolk, VA, North Carolina Railroad Museum, North Carolina Transportation Museum, Pasquotank-Camden Library, Elizabeth City, NC, Port o' Plymouth Roanoke River Museum, Shepherd-Pruden Library of Edenton, NC, Sheppard Memorial Library, Greenville, NC, Smithsonian Institution, Suffolk-Nansemond Historical Society, Swem Library of the College of William and Mary, Tyrrell County, NC Public Library, Wake County, NC Public Library,

Williamsburg, VA Regional Library, and Wilson County, NC Public Library.

Although we have tried to remember all the people and organizations who have contributed to this book, we have probably inadvertently failed to mention some who have helped us. Our sincere apologies to these people.

In assembling material from the many sources we have mentioned, we have tried to resolve any cases of conflicting information so that we can present only verified facts. When this has been impossible, we have worded our text in such a way to indicate that some doubt remains. In spite of this, we feel there are probably a few instances where inaccuracies have crept in. The authors accept full responsibility for any such errors.

Last but certainly not least, we thank our families for their patience over the seemingly interminable time span necessary to produce this book.

Contents

Introduction

In early 1982, a joke made the rounds of railfan circles. It went like this:

"Southern Railway and Norfolk and Western Railway are talking about merging. Guess what they are going to call the new company?"

"I don't know. What?"

"Norfolk Southern Railway."

Snicker, snicker!

Did you understand why this prophetic statement was a joke at the time? Probably you do, if you have enough interest in Norfolk Southern to be reading this. You probably know that at the time, Norfolk Southern had existed as a railroad name for almost one hundred years.

But perhaps you didn't know that. For in spite of the fact that for most of its existence, the railroad bearing the name Norfolk Southern was big enough to be considered a Class I road, it was certainly one of the least known of such roads.

There are many facts which contributed to the obscurity of the NS. First, although it was a Class I road, it was one of the smallest of them. So people who liked to look for bigness did not look to the Norfolk Southern. But on the other hand, it was far too big to attract the attention of most people who searched out the small, quaint and picturesque short lines. These people did not know what they were missing because the NS was built up from a multiplicity of short lines like this. And in spite of growing to Class I status, it never was able to eliminate entirely that image. One might call it "The world's longest short line," although in truth it was what today would be called a regional railroad.

Another factor which kept the NS from widespread attention was the fact that by the standards of most Class I roads, and even by the standards of some short lines, NS suffered from light traffic density. So people who liked to go to a spot to watch a steady procession of long trains went to places such as Tehachapi, Horseshoe Curve, and the Blue Ridge Grade, and gave no thought to any place on the NS. The lack of traffic on the NS was largely a result of the sparse population of most of the places through which it went, and that in turn meant that few people got a first hand look at the railroad without going out of their way to see it. Even the few large cities on the line, Norfolk, Charlotte, Raleigh, Fayetteville, Wilson, etc., were served by other roads which were bigger, had more traffic, and had been there longer.

The original Norfolk Southern certainly was not one of the more profitable roads. This caused many people to write it off as a backward and impoverished road unworthy of attention. But paradoxically, it was perhaps too successful for some people. Some unsuccessful railroads such as the New York, Ontario, and Western, the Colorado Midland, and the Rio Grande Southern have attracted and continue to attract extremely dedicated groups of followers, who have gone to great pains to preserve information on all aspects of their favorites. Unlike those roads, the original Norfolk Southern did not come to an end with a bang on a day of abandonment. In fact, the NS did not even end with the whimper of gradual decrease of trackage over the years until nothing was left. While several of the former NS lines have been abandoned, over half of its peak track mileage remains in service today in one form or another, and more than eighty percent of the trackage remaining when it ceased to have usefulness as a through route is still in service. So people who are looking to restore the memory of lost railroads have not looked to the NS either. But the day may come, and possibly not too far in the future, when the last vestiges of the old NS will disappear. We hope this book will preserve a record of the company before memories, documentation, and images of the railroad disappear as well.

Although the NS was well behind most class I railroads in statistics, it took no back seat to any of them in the loyalty of its employees, customers, and friends. This was probably due in part to the fact that the road and its employees continually had to battle against adverse conditions. These adverse conditions were not such obvious ones as mountains to cross or blizzards to fight, but were mainly the lack of resources. As we will mention repeatedly in the text to follow, the railroad's investors did not provide sufficient capital to build the road to top quality standards initially, and the income from operations was not sufficient to upgrade the line to these standards in all respects later on. As a result, NS employees became experts at making do with what little could be afforded. This most likely contributed to a feeling of kinship similar to that often found in communities afflicted by natural disasters (of which the NS had its share as well). At any rate, NS employees did have a loyalty similar to a family. Often this was literally a family loyalty, as employment on the railroad was passed down from father to son in many instances.

While most Class I railroads have been well documented, with many books of various types written about their history, geography, operations, and equipment, only one book has been published on the original Norfolk Southern. This is *Norfolk Southern Railroad, Old Dominion Line, and Connections*, by Richard E. Prince. (Note that Old Dominion Line was the name of a steamship line which connected with the NS and was covered in the book, not a nickname for the railroad). While Mr. Prince's book offers an excellent history of the road up to the date of its publication, 1972, and a very good detailed record of the road's steam locomotives, it does not include any information on diesel operations, and does not cover the history of the final days of the NS as an independent railroad and its subsequent absorption into Southern Railway in 1974. We have prepared this volume primarily to document those aspects of the railroad's history. But we have not confined ourselves exclusively to them, as Mr. Prince's book is out of print and has become a scarce collector's item, which now sells for many times its original cost, if one is lucky enough to find a copy for sale.

When we began the project of preparing this book, we had serious reservations about our ability to find sufficient photographs to fill a pictorial history book on the railroad. Now, however, several years later, we find we have been able to accumulate so many photographs of the line that we have had to leave out many we would have liked to include in order to keep the size of the book down to what can be published and sold for a reasonable price. We found that although few people assembled large collections of photos of the Norfolk Southern, many people have smaller collections, which they have generously permitted us to use.

In selecting photos for use in the book, we have tried to document all aspects of activity of the railroad, including history, operations, equipment of all types, fixed plant, and people. It is not possible in a book of this size to provide a comprehensive coverage of any of those aspects of a railroad as large as the NS without neglecting the others. As a result, we have provided more a sampler of all these items than a definitive coverage of any of them. Hopefully, this will arouse enough interest in the NS to create a demand for publication of additional material in the future. We have also given preference in selecting photos to be included to those which have not previously been published, although we have included some previously published because of the importance of the subject matter and/or high quality of the photo.

In summation, our purpose for this book is to shed some light on the original Norfolk Southern Railroad so that this enterprise which was of so much importance to the economic development of southeastern Virginia and Northeastern North Carolina is not forgotten.

Opposite page: The freight yards on the Pasquotank River waterfront at Elizabeth City, North Carolina, probably photographed sometime early in the twentieth century. This is where the first Elizabeth City and Norfolk train arrived on May 26, 1881. The view looks northward toward Norfolk. This was the southern end of the railroad for its first seven months. The first Elizabeth City passenger station called the River Station is just out of the picture to the left of the passenger train. Shipping connections from this location, including the Norfolk Southern water routes to New Bern and other ports, were of great importance to the railroad in early days. The freight station in the foreground served the railroad's freight business until a new station was built in 1971. Note the train on the curved track in the left distance. This track was built as part of the extension to Edenton in December 1881. Not long afterward, a line bypassing this area was built for through trains and was called the "New Main Line," with the line into the yard from the north and around the curve toward Edenton becoming the "Old Main Line." A curved track forming a wye can be seen just to the right of the passenger train at left. The entire yard area shown is now the campus of Roanoke Bible College. (Museum of the Albemarle collection)

Above: Another view of the Norfolk Southern waterfront yard at Elizabeth City, probably taken on the same day as the previous photo but from a different angle. The roof of the River Passenger Station, Elizabeth City's first station, appears at the left of the photo, with a corner of the freight station on the right. (Museum of the Albemarle collection)

Chapter 1

The Early Years

Excitement was high in Elizabeth City, North Carolina on Tuesday morning, May 26, 1881. The railroad was coming to town! By 11:30 A.M., the announced arrival time of the first train, a large crowd had gathered at the new depot by the Pasquotank River. Not long afterward, shrieks of a steam whistle proved that a train was indeed coming. And soon the waiting throng was treated to the sight of a locomotive bedecked with flags and banners, and bearing the name of the Elizabeth City and Norfolk Railroad, chuffing up to the station. It was greeted by a one hundred gun salute, a concert of patriotic airs by Cook's Elizabeth City Brass Band, and cheers from the onlookers.

Passengers on the train included most of the officers and directors of the railroad, many influential citizens of the Norfolk area, and reporters from Norfolk, New York, and Baltimore newspapers. As they alighted from the train, they were greeted by a reception committee of Elizabeth City's leading citizens.

The keynote welcoming speech was delivered by Colonel R. B. Creecy, editor of the *Elizabeth City Economist*, who gave a special welcome to those "who have come to put tar on your heels, and mean to stick." (Perhaps some of the railroad's later problems could have been avoided if its officers had stuck around North Carolina instead of sliding quickly back to their Wall Street offices.) Col. Creecy's speech was answered by speeches of thanks by railroad president William H. Philips and several of the other railroad officers.

The speeches were followed by a sumptuous banquet at the Albemarle House, a local hotel. Then the company was treated to a steamboat cruise down the Pasquotank River and back, following which the visitors boarded the train for the trip back to Norfolk.

On the following Monday and Tuesday, May 30 and 31, 1881, an even more gala celebration of the completion of the railroad took place in Norfolk. A special train carrying several hundred North Carolinians arrived at the EC&N's Berkley, Virginia, terminal, across the Elizabeth River from downtown Norfolk, late Monday afternoon. Today Berkley is part of the city of Norfolk, but in 1881 it was a separate town. The passengers were ferried to the Old Dominion Steamship Company's dock in Norfolk, then proceeded to Norfolk City Hall, where they were greeted by a welcoming speech from Mayor William Lamb.

After spending the night in various downtown hotels, as arranged by the welcoming committee, the guests on Tuesday were given a cruise across Hampton Roads on the venerable Old Dominion Line steamboat *Nathaniel P. Banks*. Then followed a banquet, band

concert, and of course several speeches. As might be expected, the speeches were filled with optimistic predictions of the economic growth of the area which the railroad would produce, and of the rapid expansion of the road which could be expected. One speaker went so far as to predict that within ten to twenty years, travelers would be able to ride from Norfolk to Mexico City without changing cars!

Getting a railroad to Elizabeth City had been a long, slow process. The city itself had come into being soon after the start of construction of the Dismal Swamp Canal in 1793. The canal connects Deep Creek, which flows into the Elizabeth River and on into Norfolk harbor, with Joyce's Creek, a tributary of the Pasquotank River, which

A view of the Norfolk Southern Berkley yards in Norfolk, Virginia about the time of World War I. The special train of dignitaries from Elizabeth City arrived here on Monday, May 30, 1881. Downtown Norfolk lies across the Eastern Branch of the Elizabeth River, out of the picture in the right distance. In the railroad's first few years, Norfolk-bound passengers detrained here in Berkley for a ferry trip to the downtown station across the river. Freight traffic by water to the wharves in this area continued to be important until the time of World War II. Today most of this area is occupied by Norshipco(Norfolk Shipbuilding and Drydock Company). The Seaboard Air Line's wharves across the Southern Branch of the Elizabeth River in the city of Portsmouth are in the left background. (Harry C. Mann collection, Library of Virginia)

flows into Albemarle Sound. Elizabeth City is situated at "the narrows" where the Pasquotank narrows down before widening considerably in its course to the Sound. Since in the early days, only very small boats could negotiate the narrow and shallow canal, the Elizabeth City location was desirable for a port where transloading into bigger vessels could take place. The city was named for Elizabeth Tooley, who operated an inn at the location before it was incorporated as a city.

The canal was a big boon for the economy of the Albemarle area of northeastern North Carolina, as it provided access to Hampton Roads, a major harbor. Elizabeth City grew rapidly as a result of the commerce created by the canal. This growth slowed in the 1850s, even though the canal had been deepened and widened in 1828, because a newer, deeper, and wider canal had been opened. This was the Albemarle and Chesapeake Canal, which connects Deep Creek with Currituck Sound, bypassing Elizabeth City. The Civil War further depressed the economy of the region. Elizabeth City

businessmen tried unsuccessfully to get the government to make further improvements in the Dismal Swamp Canal, but by this time railroads were becoming the favored mode of transportation.

On January 20, 1870, the Elizabeth City and Norfolk Railroad Company was chartered in North Carolina to connect the two cities of its name. The initial board of directors was made up mainly of business leaders from those two cities. A notable early investor in the company was John L. Roper. He was a native of Pennsylvania who moved to Norfolk after the Civil War to aid in the reconstruction of the area (and of course to profit from it.) He went into the lumber business, becoming a partner in the Baird and Roper Lumber Company, which became the John L. Roper Lumber Company after Mr. Baird died. The company bought huge amounts of timber lands in southeastern Virginia and northeastern North Carolina, and built a large sawmill at Gilmerton, VA, south of Norfolk. It was intended that the EC&N would be much more than a logging railroad, but no doubt Mr. Roper foresaw that the railroad would benefit his lumber business greatly. The fortunes of the railroad and lumber company would be closely related for more than fifty years, as we will see.

Chartering the railroad was not difficult, but getting it built was another matter. You will recall that the first train did not run until 1881, eleven years after the charter was granted. The main reason for the delay can be inferred from a small portion of Norfolk Mayor Lamb's speech of welcome on May 30, 1881. He said, "Quietly, and without cost to us, northern gentlemen of capital, energy, and enterprise have come among us and built this road . . . " In other words, nothing happened

Excursion trains were a good source of income for the Norfolk Southern in early years, particularly after the Virginia Beach lines were added to the system. Churches in Elizabeth City, Edenton, and elsewhere often operated excursions to the beach on summer weekends, sometimes requiring ten or more cars to handle the crowds. No specific information is available about this photograph, but it appears to be an excursion of some sort.
(Tal Carey collection)

until the local promoters had enticed northerners with necessary capital to finance the venture. Evidence of this is the fact that by the time the road was opened, all directors of the corporation were New Yorkers, rather than the local investors who had started the company. Finally, though, the road was built. The last spike (certainly not a gold one) was driven on May 12, 1881, at Shingle Landing Creek near Moyock, NC, roughly halfway between Norfolk and Elizabeth City. There was no ceremony at that time as everybody was busy preparing for the celebrations we have described.

On June 1, 1881, the EC&N was opened for public business. One train was scheduled each way daily except Sunday between downtown Norfolk and Elizabeth City. The schedule allowed three and one-half hours for the 46-mile trip. This included 30 minutes for a ferry trip across the Elizabeth River from the new passenger and freight station at the foot of Church Street in Norfolk to the end of track in Berkley. It appears the trains were mixed trains, as early advertisements in the Norfolk *Landmark* say that freight was received until 4:00 P.M., with the above-mentioned train scheduled to leave at 5:00 P.M..

People along the line were quick to take advan-

tage of the new railroad. Several Norfolk groups advertised excursion trains to Elizabeth City even before the first train ran. Unfortunately, some entrepreneurs soon found less legitimate ways of using the railroad in their promotions. Only two days after public opening of the line, one John Giddings of Norfolk was arrested for selling bogus excursion tickets.

Although completion of the line from Norfolk to Elizabeth City fulfilled the objective of its original incorporators, by 1881 more ambitious goals were envisioned by the officers of the company. Even as the celebrations described earlier were taking place, work was under way on an extension to Edenton, NC. This historic town, which served as colonial capital of North Carolina for more than twenty years, was another important center for water transportation, being situated near the point where the Chowan and Roanoke Rivers join to form Albemarle Sound. The title of Edenton's major newspaper from 1886 to 1897, *The Fisherman and Farmer*, indicates that these activities were also important at that time.

An attempt to promote a railroad to Edenton had been made as early as 1834. In that year, Jonathan H. Haughton, the Edenton representative to the North Carolina General Assembly, introduced a bill to charter the Albemarle Railroad, to run from Edenton to a connection with the Portsmouth and Roanoke Railroad (later to become the Seaboard Air Line) at a point near Suffolk, Virginia. The response in Edenton to this development was underwhelming. At a town meeting held to discuss it, it was reported that almost 80 percent of the attendees expressed opposition to the railroad.

Most of these people wanted shipping to be encouraged instead. They wanted the federal government to open up Roanoke Inlet, which had been Edenton's means of access to the ocean until it was closed by a storm in 1795. The charter for the railroad was passed anyway, but when subscription books for sale of stock were opened at Edenton, Norfolk, and Suffolk, the number of shares sold was a flat zero.

Several other attempts to start a railroad out of Edenton were equally unsuccessful, but by 1881, a major shift in thinking had taken place. By this time, railroads were great successes almost anywhere they were built. Elizabeth City, which was already growing as a port at Edenton's expense, would surely take away more business if the railroad stopped there. So, a few days after the EC&N was opened, the citizens of Edenton voted to offer a sizeable amount of land to the railroad for right-of-way and waterfront terminal facilities if they would extend their line to Edenton. This was accepted gladly by the company, and the extension was completed in early December of 1881. On December 13, a special excursion train arrived in Edenton to open the extension, to be greeted by the usual cheers, band concerts, banquet, and speech mak-

Above: The waterfront freight yards in Edenton, the southern terminus of the railroad from December 1881 until June 1891. Steamboat connections from the wharf on the right for points on Albemarle Sound and the Chowan and Roanoke Rivers kept this yard very busy in those years. The ferry to Mackey's Ferry also operated from the wharf on the right until the opening of the Albemarle Sound bridge in January 1910. At that time, the main line was relocated about one-half mile east, out of the picture to the left. The passenger station at the left of this photograph was then replaced by a new one on the new main line, but this yard continued to be important for water traffic connections for several years afterward.(North Carolina Division of Archives and History)

Right: This early view of downtown Goldsborough, NC (now Goldsboro) shows why the EC&N was anxious to extend its tracks there. The view looks southwestward across Center Street. An Atlantic and North Carolina Railroad train is ready to leave for New Bern and Morehead City in the foreground. Behind it is a Wilmington and Weldon Railroad (later Atlantic Coast Line) train headed toward Wilmington. The third track in the photo was used by the North Carolina Railroad (later Richmond and Danville and then Southern Railway) to Raleigh, Greensboro, and Charlotte. The EC&N and later the NS could connect with all these lines if it got to Goldsborough, but it did not make it there until 1906 when it assumed the lease of the A&NC. Shortly after that, a new Union Station was built several blocks west of this spot to reduce congestion on one of Goldsborough's main streets. (Wayne County, NC, Public Library)

17

ing. Regular service began on December 19.

The extension to Edenton did not satisfy all the company's ambitions. The next goal contemplated was Goldsborough, North Carolina, roughly 100 miles away. This city (now spelled Goldsboro) was an important railroad junction. It had been founded to be a division point on the Wilmington and Weldon Railroad and was named after Matthew Goldsborough, a surveyor of that railroad. Here, the EC&N could make connections with the Wilmington and Weldon (which later became the Atlantic Coast Line), as well as the Richmond and Danville Railroad (later Southern Railway) and the Atlantic and North Carolina Railroad for all points south and west. Eventually this city was reached, but much later, and indirectly, as we will see.

Since the company already had plans to expand far beyond its original terminus at Elizabeth City, it was decided to change the name from Elizabeth City and Norfolk Railroad to Norfolk Southern Railroad. The change became effective on February 1, 1883. So came into being a railroad name which has remained in existence to this day (if we overlook a temporary change to Norfolk and Southern), although the character of the railroad bearing the name has undergone major changes throughout the years.

The change of name did not please some citizens of Elizabeth City, to say the least. A public outcry greeted the news of the renaming, led by none other

A view of the Jamesville and Washington Railroad headquarters at Dymond City, NC, December 23, 1888. The J&W was built in 1877, and had been operated under lease by the Norfolk Southern from January 1883 to April 1884, but then resumed independent operation. This operation did not prove successful, and the company was out of business within twelve years. Dymond City, about halfway between Washington, NC, on the Tar River, and Jamesville, NC, on the Roanoke River, was named for J. J. Dymond, an English investor in the company, and did not survive for long after abandonment of the railroad.
(North Carolina Division of Archives and History)

than Col. R. B. Creecy, editor of the *Elizabeth City Economist*, who had been so enthusiastic in greeting the first train less than two years before. On January 23, 1883, he editorialized that "It (the railroad) will go no further south," and "All this talk about 'Southern' is mere fraud and clap-trap. It's a Wall Street dodge at the expense of Elizabeth City . . . " Shortly afterward, he reported, "We hear considerable mention of a new railroad, to be called the Elizabeth City and Northern Railroad from this town . . . along the canal bank to the junction with the Norfolk and Western Road a short distance beyond Deep Creek." Col. Creecy also urged people to boycott the Norfolk Southern by using canal transportation instead whenever possible. None of this prevented the name change, however, and no more was mentioned about a competing Elizabeth City railroad. Eventually, Col. Creecy had to admit that a railroad without Elizabeth City in its name was better than no railroad at all.

Even before the official change of name, the EC&N had moved to extend its rail lines south, contrary to Col. Creecy's prediction. On January 1, 1883, the EC&N began to operate the Jamesville and Washington Railroad by lease. This road, which had opened December 1, 1877, connected Jamesville, North Carolina, on the Roanoke River, with Washington, North Carolina, on the Pamlico River (known as the Tar River upstream from Washington). It had been built primarily as a logging road, but by 1881 was a common carrier and also operated a steamboat from Jamesville to Edenton. Thus, the EC&N, the J&W, and the steamboat provided a through route from Norfolk to Washington, where connections were made with other steamboat lines to the south.

Apparently the lease of the J&W to the EC&N was considerably less than a rousing success. Barely more than a year after its inception, the J&W bondholders foreclosed and the line was sold, ending the lease and returning the line to independent operation. A few years later, the J&W advertised themselves to be part of a "South Atlantic Air Line" with the Suffolk and Carolina and Atlantic and Danville Railroads, providing a through route from Norfolk to Washington. Little came of this, however, and the "Jolt and Wiggle" finally expired in 1896.

In 1884, the New York, Philadelphia, and Norfolk Railroad completed its line to Cape Charles, Virginia, and began steamboat operation across Chesapeake Bay from Cape Charles to downtown Norfolk. This was an event which would have an

Right: Hogsheads of tobacco and bales of cotton are being transferred from river craft to railroad cars at the Elizabeth City docks in this photo taken about 1905. Scenes such as this were regular occurrences at Elizabeth City from the time the railroad opened in 1881 until through rail traffic began to supplant the water-rail connections around the time of the opening of the Albemarle Sound bridge in 1910. Similar scenes also took place at Norfolk, Edenton, Belhaven, Plymouth, and Washington as soon as the railroad reached those cities and established water connections. Note that N&S car number 567 is a ventilated boxcar, very common on the N&S in those days. (Museum of the Albemarle collection)

important bearing on the development of the new Norfolk Southern. The NS quickly realized the value of having the "Nip 'n' N" as a northern connection. This provided much faster service than all-water routes northward out of Norfolk. Passengers appreciated the reduced travel time, but of considerably greater importance to the NS was the advantage gained in the ship-

Below: Facilities of the Albemarle and Pantego Railroad at Lees Mills, NC, December 22, 1888. Lees Mills would soon be renamed Roper for the John L. Roper Lumber Company, which built a large sawmill there. The A&P was combined with the Norfolk Southern Railroad in June 1891 to form the new Norfolk and Southern Railroad. The A&P ran from Mackey's Ferry to Belhaven through Roper. Trackage from Roper to Bishop Cross was removed in 1937, having been superseded by the line from Pinetown to Belhaven via Bishop Cross. The track from Mackeys to Roper remained in place for several years, but was used mostly for car storage. Records indicate that the A&P owned three locomotives which were taken over by the N&S, which may have included the one in the photograph, but there is no record of their history after that. (Madlin Futrell photo, North Carolina Division of Archives and History)

ment of perishable agricultural products and seafood to northern markets. In 1887, a formal agreement between the NS and the NYP&N established the Eastern Carolina Despatch fast freight line for this traffic.

These products formed a large and growing part of NS business. As the John L. Roper Lumber Company and others cut the forests of southeastern Virginia and northeastern North Carolina, rich farmland was opened up. The NS soon was making sales pitches at agricultural exhibitions, and publishing booklets urging farmers to relocate to the area and benefit from the fertility of the soil. Of course, it was assumed that they would ship their crops by NS.

The opening of the NYP&N meant more to the NS than just a new connection. The NYP&N was backed by the mighty Pennsylvania Railroad, and was headed by Alexander J. Cassatt, a former executive of the PRR and later its president. The PRR invested badly needed capital into the NS. Cassatt became a member of the NS board of directors for a short time a few years later. Also a few years later, when the NS felt the need for a newer and larger steamboat for its Elizabeth City to New Bern run, the PRR helped finance the new ship, called the Neuse, and registered it in the name of the Wilmington Steamship Company, a PRR subsidiary. Later, when the NS could afford it, full ownership was purchased by the NS.

The early years of the NS showed an encouraging volume of business, and the road was making money. In 1883, for example, gross earnings were

approximately $210,000, while operating expenses totaled about $140,000. Unfortunately, the road had very high bonded indebtedness, so that interest payments for that year left a surplus of only $319! Throughout the 1880s, earnings continued to rise, but expenses rose even faster, so that interest payments could no longer be met and the road went into receivership in 1889.

In 1891, the company was reorganized under the name Norfolk and Southern Railroad Company. The new company had much less bonded indebtedness so that interest payments were reduced. It also included additional trackage, as the Albemarle and Pantego Railroad was absorbed into the new company. This road had been built by the John L. Roper Lumber Company in 1887 south from Mackey's Ferry, North Carolina (now known as Mackeys), on Albemarle Sound, into the company's timber lands between Albemarle and Pamlico Sounds. By the time of its inclusion in the new N&S,

Right: The steamer Neuse *was the finest, possibly excepting the ferry* John W. Garrett, *of the more than twenty vessels owned by the Norfolk and Southern Railway over the years. The* Neuse *went into service between Elizabeth City and New Bern in 1890. Sometime around 1907, the northern terminal of its route was shifted to Belhaven. Soon afterward, with the Norfolk Southern having completed an all-rail route from Norfolk to New Bern, the vessel was withdrawn from this service and sold to the Baltimore, Chesapeake, and Atlantic Railway, a Pennsylvania Railroad subsidiary, which renamed her the Piankatank. (Hugh Wood photo, North Carolina Division of Archives and History)*

Below: Car ferry John W. Garrett *had been built for cross-harbor service by the Baltimore and Ohio Railroad in 1887, and was named for the late former president of that railroad. It became surplus to the B&O with completion of their rail line through Baltimore, and was sold to the Norfolk and Southern in 1899. The* Garrett *ferried cars across Albemarle Sound between Edenton and Mackey's Ferry until the Albemarle Sound bridge was put into regular service January 17, 1910. It was then sold to the St. Louis-San Francisco Railroad for car ferry service across the Mississippi River at St. Louis. (Harry C. Mann collection, Library of Virginia)*

The deck of the car ferry John W. Garrett. *Note the sign to the far right identifying the "lunch room (colored)." Of course, there was a separate white lunch room. (Willard E. Jones collection)*

it had been extended to Belhaven, North Carolina, a newly established port city on the Pungo River which flows into Pamlico Sound.

The A&P brought more to the N&S than just a railroad. It also owned a tugboat, the *George W. Roper*, named after John L. Roper's son. This tug ferried a car float between Mackey's Ferry and Edenton, so that a through rail-and-water route from Norfolk to Belhaven became available to the N&S. The A&P also owned and operated other steamboats on Albemarle and Pamlico Sounds, and a hotel in Belhaven, all of which came under ownership of the N&S. The A&P also contributed a new member to the N&S board of directors, John L. Roper himself. He remained on the board for only a year, but his name will reappear later in these pages.

Between 1891 and 1899, the Norfolk and Southern operated 104 miles of track, in two segments separated by a nine-mile car ferry operation. One passenger train in each direction ran daily except Sunday over the length of the route, with a second train in each direction between Norfolk and Edenton. The run from Norfolk to Belhaven was scheduled to take seven and one-half hours for the 113-mile trip, including one and one-half hours for the ferry operation. At least by this time passengers were spared a ferry trip across the Elizabeth River in Norfolk. By 1888, the N&S operated its passenger trains out of the Norfolk and Western's downtown Norfolk station, using trackage rights over the N&W to Berkley Junction (today called NS Junction), where the two railroads crossed. Connecting trains from Berkley Junction to Berkley served passengers from that area.

As you probably realize from what we have written so far, throughout these early years, water transport was at least as important to the N&S as rail transport. The importance of water operations is indicated by the fact that in 1881, when the EC&N was first opened, a tugboat purchased for Norfolk harbor operations was named *William H. Philips* after the road's president. The first steam locomotive only rated the name of company treasurer W. G. Dominick.

All train schedules in the early days were coordinated with connecting steamboat lines at Norfolk, Elizabeth City, Edenton, and Belhaven. Soon the railroad found that this could be facilitated if the railroad owned and operated the steamboat lines itself, so it bought several of these. We have already mentioned the *Neuse*, the steamboat which the PRR helped to finance. This was only one of more than twenty steamboats and tugs which were owned by the railroad at one time or another. Steamboat lines operated by the company in the 1890s totaled more than 400 miles, compared to only 104 rail miles. The company even operated steamboats on two different routes between Norfolk and Elizabeth City in competition to its own rail route. One of these routes was by the Dismal Swamp Canal, and the other was by the Albemarle and Chesapeake Canal.

By the mid-1890s, seven railroads other than the N&S had established operations in the Norfolk-Portsmouth area, but the N&S had a rail connection with only one, the Norfolk and Western. Interchange by water kept the harbor filled with tugs, barges, and lighters, including the *William H. Philips*. In 1898, the Norfolk and Portsmouth Belt Line Railroad was built to provide rail connections between the other railroads of the area. The Belt Line was owned in equal shares by these railroads, including the N&S.

We have also mentioned the ferry between Edenton and Mackey's Ferry. This remained part of the main line until Albemarle Sound was finally bridged in 1910. In 1899, the railroad was presented with an opportunity to upgrade the service when the ferryboat *John W. Garrett* became available. This craft had been built by the Baltimore and Ohio Railroad in 1887 for service in Baltimore harbor, and was named for its longtime former president. With the opening of the rail tunnel in Baltimore, it was no longer needed by the B&O, and was bought by the N&S.

During most of the last decade of the nineteenth century, the Norfolk and Southern put its plans for expansion of rail lines on hold, and concentrated on upgrading the service on existing lines. It was reasonably successful in doing this. Between 1892 and 1899, net earnings more than doubled, and the road was finally able to pay dividends to its stockholders. With the coming of the twentieth century, however, the railroad began to expand rapidly. In the next fifteen years, the track mileage operated by the company would increase by almost 800 percent.

The crew of the *John W. Garrett* on its deck. Crew members who can be identified include, seated left to right, Captain Samuel F. Williams, James Durfey, George Cuthrell, and Tom Jones. As you can see, shipments of logs were still an important part of the railroad's business while the *Garrett* was in service.
(Philip McMullan collection)

Above: The Virginia Beach oceanfront about 1900, showing the Norfolk and Southern-owned Princess Anne Hotel at the far right. The train shed serving the hotel is in the center of the photo, with the square tower of the depot just to its left. The tracks were behind the train shed. The building at far left is the dance pavilion. The Princess Anne Hotel was built by Norfolk Southern predecessor Norfolk and Virginia Beach Railroad and operated by that company and its successors until the hotel burned to the ground in 1907. The depot and train shed were also destroyed in that fire. (Robert C. Reisweber collection)

Right: Locomotive Number 3 of the Norfolk and Virginia Beach Railroad was this 4-4-0, shown in a 1884 photograph. It had been built by the Virginia Iron Works of Norfolk, and was three-foot gauge. It was named James H. Hopkins after an early president of the railroad. No information on its disposition is available, but it apparently was not used on the road after the track was widened to standard gauge in 1897. (Harold K. Vollrath collection)

Chapter 2

The Virginia Beach Lines

The first extension of N&S rails in this expansion period occurred on January 25, 1900, and was not in the southward direction which had been anticipated for many years. On that date, the N&S purchased the Norfolk, Virginia Beach, and Southern Railroad, which ran eastward out of Norfolk to the Atlantic Ocean at Virginia Beach.

The NVB&S had its beginnings on March 23, 1872, when the Norfolk and Sewell's Point Railroad was incorporated. As the name implies, it was proposed as a line between downtown Norfolk and Sewell's Point, where the Elizabeth River enters the waters of Hampton Roads, but the charter allowed some flexibility by specifying that the road should be built from Norfolk "to Sewell's Point or some other point in the Counties of Norfolk or Princess Anne on the bay or coast." Princess Anne County is now the City of

Virginia Beach, but was mostly sand dunes and farmland in 1872. The name Sewell's Point has been spelled several different ways over the years. The spelling used here is that used in the 1872 charter. Today, Sewell's Point is part of the City of Norfolk and is the site of the U. S. Navy Operating Base, but in 1872 it was a relatively undeveloped part of Norfolk County.

Like the Elizabeth City and Norfolk Railroad of the 1870s, the Norfolk and Sewell's Point Railroad was able to raise little money, and so actual construction was long delayed. By the early 1880s, however, enough financing was available that construction could begin. By this time, the company had definitely decided to make the Virginia Beach oceanfront its destination, and on January 14, 1882, the name of the company was officially changed to the Norfolk and Virginia Beach Railroad and Improvement Company. Marshall

Parks was the main driving force behind the company at this time and became its president. Parks had been president of the Albemarle and Chesapeake Canal Company for many years.

The "Improvement" part of the name showed that the company planned to do more than just build and operate a railroad. Parks also was a leader in the development of Virginia Beach as a resort. He had been instrumental in forming the Seaside Hotel and Land Company in 1880, which company was taken over by the NVBRR&ICo soon after the company adopted its new name. This made the railroad the owner of 1600 acres of prime waterfront property, on which were built the Virginia Beach Hotel, which later became the Princess Anne Hotel, the first large hotel on the ocean-front, and several "cottages", which in fact were small hotels.

The charter changing the name of the railroad gave the company five years to complete construction, but the flat land made construction easy and fast, so that even with finances tight, it was actually finished only eighteen months after the charter was granted. The first train ran on July 16, 1883. The line was steam powered and was three-foot gauge.

In the earliest days, the western end of track of the N&VB Railroad was on the east bank of Broad Creek, which flows into the Eastern Branch of the Elizabeth River three miles east of downtown Norfolk. Passengers going from Norfolk to the Beach had to start with a boat ride covering this distance before they could board the train. Before long, however, the company built a bridge across Broad Creek and extended track into the Norfolk and Western station at the end of East Main Street in downtown Norfolk. Recall that a few years later, NS passenger trains would use this station also.

The Virginia Beach line had one thing in common with the N&S in early years—financial instability.

Combine number 15 of the Norfolk, Virginia Beach, and Southern Railroad. This appears to be a builder's or railroad publicity photo to advertise the railroad's newest equipment. Since the NVB&S was only in existence from 1896 to 1900, it was probably taken in that time period or very soon afterward. The location is not known definitely, but may be where tracks crossed Lake Holly and curved northward to the Princess Anne Hotel. (Railroad Museum of Pennsylvania, Pennsylvania Historical and Museum Commission)

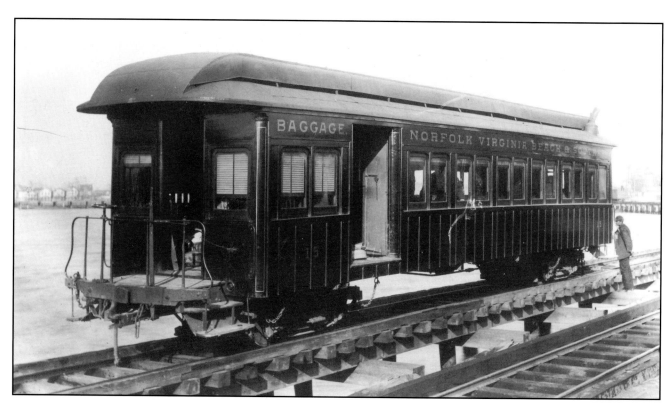

Chesapeake Transit Company car number 15 on the trestle over Lynnhaven Inlet. This trestle became part of the Norfolk and Southern North Route to Cape Henry and Virginia Beach when the two railroads merged in 1904. The trestle was given a solid deck in 1926 so that the newly formed Norfolk Southern Bus Company could operate buses over it, as there was no highway bridge over Lynnhaven Inlet at that time. Car number 15 later became an open trailer with the same number on the roster of the Norfolk Southern. (Mrs. John H. Kelly, Jr. collection)

The N&VBRR&ICo. went into receivership in 1884 and again in 1886. In 1887, it was reorganized as the Norfolk and Virginia Beach Railroad Company. On January 29, 1891, this company agreed to merge with the Danville and Seaboard Railroad Company to form the Norfolk, Albemarle, and Atlantic Railroad. The Danville and Seaboard had been chartered in 1887 to build a railroad from Danville, VA to "some point at or near the seaboard at or near Norfolk", some two hundred miles away, but apparently never did any actual construction. Considering that by the time of its merger, it had sold only ten thousand dollars of stock out of an authorized five million dollars' worth, the lack of construction is hardly surprising.

It was not long before the new NA&A railroad was in financial difficulties. On April 25, 1896, the company was sold at public auction to a committee of bondholders, who announced their intention to form a new corporation called the Norfolk, Virginia Beach, and Southern Railroad Company. By this time, the Vanderbilt family and the New York Central and Hudson River Railroad had acquired substantial holdings in the company.

In 1898, the NVB&S completed a branch line from Clapham Junction, near Euclid Station, 22 miles south to Munden, Virginia. Munden is located on the North Landing River which leads into Currituck Sound. The NVB&S operated the steamboat *Comet* from Munden 33 miles down the sound to Poplar Branch, North Carolina. This operation attracted sportsmen from a wide area, as the hunting and fishing in the Currituck Sound area were quite popular. The N&S inherited this business along with five other steamboats previously owned by the NVB&S. Two of these five

Norfolk and Southern construction car number 4 was presumably used in the electrification of the route to Virginia Beach in 1904, and no doubt was used for maintenance of the electric lines after that. Location of the photo is not known. (Allan H. Berner collection)

boats, the *Thomas Newton* and the *C. W. Pettit*, operated on the Dismal Swamp Canal and Albemarle and Chesapeake Canal routes mentioned earlier. Later that year, the NVB&S converted its lines from narrow gauge to standard gauge.

The NVB&S remained in business only until January 1900, when it was bought out by the N&S. While officially the Norfolk and Southern purchased the NVB&S, in actuality it was more of a merger. In fact, the new president of the N&S was John Carstensen, who had been secretary-treasurer of the NVB&S, and who was also comptroller of the NYC&HR. Chairman of the Board Chauncey Depew and Treasurer E. V. W. Rossiter of the NYC&HR also took seats on the board of directors of the N&S, showing the strong influence of the New York Central and the Vanderbilts on the new ownership. Only three directors of the old N&S retained their seats on the board. One of these was Alexander J. Cassatt, indicating that the Pennsylvania Railroad influence still existed to a degree. One wonders if Depew and Cassatt got along better at board meetings than NYC and PRR executives did seventy years later when the Penn Central was formed. However, their common membership on the board did not last long, as we will see.

Not only was the geographic direction of the

NVB&S a change of thinking for the N&S, but also the type of business was different. Until this time, the N&S had been promoting industrial, commercial, and agricultural development along its line, accepting whatever passenger traffic this might bring. Now it had acquired a line whose main purpose was to move passengers.

After the Norfolk and Southern acquired the NVB&S, management recognized that its track offered an entrance into downtown Norfolk that could be used for its mainline passenger trains as well. A new branch 7.6 miles long was constructed from Clapham Junction on the Virginia Beach line to Providence Junction on the Berkley to Elizabeth City main line. The branch opened for business on January 1, 1904. Passenger trains from Norfolk to Edenton and Belhaven then began their journey at the Park Avenue station on the Virginia Beach line and utilized the new branch. This enabled the N&S to discontinue use of the N&W station and the trackage rights leading to it. Virginia Beach trains had already discontinued use of the N&W station in favor of the Park Avenue station, 0.6 miles to the east, at an earlier date.

The new Virginia Beach line added significant business to the N&S, but it was not long before competition for the business arose. On March 3, 1898, the Chesapeake Transit Company had been chartered to build a line from Norfolk to Cape Henry and Virginia Beach. The line was opened for business in December 1902. The charter optimistically permitted the road to be extended all the way to the West Virginia border, but it never came close to there. The CT route to the currently developed area of Virginia Beach was some six miles longer then the direct N&S line, but the last six miles from Cape Henry ran along the oceanfront, which had potential for new development. Also, the CT was an electric line, which was preferred by many riders to the conventional steam-powered trains of the N&S. The CT was owned by a syndicate of bankers including Flint, Bacon, and Company and Colonial Trust Company of Pittsburgh.

The N&S moved quickly to meet the competition. Construction was started on an extension of the road northward from the Virginia Beach end of track to

Cape Henry, paralleling the CT route. Also, the main line from Park Avenue Station to the oceanfront was converted to electric operation, although neither the Cape Henry extension nor the Currituck Branch to Munden were ever electrified.

Competition between the N&S and the CT did not last long. In April 1904, the Vanderbilt interests sold their stock in the N&S to the owners of the CT. A. H. Flint, of Flint, Bacon, and Company, replaced John Carstensen as president of the N&S. Depew and Rossiter, representing the Vanderbilt interests, resigned from the N&S board of directors and were replaced by representatives of the syndicate owning the CT. Alexander Cassatt had left the N&S board of directors two years earlier.

With control of both companies in the same hands, a merger agreement was immediately drawn up. But N&S minority stockholder Walter S. Johnston, acting through noted attorney Elihu Root, a former U.S. secretary of war, obtained a court injunction blocking it. He argued successfully that the scheme as publicly announced was illegal. The attorney representing the CT syndicate admitted this was the case, and that the scheme had been abandoned on advice of counsel. Supreme Court Justice Greenbaum went so far as to restrain the syndicate from any other attempts at merger. Eventually the syndicate had to buy out all Johnston's stock to clear the way. On November 21, 1904, the merger into a new Norfolk and Southern became effective.

Even before the merger was complete, the N&S had torn up its line paralleling the CT line to Cape

Above: City Hall Avenue in Norfolk about 1915. Norfolk Southern's Electric Division lines operated from here until 1919. It is impossible to identify the cars shown in the photo, but it appears the two-car train curving to the left in the background may be a NS train. The track they are on was owned by the Norfolk and Portsmouth Traction Company, but was used by the Norfolk Southern electric trains to the beach. The other two cars may be NPTC cars. The NS downtown ticket office was in the Monticello Arcade, just to the right of the cars. The building to the left of the photo is the Monticello Hotel, a major downtown landmark for many years. The domed building in the background is the Norfolk City Hall and Courthouse, which now houses the memorial to General Douglas MacArthur, whose mother grew up in Berkley a few blocks from the NS Berkley yards. NS abandoned use of the tracks in the photo in 1919 when requested to pay for street improvements, moving electric operations to the Terminal Station. (Harry C. Mann photo, Library of Virginia)

Below: The Norfolk Southern downtown ticket office in the Monticello Arcade about 1915. Note that tickets for both the electric lines to Virginia Beach and steam lines to the south were sold here, although the steam trains departed from Terminal (Union) Station, about one-half mile east. Also note that there were separate white and colored ticket offices at that time. Monticello Arcade still exists, but it has not contained a Norfolk Southern ticket office for many years. (Harry C. Mann photo, Library of Virginia)

Left: Seventeenth Street station in Virginia Beach. This became the most important of several stations along the oceanfront after fire destroyed the Princess Anne Hotel and the adjacent station. (Edgar Brown collection)

Below: Another view of Seventeenth Street station, showing a three-car train of two motor cars and trailer car number 65. (Harry C. Mann photo, Library of Virginia)

Henry, anticipating the merger. Soon connections between the two roads were built at both the Norfolk and Virginia Beach ends, so that a complete electrically operated loop was created. The former CT line became known as the North Route, and the former NVB&S line became the South Route. The connecting track in Norfolk ran 0.8 miles in what is now Norchester Street, between points called North Junction and South Junction. Shops for the electrically powered equipment were established at South Junction. A power plant to supply electricity for the line was located at Bayville, about halfway between North Junction and

Norfolk Southern perishable station at Diamond Springs on the North Beach Route in 1937. In those days, most of the land between Norfolk and Virginia Beach was still farmland and provided considerable agricultural business for the railroad.
(John W. Barriger III photo, Barriger Railroad collection, St. Louis Mercantile Library)

Cape Henry on the North route.

The Chesapeake Transit Company's first Norfolk terminal was at Princess Anne Road, about a mile north of downtown Norfolk, but on June 29, 1903, the company began to use trackage rights over the Norfolk and Atlantic Terminal Company, which later became part of the Norfolk and Portsmouth Traction Company, to reach the Monticello Arcade on City Hall Avenue in downtown Norfolk. This became the main Norfolk terminal for Norfolk and Southern Virginia Beach trains after the merger. Other runs continued to leave from Park Avenue station, as did the steam trains to the south. In 1919, the city of Norfolk requested the railroad to pay for improvements to streets containing tracks leading to the Monticello Arcade. Rather than doing this, the company shifted the terminal for electric operations to the Norfolk Terminal Station, from which steam operations had been conducted since 1912.

By the summer of 1907, the schedule showed seventeen trains each way daily over the South Route, with fourteen each way daily over the North Route. In

addition, on summer weekends, special excursion trains were often run. When the traffic was at its heaviest, there were times when there was insufficient electrically operated equipment available to handle all trips. Some steam-powered passenger trains were operated at these times.

To this point, we have discussed the Virginia Beach lines as passenger operations, which is what they were primarily built to be. But we should not overlook the freight business over these lines. Agricultural products and seafood, such as the famous Lynnhaven oysters, provided significant revenue for the company, as did other categories of freight. In the early days, what is today the heavily developed city of Virginia Beach was mostly farmland. In particular, the Munden Branch went through an area which produced large shipments of potatoes over the railroad for many years. Even today, the area surrounding the southern end of the former right-of-way to Munden is still mainly farmland, although the line itself is long gone and no longer produces any revenue for the railroad.

Today, as we look at the large modern hotels and motels that line the Virginia Beach oceanfront, and the auto-clogged streets behind them, it is hard to realize how important the railroad was to the development of the Beach. Of course, in 1900 it was impractical to get to the beach from more than a few miles away other than by railroad. And, as we have noted, the railroad owned the major accommodations and most of the oceanfront property. When Virginia Beach was incorporated as a town in 1906, it was fitting that Bernard P. Holland, superintendent of the N&S electric lines at that time, became the first mayor.

The Princess Anne Hotel was destroyed by fire in 1907, and the railroad did not attempt to build a replacement hotel, but in 1912 it built the Seaside Park Casino about 1.5 miles north of the Princess Anne Hotel site, and built a new station right behind it. The casino contained a bathhouse, restaurant, and the Peacock Ballroom, where nationally known dance bands entertained. The casino was operated by the railroad until it was sold in the 1920s. It continued to be a major attraction of the beach and an important source of passenger revenue for the railroad until passenger service ended in 1947.

A fine new hotel, the Cavalier, was built near the oceanfront north of Seaside Park in 1927. This was not built by the railroad, but the railroad was always closely associated with it. The road opened a station opposite the hotel and started direct service, including a New York-to Virginia Beach Pullman run to the new station, operated in conjunction with the Pennsylvania Railroad and the Norfolk and Western. This service lasted until the early days of World War II, when the Cavalier was taken over by the Navy as a training facil-

Seaside Park Casino in Virginia Beach, built by the Norfolk Southern Railroad in 1912, and operated by it until sold in 1926. Building to the left of the photo is the Peacock Ballroom, where nationally known bands performed. The depot and water tank are shown behind the rightmost building, with the passenger canopy and wye track in the center rear. The main track ran along what is today Pacific Avenue. The casino occupied the oceanfront between 30th and 33rd streets. It was destroyed by fire in 1955. (Mrs. John H. Kelly, Jr. collection)

2-8-0 number 208 brings Pullman Mountain Springs to the Cavalier Hotel in Virginia Beach. The exact date of this photo is not known, but an associated photo indicates it was shortly after World War II. That would make it a special operation, but a regular daily Pullman run from New York came directly to the Cavalier until early in that war. This run had usually been powered by an electric freight motor before the end of electrification, but would have used a steam locomotive like this after 1935. Pullman Mountain Springs was a ten section-lounge-observation car built in 1923. Similar cars of the Mountain series were assigned to the Pan American and Capitol Limited, but Mountain Springs was apparently never assigned regularly to a specific train. It was transferred to storage and porter car number S-54 in 1958. (William Robson collection)

ity. The railroad also brought many privately owned passenger cars to the hotel, parking them on a nearby siding. Long time residents of the area recall that former Prime Minister of Canada Mackenzie King's private car was parked in front of the Cavalier on several occasions.

In 1935, electric operation was discontinued over both Virginia Beach routes, and railbuses were substituted on the passenger trains. We will discuss this change in more detail in later chapters.

By 1947, it had become apparent that more and more people were using automobiles or buses to get to Virginia Beach. Schedules still showed eleven trains each way between Norfolk and the beach, but now only one trip, train number 101, used the North Route. This run left Park Avenue at 6:50 A.M., arrived at Cape Henry at 7:30 A.M., then proceeded around the loop, returning to Park Avenue via the South Route at 8:45 A.M. as train number 54. This trip was apparently operated mainly for mail and express business along the North Route.

On November 8, 1947, the last railbus runs to the beach were made. In 1950, the tracks paralleling the oceanfront from Cape Henry to Lake Station were removed, and the right-of-way was paved over, becoming Pacific Avenue, one of the most important thoroughfares in Virginia Beach. No evidence remains to show that a railroad ever operated along this route.

Recently, Norfolk Southern Corporation and the city of Norfolk have reached an agreement to transfer ownership of the portion of the South Route right-of-way within the city limits to the city. A light rail line will be constructed on part of that right-of-way. It would seem logical to extend that light rail line all the way to the Virginia Beach oceanfront, but in 1999, Virginia Beach voters rejected a proposal to do so. But it now appears that passenger rail will return to at least the Norfolk portion part of the route.

Above: View of a train crossing the Trent River bridge entering New Bern. The photo is not dated but could be either shortly before or shortly after the Norfolk and Southern takeover of this line from the Atlantic and North Carolina Company in 1906. In either case, the appearance of the train would have been very similar in early years of Norfolk and Southern operation. The brick and granite piers and abutments of the bridge seen in the photo date to the original construction of the line in 1858, and remain in place today, but the original wood truss structure was burned by the Confederates in March 1862 to prevent its use by the Union Army. The Union Army quickly built a temporary wood trestle replacement, and the bridge retains that form today.
(North Carolina Division of Archives and History)

Opposite page: Washington and Plymouth Railroad operated this unusual narrow gauge 4-4-2 between Washington, NC and Plymouth, NC. It did not survive the takeover of the railroad by Norfolk and Southern in 1904 and the rapid conversion to standard gauge.
(Railroad Museum of Pennsylvania, Pennsylvania Historical and Museum Commission)

Chapter 3

Expansion to Raleigh and New Bern

Even as the Norfolk and Southern was completing development of its lines to Virginia Beach, events were taking place in northeastern North Carolina which would have considerable effect on the N&S. After years of painfully slow growth of rail lines in the area, more and more people suddenly became interested in accelerating this growth. Today, almost 100 years later, it is hard to sort out which people were working together and which were competing with each other, but it appears that shortly after the turn of the century, at least five groups became actively engaged in building new common carrier rail lines in the area independent of each other.

Not surprisingly, one of these groups was the management of the Norfolk and Southern itself. You will recall that even in the earliest days of the railroad, expansion southward had been a long term goal. The management of the company had almost completely changed since those days, but that goal had not.

The first step N&S management took in its southward expansion was the purchase of the Washington and Plymouth Railroad, completed on March 10, 1904. The W&P had been built as a three-foot gauge logging railroad about 1889 by the Roanoke Railroad and Lumber Company, but on April 23, 1902, it was opened with the usual festivities as a common carrier railroad between Washington, North Carolina and Plymouth, North Carolina, on the Roanoke River about fifteen miles downstream from Jamesville. So the W&P provided the N&S

with a replacement line for the Jamesville and Washington Railroad, lost to the NS twenty years earlier and now nothing more than a memory. As soon as possible after taking over the W&P, the N&S converted it to standard gauge and built an extension from Plymouth to Mackey's Ferry, so that a through route was established from Norfolk to Washington, although one which was still dependent on the ferry across Albemarle Sound. This route was 135 miles long.

Washington was another important port for traffic on the Carolina sounds and rivers by this time. It had been the terminus for one of the earliest steamboat lines connecting with the N&S. It has often been called "Little Washington," but most people in the area would prefer it to be known as "The Original Washington," as it was incorporated and named for the famous General in 1776, long before he became president, and while "Big Washington" was still Maryland swampland.

A second group of investors which would become of great importance to the future of the N&S was in the process of forming the Howland Improvement Company while the N&S was buying the Washington and Plymouth. This company was named for Richard S. Howland of Asheville, North Carolina, a

major investor, but most of the money came from a group from New York City and Providence, Rhode Island, headed by Marsden J. Perry of the latter city. The company was soon renamed the Atlantic and North Carolina Company, and had been formed to operate the Atlantic and North Carolina Railroad under lease.

The Atlantic and North Carolina Railroad had been placed in operation from Goldsboro, North Carolina (then known as Goldsborough) through New Bern to Morehead City, North Carolina in 1858, making it the oldest rail line ever to become part of the N&S. It had been built by the Atlantic and North Carolina Railroad Company, of which the State of North Carolina was the largest stockholder. It was promoted by former North Carolina Governor John Motley Morehead, who envisioned that a major seaport might develop on Bogue Sound if a railroad were built there from Goldsboro. Goldsboro by this time was already an important rail junction, as it was the location where the Atlantic Coast Line's north-to-south route met the North Carolina Railroad, another state-owned railroad which had been leased to the Richmond and Danville Railroad on September 11, 1871. The R&D later became part of Southern Railway, which negotiated a new 99-year lease on January 1, 1896. The North Carolina Railroad was a major route to the western part of the state. You will recall that the NS had intended to extend its route to Goldsboro from its earliest days.

The A&NC Railroad was built to Bogue Sound as planned, and a new seaport city was built there. It was named Morehead City after Governor Morehead. Although the A&NC and its Goldsboro connections provided convenient access to most of the interior parts

of the state, Morehead City never became as large a port as Governor Morehead and its other promoters expected. It was surpassed by Wilmington, North Carolina, a few miles south, which was served by both the Atlantic Coast Line and the Seaboard Air Line. It has continued to serve as a port to this day, however, and is still served by the rail line built by the A&NC Railroad Company.

The city of New Bern, an intermediate station on the A&NC Railroad, was also of considerable importance. The town had been established in 1710 by immigrants from Switzerland and Germany, who named it for Bern, Switzerland, from which many of them came. The Swiss influence was soon wiped out by Indian raids which killed or drove off most of the early settlers, but the town was repopulated by settlers of English descent who retained the original name. Its growth was enhanced in the mid-eighteenth century when it became the colonial capital of North Carolina. It lost this distinction to a more central location, which became the city of Raleigh, in 1791, but it continued to grow rapidly as a center of industry, mainly lumber and naval stores. For the first third of the nineteenth century, it was the largest city in North Carolina. Located at the confluence of the Neuse and Trent Rivers, it was also an important location for water traffic. It had been the southern terminus of the most important of the Norfolk Southern steamboat lines from the earliest days of that company.

Although the State of North Carolina had bought more than two-thirds of the stock of the Atlantic and North Carolina Railroad Company when it was formed, the company charter limited the state to only

Above: An early view of the Norfolk Southern bridge across the Newport River between Morehead City and Beaufort. This was part of the extension between those cities begun by the Atlantic and North Carolina Company just before it became part of the Norfolk and Southern. The N&S completed the extension. (North Carolina Division of Archives and History)

Below: Locomotive number 2 of the Suffolk and Carolina Railroad. This locomotive was built by Thomas W. Godwin and Company of Norfolk, VA., also known as Virginia Iron Works, about 1880, and was 3 foot 6 inch gauge. This appears to be a builder's photo taken at the Virginia Iron Works. W. H. Gay, for whom the locomotive was named, was the founder of the Gay Manufacturing Company, a lumber company which built the S&CRR as a logging road for their mill in Suffolk. Small rod-driven locomotives such as this were very common on the logging railroads of eastern Virginia and North Carolina. In this flat country, there was no need for the better known geared locomotives used on logging lines in more rugged locations. (Suffolk, VA. News-Herald)

one-third of the stockholders' votes, with private investors holding two-thirds of the voting rights. Apparently this was done to prevent political influence from having too much effect on day-to-day operation of the railroad, but the arrangement turned out to be impractical. By 1904, at least two attempts had been made to lease the line to private operators, only to see them fail, and on one occasion the state legislature attempted to take complete control of the road but was prevented by an injunction obtained by one of the private stockholders.

In September 1904, the A&NC was again leased, this time to the new A&NC Company. Immediately after beginning to operate the A&NC RR, the A&NC Company began to build a three-mile extension from Morehead City to Beaufort under the name Beaufort and Western Railroad. Beaufort was a much older port town on Bogue Sound, but one which had little available land to provide for the port expansion which the promoters of Morehead City expected to require. Since this line was built by the private leasing company, it did not become part of the state-owned Atlantic and North Carolina Railroad Company.

In September of 1905, word began to spread around southeastern Virginia and Northeastern North Carolina that some unknown investors were buying up large amounts of Norfolk and Southern stock. There was considerable speculation as to who might be responsible. One guess was that Henry Huttleston Rogers was buying it to combine the N&S with the Tidewater Railway, which he was building west from Norfolk, and which later became the Virginian Railway. Another suggestion was that George Gould was buying the N&S and would combine it with the Wabash Railroad. Before long, however, it became known that the owners of the Atlantic and North Carolina Company were buying up the largest part of the N&S stock.

A short time later, the same group began to acquire an interest in the Raleigh and Pamlico Sound Railroad. This company had first been chartered as the Raleigh and Eastern North Carolina Railroad in 1903 by a third group of investors, mostly from Raleigh, including J. M. Turner, E. B. Barbee, and C. B. Barbee.

By this time, as we have noted, Raleigh had been the state capital for more than 100 years and was growing rapidly as a commercial center as well. It was natural for Raleigh businessmen to want rail connections with the eastern part of the state. They also successfully solicited investment from businessmen in the cities of Stantonsburg, Wilson, Farmville, and Greenville, through which they planned to build their line. The name of the company was changed in February 1905 to the Raleigh and Pamlico Sound Railroad. By that time, the line had been constructed from Raleigh to Knightwood (now Knightdale), and was being pushed eastward. When it became known that the owners of the A&NC Company were investing in the line, it became obvious that they intended that the line should connect at Washington with the N&S, which they were also buying, and at New Bern with the A&NC, which they already operated.

While all this was going on, a fourth group was starting to develop another rail system in the area. This group was headed by New York banker Rudolph Kleybolte. They formed the Virginia and Carolina Coast Railroad company in July 1905, and announced plans to complete a line from the Hampton Roads area to Beaufort, North Carolina. They proposed to do this mainly by buying up other railroads, including several logging roads operated by lumber companies.

The V&CC took its first step in forming its line by buying the John L. Roper Lumber Company, soon followed by the purchase of several other lumber companies in the area which were merged into the Roper Company. This gave the V&CC a network of roughly 150 miles of logging railroads, some of which were planned to be parts of the new railroad's main line.

Soon after this, the V&CC took an even bigger step toward completion of its proposed line when it bought the Suffolk and Carolina Railroad. This road had been built beginning in 1873 by the Gay Manufacturing Company, which owned a sawmill in Suffolk, Virginia. At first, the S&C was a three-foot-six-inch gauge logging road leading south out of Suffolk to timber lands just across the state line in North Carolina. By 1905, however, it had been converted to standard gauge, became a common carrier, and extended to Edenton and Elizabeth City. Passenger service was offered from both Edenton and Elizabeth City to Portsmouth, Virginia, utilizing trackage rights over the Seaboard Air Line from Suffolk to Portsmouth. A ferry connection provided service to Norfolk. The schedule was a few minutes slower than the N&S

schedule between Norfolk and Edenton, but close enough to compete for business. The S&C also owned several steamboats which traveled the rivers and sounds out of Edenton in competition with the N&S steamboat lines.

At roughly the same time, the V&CC bought the Pamlico, Oriental, and Western Railroad. This company had been formed in 1891 by a fifth group of investors to build a line from New Bern eastward to Bayboro, then southeastward to Oriental, North Carolina, a small port city on Pamlico Sound. The group that formed this company included some of the stockholders of the Atlantic and North Carolina Railroad Company (the state-owned company, not the privately-owned A&NC Company) As was so often the case with NS predecessor roads, however, capital was scarce and construction progress was delayed by this fact. By the time of the V&CC takeover in 1905, the line had been completed only as far as Bayboro, about 17 miles.

The V&CC immediately started to expand its system by beginning construction of a new line from Mackey's Ferry to Columbia, North Carolina, on the

The first train through Grantsboro on the Pamlico, Oriental, and Western Railroad in 1905. The diminutive 0-4-4T Forney was locomotive number 1 of the PO&W, and became third Number 1 of the Norfolk and Southern in 1907, the smallest steam locomotive ever owned by the N&S. It had been built as second number 242 of the Manhattan Railway by Pittsburgh Locomotive Works in 1894 and was sold to the PO&W in 1904. Note that the digits 4 and 2 of its original number can still be seen on the dome. It was sold to the Mottu Land and Lumber Company in 1912. The PO&W became the N&S Oriental Branch.
(North Carolina Division of Archives and History)

Above: The first train in Columbia on the Norfolk and Southern Columbia Branch in 1908 was a cause for considerable celebration in the town and brought out many people eager to pose on the locomotive. N&S fireman Dude Dunbar (by the cab door) worked on the Columbia trains for many years. Notes on the photo identify the other people standing on the locomotive as "sis, Eva, big hat", Bertie Armstrong, Mae Carawan, Sanderlin Carawan, Mr. Duncan. As far as is now known, none of these people were railroad employees. N&S locomotive number 41 came to the road from the Atlantic and North Carolina, where it had been number 19, and was retired in 1932. (Collon Snell collection)

Below: The station at Beaufort, NC was built by the N&S as part of the railroad's extension to that city in 1906. It was turned over to the Beaufort and Morehead Railroad in 1937. It is still in existence although rails no longer run to downtown Beaufort. (D. P. McDonald collection)

south shore of Albemarle Sound 22 miles east of Mackey's Ferry. The Suffolk and Carolina already offered ferry service from Edenton to Mackey's Ferry as one of its water routes. Completion of the rail line to Columbia would put the V&CC into further competition with the N&S, which operated an all-water route from Edenton to Columbia.

As you can see, the lines purchased by the V&CC were already competing with the N&S, and their proposed extensions, if completed, would heighten the competition. It has been suggested that the main purpose of the V&CC owners in proposing these extensions was to force the N&S to buy them out. Whether this was true cannot be determined at this late date, but if it was their purpose, they were very successful, for on November 23, 1906, the Norfolk and Southern Railroad and the Virginia and Carolina Coast Railroad were combined into a new Norfolk and Southern Railway Company. The Atlantic and North Carolina Company, the Raleigh and Pamlico Sound Railroad Company, the Pamlico, Oriental and Western Railroad, and the Beaufort and Western Railroad were also merged into the new N&S Railway Company at the same time.

One of the leading figures in the new company was Frank S. Gannon. He had been third vice-president and general manager of the Southern Railway, then vice-president of the New York metropolitan street railways, before he turned his attention to the development of the lines in eastern North Carolina. He had been one of the founders of the Atlantic and North Carolina Company and was its vice-president. At the time of the formation of the new N&S Railway, he was also on the board of directors of the V&CC, the PO&W, and the John L.

Roper Lumber Company, showing that all those companies were closely allied even before the formal merger took place. Mr. Gannon became president of the new N&S Railway. Marsden J. Perry, president of the A&NC Company and of the Union Trust Company of Providence, Rhode Island, became chairman of the board, a post he held until 1925. The first board of directors of the N&S Railway also included a familiar name, John L. Roper. Mr. Roper had retired from active management of his lumber company a few years before but retained his financial interest. Mr. Roper's son George W. Roper was by this time the manager of the lumber company and also a director of the N&S Ry.

Immediately after the formation of the new Norfolk and Southern Railway, the company proceeded to complete the track extensions that were in progress. This included the V&CC extension to Columbia, the PO&W extension to Oriental, and the Beaufort and Western to Beaufort. This latter line was owned outright by the N&S as it had been by the A&NC Company. Not long after this, the N&S attempted to purchase the A&NC Railroad Company. This would have made the N&S owner of all the track it operated, but it did not happen. The state-controlled company continued to own the track, as it does today.

In March 1913, Norfolk Southern was granted a charter to extend the Beaufort and Western line to Cape Lookout, ten miles east of Beaufort. It was envisioned that a ship refueling station and harbor of refuge would be built there. This was never done, however, and the extension was never constructed.

The most important construction project for the new N&S was the completion of the line eastward from Raleigh, which had been begun by the Raleigh and Pamlico Sound. Completion of this line to Washington and New Bern would connect all parts of the new system and permit through service to both New Bern and

Above: An early view of the Norfolk and Southern bridge over the Pamlico (or Tar) River at Washington, NC. At this time, the bridge was 4,497 feet long, but later it was shortened to 3,897 feet by fill at the south end. As the photo shows, it included a swing span for water traffic. The bridge was placed in service in 1907 as part of the railroad's extension to Raleigh and New Bern. The bridge looks little different today than it did when first built, but has required extensive repairs several times over the years as a result of storm damage, the most recent from Hurricane Floyd in September 1999. (Winstead collection)

Below: Norfolk Southern 2-6-0 number 103 and a work train are in the process of "building the missing link" near Vanceboro, according to writing on the photo. This is on the New Bern Branch, which would date the photo to 1907. (North Carolina Division of Archives and History)

Raleigh from Norfolk. Fortunately for the N&S, the most difficult part of this extension had already been completed. The Pamlico, Oriental and Western had built a trestle more than a mile long across the Neuse River from New Bern to the town of Bridgeton. By connecting the new line to the PO&W at Bridgeton, another crossing of the Neuse River could be avoided.

Above: Union Station, Raleigh, NC. The station was built in 1892. It served the passenger trains of Norfolk Southern throughout the history of its passenger service in Raleigh, from 1908 to 1948. It was also used by the Southern Railway, and by Seaboard Air Line until that road built its own station in 1942. It served the Raleigh and Southport Railroad before that road was merged into the NS. (North Carolina Division of Archives and History)

Below: A view of the trackage leading to Raleigh Union Station (building to left of center). Tracks curving to the left are the Seaboard Air Line main tracks to Richmond and Portsmouth, VA. Tracks curving under the bridge at right are those of the Southern Railway (leased from the state-owned North Carolina Railroad) to Goldsboro, NC. NS tracks crossed both those roads at Boylan Tower, just behind and to the left of the photographer, and had trackage rights from there into the station. (Raymond Carneal photo, Marvin Black collection)

these lines, the N&S had increased its total track mileage to 608.

The first passenger trains to Raleigh used a temporary station which was built at Jones and Saunders Streets. It was not long before the N&S obtained trackage rights to operate out of Raleigh Union Station where connection could be made with trains of the Southern Railway and the Seaboard Air Line for points south.

Soon after this, the N&S completed another line between Pinetown, North Carolina, on the main line, and Bishop Cross, North Carolina, on the Belhaven Branch from Mackey's Ferry. This permitted trains to operate to Belhaven from Chocowinity, North Carolina. The latter town was the point where the line to New Bern left the Norfolk-Raleigh line, and quickly became an important operating center for the railroad, a status it retains today. Chocowinity is the name of a nearby creek, and is an Indian word meaning "fish from many waters."

In 1917, the station at Chocowinity was renamed Marsden in honor of the Chairman of the Board of the railroad, but the town retained its name.

Construction on this line was completed in time for several excursion trains to be operated to the state fair in Raleigh on October 17 and 18, 1907. These trains originated in New Bern, Plymouth, Greenville, and Wilson, giving citizens of those localities and intermediate points a chance to try out their new railroad while visiting the fair. Regular service began on October 24, 1907. With completion of

Eventually, around 1965, the station was renamed Chocowinity. It seems the U. S. Postal Service had a problem with mail addressed to "Norfolk Southern Railway, Marsden, North Carolina." Since there was no post office named Marsden, they often sent it to Marston, North Carolina and delivered it to the Seaboard Air Line, the only railroad in Marston. It would eventually get to the right place, but after considerable delay. Employees were not overjoyed by the change back to Chocowinity. When the name had to be spelled out, such as when reading train orders over the telephone, it took almost twice as long to spell Chocowinity as it had to spell Marsden. Perhaps this explains why it had been renamed Marsden earlier.

Above: Logging operations of the John L. Roper Lumber Company at Twenty-Mile Siding on the Norfolk and Southern Railroad. The John L. Roper Lumber Company was one of the largest lumber companies in the country when this photo was made about 1907. At the time, it was totally owned by the N&S. Twenty-Mile Siding was so named because it was twenty miles from Mackey's Ferry, the north end of the line of the Albemarle and Pantego Railroad, which became the N&S Belhaven Branch. The locomotive at the left is probably owned by the N&S. The lumber company had a sizeable fleet of locomotives in its own name, but most were smaller than this.
(Yale University College of Forestry collection)

The merger that formed the Norfolk and Southern Railway not only expanded the railroad business, but it also put the company into the lumber business in a big way. As we have noted before, the Virginia and Carolina Coast had bought all the stock of the John L. Roper Lumber Company, and had also bought several other lumber companies and merged them into the Roper Company. This created a huge operation including sixteen saw, planing, and shingle mills, roughly 150 miles of logging railroads, 23 locomotives, and 600,000 acres of timberlands, with timber rights on more than 200,000 additional acres. A very large and modern mill

Below: A John L. Roper Lumber Company train on its way to deliver logs to the company mill in New Bern about 1907. It appears this train is crossing the Norfolk and Southern bridge across the Neuse River, but it may be on a separate lumber company trestle across either the Neuse or Trent Rivers at New Bern.
(Yale University College of Forestry collection)

was under construction at New Bern, near the N&S tracks at the end of the Neuse River trestle. The Roper Company mills at Belhaven, at Roper, on the Belhaven Branch, and at Oriental, the end of the former PO&W, were also served by the rails of the N&S.

As we have also noted earlier, by this time John Roper's son George

ran the lumber business and sat on the N&S board of directors along with John Roper. Another son of John Roper, William B. Roper, was secretary and treasurer of the Roper Lumber Company. Apparently the Roper family had some differences with the other officers of the N&S, however, because by 1910 all the Ropers had severed their connections with both the railroad and the John L. Roper Lumber Company.

The lumber company remained a wholly owned subsidiary of the railroad until 1942, but the owners of the railroad became disenchanted with being lumber manufacturers because the business was no longer contributing much in the way of profit. By 1922, the company had sold all its sawmills. The John L. Roper Lumber Company then became a real estate holding company, still owning the timber lands, which were gradually sold off over the years.

At its formation, the Norfolk and Southern Railway was still a big steamboat operator, as the N&S Railroad had been. This business grew somewhat with the merger as the lines operated by the Virginia and Carolina Coast, most of which came from the Suffolk and Carolina, were operated by the new company. But by this time, the railroad owners were much more interested in rail operations. The company began to discontinue steamboat routes and sell off the boats. By the end of 1913, all the boats had been sold off except the tug *Lynnhaven*, which continued to move freight across Norfolk harbor until 1944.

Although the N&S sold all its boats and ceased water transport operations, this does not mean that shipping connections were no longer of any importance to the railroad. On the contrary, the railroad continued to connect with navigation companies on the rivers and sounds out of Elizabeth City, Edenton, Plymouth, Washington, New Bern, Beaufort, and Morehead City for many years. Also, shipping lines northward out of Norfolk were still very important connections. This remained the case until World War II, when most boats belonging to these lines were diverted to war-related transport. By the end of the war, little remained of the NS's water transport connections, and would never be

reestablished.

The NS Railway also took over the operation of the Atlantic Hotel at Morehead City at its formation. Prior to that time, the hotel, which was built in 1880, was operated by the Atlantic and North Carolina Company. The N&S continued to operate the Atlantic Hotel until it burned on April 15, 1933. During that time, it was one of the leading resort hotels in North Carolina. The NS made no attempt to rebuild it after the fire, but several years later the old wooden business car *Virginia* was permanently located near the Morehead City station and the old hotel site, and was made available to company officials for vacations.

With the completion of lines to Raleigh and New Bern, through passenger service between those cities and Norfolk was initiated. Train numbers 1 and 2 were the only through runs, and had separate sections for Raleigh and New Bern. The Raleigh runs required just over ten hours for the 243-mile trip. The New Bern sections took seven hours 20 minutes for the 171 mile runs.

A ferry trip on the *John W. Garrett* from Edenton to Mackey's Ferry was still part of this service. This trip still required one hour and 15 minutes for the nine-mile run, which reduced the overall average speed, but it did give the passengers time to enjoy a leisurely lunch in the dining room of the *Garrett* while admiring the view of the sound. The schedules of trains numbers 1 and 2 were set up so that the *Garrett* left Mackey's Ferry a few minutes after noon with number 2's northbound cars, carried them to Edenton, then dropped them off and picked up number 1's waiting cars to take them to Mackey's Ferry. Engines were not ferried, but fresh ones were made available to continue the runs as soon as the cars could be coupled up. The schedules of train numbers 1 and 2 were also coordinated with the schedules of Old Dominion Line steamships running between Norfolk and New York.

Railroad management had long recognized that the ferry operation in the middle of the through passenger runs was very undesirable. Plans were soon announced to replace it with a bridge across Albemarle Sound. Construction got under way quickly, but as usual, financial problems hampered progress.

The financial structure of the new N&S Railway was not strong enough to support the integration of all the new additions to the system, the purchase of new equipment required to operate them, and to undertake a construction project as big as the Albemarle Sound bridge. On top of that, a general

An early view of the Albemarle Sound bridge with McKeen car number 90 on it. Regular service over the bridge started on January 17, 1910. The McKeen car shown was used in North Carolina until 1914, after which it was used mainly on the unelectrified Currituck Branch in Virginia Beach. (Robert C. Reisweber collection)

financial panic hit in 1907. The N&S was forced into receivership on July 1, 1908. The company was reorganized, again becoming the Norfolk Southern Railroad Company, which took over operation on May 4, 1910.

The financial problems of the N&S slowed construction of the sound bridge, but did not halt it. When the road went into receivership, receivers Thomas Fitzgerald, Hugh M. Kerr, and Harry K. Walcott applied to federal Judge Waddill for one million dollars in receivers' certificates to complete construction. This was granted and construction resumed.

The bridge was finally completed and the first train was run across it on January 1, 1910. Regular operation across the bridge commenced on January 17, 1910. The Albemarle Sound bridge was one of the longest bridges in the world, extending for 26,668 feet in length, or just over five miles. More than 2000 cypress and pine bents were included in the trestle portions. A drawspan 152 feet in length permitted passage of large vessels through the sound, and a steel girder swing span 94 feet in length was provided for smaller vessels. There were also five fixed steel girder spans which, with the two drawspans, divided the wood trestle into eight sections separated by steel firebreaks. Rail used in the bridge was primarily 75-pound steel. The north end of the bridge was at Skinner's Point, about four miles southeast of Edenton. This point was later renamed Waddill in honor of the judge who made the completion possible. South end was at Mackey's Ferry, near the ferry terminal.

Completion of the sound bridge ended the usefulness of the *John W. Garrett* to the railroad, and it was sold to the Frisco Lines, which put it into service cross-

Ferry station and the Albemarle Sound bridge, to permit the ferries to reach their southern terminal on the creek.

As soon as the Albemarle Sound bridge was completed, the NS upgraded its passenger service. Train numbers 5 and 6, which had been afternoon accommodation trains between Norfolk and Edenton, became overnight trains between Norfolk and Raleigh and carried a Pullman sleeping car between those points. These trains also carried a Norfolk-New Bern-Goldsboro Pullman sleeper between Norfolk and Washington, where it was placed on a connecting train. Train numbers 1 and 2 continued to be the main day trains between Norfolk and New Bern, with the Chocowinity-Raleigh sections now being called trains numbers 11 and 12. A Pullman buffet parlor car was put into service between Norfolk and Raleigh on these runs. Train numbers 3 and 4 then

Above: An aerial view of Norfolk Terminal Station (Union Station) about 1920. The station head-house housed corporate offices of the NS from its construction in 1912 until 1961, when the rail-road was forced to move to Raleigh by news of the impending demolishment of the building. NS passenger service had left this station in 1940 because traffic was not sufficient to justify the fees charged. Note the three-masted schooner in the upper right of the photo. Today this area is the site of Harbor Park, the home of the Norfolk Tides of the International Baseball League. About the only recognizable feature of this photo which could be seen in an aerial view today is the Elizabeth River. Even the bridge across it has been removed and replaced by a new one farther downstream. The last train to use Terminal Station, Norfolk and Western train number 16-22, arrived at 6:55 AM on December 26, 1962. The building was demolished in February 1963.
(Norfolk Public Library)

Below: Norfolk Southern freight motor number 2 and passenger cars at Terminal Station. NS moved the Norfolk terminal for the electric division here in 1919 to avoid being assessed for street improvements in downtown Norfolk. The cars coupled to number 2 are probably New York to Virginia Beach cars which came in over the Norfolk and Western. These cars were usually pulled to the beach by the electric freight motors. (Tal Carey collection)

ing the Mississippi River. A ferry for highway vehicles continued to operate between Edenton and Mackey's Ferry until a highway bridge was built across the sound in the 1930s. This required the railroad to build a bridge with a swing span across Mackey's Creek (also known as Kendrick's Creek), between Mackey's

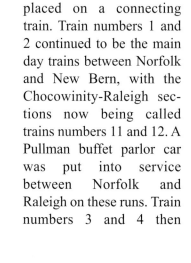

served as morning accommodation trains between Norfolk and Edenton.

A short time later, these schedules were adjusted somewhat. Train numbers 1 and 2, now known as the *Carolina Express*, ran between Norfolk and Raleigh, and trains numbers 11 and 12 became Chocowinity-New Bern connections. The parlor cars were then shifted to run between Norfolk and New Bern. Train numbers 3 and 4 were now the overnight Norfolk-Raleigh trains, called the *Midnight Expresses*, carrying the sleeper between those points. The Norfolk-New Bern-Goldsboro sleeper was then terminated at New Bern, with connecting coach service between New Bern and Goldsboro, and also between New Bern and Beaufort. Train numbers 5 and 6 once again became Norfolk-Edenton accommodation trains. All the branch lines also had passenger service, but many of these were mixed trains.

In 1911, the NS announced a major improvement in their passenger facilities in Norfolk. The company, together with the Norfolk and Western Railway and the Virginian Railway, formed the Norfolk Terminal Railway Company to build a new station in downtown Norfolk. This was officially named Norfolk Terminal Station, but was often called Union Station. When completed and opened on June 1, 1912, the new building not only provided modern facilities for the passenger trains of all three railroads, but also provided office space for the corporate offices of the NS and the Virginian. When first opened, the station served only the steam passenger trains of the NS, but as we mentioned earlier, the railroad shifted electric operations to Union Station in 1919 to avoid assessment for street improvements to City Hall and Monticello Avenues.

A few years before this, in 1908, the NS had obtained trackage rights over the Virginian Railway from its crossing with the steam main line at Carolina Junction, three miles south of Berkley, to its crossing of the Virginia Beach South Route at Tidewater Junction. This provided a much shorter route into the new Union

Soon after the Virginian Railway was built into Norfolk in 1907, Norfolk Southern obtained trackage rights over the Virginian from Carolina Junction to Tidewater Junction, shortening the NS route to the N&W Norfolk station and later to Terminal Station. Here Ten-Wheeler number 111 is pulling passenger train number 2 on Virginian rails at the approaches to Tidewater Junction in April 1933. The train has just crossed the East Branch of the Elizabeth River. The fireman in the cab is believed to be Arthur "Bones" Askew, well remembered by long-time former employees of the railroad. (Harold Vollrath collection)

Aerial view of Carolina Yard and shops about 1938. The main line northward to Berkley leaves the scene at the upper left. The south-bound main line to Raleigh and Charlotte runs out of the upper right edge of the photo. The turntable can be seen near the center of the scene. Above and to its left is the locomotive servicing area with coal loading conveyor, sand house, and low locomotive water tank. The tall tank to the right of this area serves the entire shop complex. The large building at center of the right edge of the photo is the locomotive shop. The Mechanical Department office building is the two-story building just below the turntable. The building with flat roof at the lower right corner was used to house the office car Virginia. (Aubrey Wiley collection)

Station than the branch from Providence Junction to Euclid, which had been used to reach downtown Norfolk before the Virginian was built.

At the same time, the NS also moved to expand its freight facilities in the Norfolk area. The company purchased a sizeable tract of land near Carolina Junction and began construction of a new yard and shop area. The Berkley yards and shops were becoming too small, and there was little room for expansion. The new tract had plenty of room for current yard and shop needs and for the foreseeable future. In fact, there was so much room that the railroad rented some of the land to its employees for nominal sums of five dollars per year each to grow crops. A few years later, the railroad

discontinued collection of the rent money, but since the railroad's need for land never matched the amount available, employees continued to be permitted to farm the excess land until the end of the NS as an independent company in 1974.

Another important construction project was begun in 1911. This was a large new brick passenger station and office building at New Bern. This building was used jointly as a passenger station by the NS and the Atlantic Coast Line, and also housed the offices of the superintendents of the NS Beaufort, Pamlico, and Raleigh Divisions. In later years, when operations were consolidated, the general superintendent of the entire railroad maintained an office in the building for several years.

In addition to all the expansions already described in this chapter, the NS in this time period became sole owner of two other railroads, but these were always operated separately from the NS proper. One was the Kinston Carolina Railroad, which ran southward out of Kinston, North Carolina, east of Goldsboro on the

Above: An early view of the New Bern station, built by the Norfolk Southern in 1911. NS 4-4-0 number 51 is headed southeastward for Morehead City at the left, with trackage from Goldsboro and Norfolk behind it. An Atlantic Coast Line locomotive at the right is headed southwest toward Wilmington. Ownership of this station was turned over to the Atlantic and North Carolina Railroad when the NS lease ended in 1935, and it became the corporate headquarters of the A&NC. NS passenger trains continued to use the station until the end of New Bern service, and the NS general superintendent's office remained there until 1938. The building still exists but is currently vacant. Efforts are under way in New Bern to preserve it.
(Special Collections Library, Duke University)

Below: Locomotive number 5 of the Kinston and Carolina Railroad was built by Lima Locomotive Works in 1905. That railroad was purchased by the John L. Roper Lumber Company in 1909, thereby coming under the ownership of the N&S, but its operations were always independent of the NS proper. Its main track ran south out of Kinston to Pink Hill and Beulaville. It was abandoned in 1929. Locomotive number 5 had 40 inch drivers and 12 inch by 18 inch cylinders.
(Railroad Museum of Pennsylvania, PHMC)

former A&NC, to Beulaville, about 31 miles. This had been built as a narrow-gauge logging road by the Gay Lumber Company, the former owner of the Suffolk and Carolina, but by 1909 the line had been converted to standard gauge. In that year, it was bought by the John L. Roper Lumber Company, which as we know was then wholly owned by the N&S. The Kinston Carolina Railroad was abandoned in 1929.

The other subsidiary was the Carolina Railroad. This was also a logging road, and operated north out of Kinston 13 miles to Snow Hill, North Carolina. It was bought by the NS in 1912 and operated under common management with the Kinston Carolina. This road hung on a little longer than the KC, finally being abandoned in 1931.

Looking back over this chapter, we see that the years from 1904 to 1911 were very momentous for the Norfolk Southern Railroad. It had almost sextupled its track mileage, begun first class passenger service, added many cities and towns to the list it served, upgraded several important facilities, and completed the biggest single construction project in its history, the Albemarle Sound bridge. But the owners of the railroad didn't even pause to catch their breath at this point, as we will see in the next chapter.

Above: Ten Wheeler number 7 of the Raleigh and Southport at an unknown date and location. When the R&S became part of the Norfolk Southern in 1911, number 7 became number 88 of the NS. It had been built by Baldwin in 1907, and was retired in 1932.
(W. R. Newton collection)

Opposite page: Fayetteville, NC was the south end of the Raleigh and Southport main line, and became the end of a Norfolk Southern branch after that road purchased the R&S. The R&S had exercised trackage rights over the Atlantic Coast Line's Sanford Branch, which formerly had been part of the Cape Fear and Yadkin Valley Railroad's main line, to get to downtown Fayetteville. NS continued to use these trackage rights, as the train in the photo is doing on July 21, 1973. It is crossing the Richmond-Jacksonville main line of the former ACL, by this time the Seaboard Coast Line, at AY tower.
(Robert Graham)

Chapter 4

On to Charlotte

Early in 1911, Attorney W. L. Mann of Albemarle, North Carolina (a small city near Charlotte, not to be confused with the Albemarle region of the state around Elizabeth City and Edenton) was studying a railroad map of his state. He noted that there was no direct rail route from Raleigh, the capital, to Charlotte, the state's largest city and a rapidly expanding center of commerce. A straight line between the two cities was about 130 miles long. The two existing rail routes, the Southern Railway via Greensboro and the Seaboard Air Line via Hamlet, were both more than 170 miles long. Mr. Mann reasoned that a new railroad closely following the straight line would be able to attract considerable through traffic away from the existing routes. It certainly did not escape Mr. Mann's attention that the straight line passed within a couple of miles of his hometown of Albemarle.

Mr. Mann discussed his idea with several of his friends, and found enthusiastic support for building such a road. Unfortunately, they were far short of having sufficient capital to build a road of that length. Mr. Mann and his friends then decided to alter their proposed route somewhat so that it would pass through the established towns of Pittsboro, Siler City, Ramseur, and Asheboro. They then visited these towns to solicit financial support. They were successful in this, and so they applied to the state legislature for a charter for their road, which they called Raleigh, Charlotte,

and Southern Railroad. This was granted on May 7, 1911.

With charter in hand, the group called a meeting to be held in Greensboro on July 28, 1911 for the purpose of organizing the company. Most of the shareholders assembled at that time, and were greeted by another man who was not a shareholder. This was Mr. E. Carl Duncan of Raleigh. Mr. Duncan proposed to the group that if they wanted the road to be built quickly, they should sell him the charter and let him and his associates build the road. It is not clear whether he told the group who his associates were, but before long it became common knowledge that they were the owners of the Norfolk Southern Railroad. Mr. Duncan had become associated with the NS through the lease of the A&NC Railroad, as he was one of the private stockholders and directors of that company. Whether they realized this or not, the RC&S stockholders agreed to Mr. Duncan's proposal, so the NS became the owner of the chartered right to extend its line from Raleigh to

Charlotte.

Not much happened to the proposed line for the next few months, but on Saturday, November 18, 1911, the *Raleigh News and Observer* devoted much of its issue to an important announcement. It was that the "big and rich" Norfolk Southern had bought the Raleigh and Southport Railroad and the Durham and Charlotte Railroad. An editorial called the news of the purchase "the biggest thing yet for Raleigh" and "the best announcement that a Raleigh newspaper has made for Raleigh and railroad development in a decade." It was obvious to all that the two roads purchased were to be used for part of the route to Charlotte.

The Raleigh and Southport Railroad had been started as the Raleigh and Cape Fear Railroad. As both names implied, it was intended to extend from Raleigh to Southport, North Carolina, located near the mouth of the Cape Fear River, which is the southernmost port town in the state. The railroad never made it there, however, as its southern end was at Fayetteville, also on the Cape Fear River about 100 miles upstream from Southport.

Since Fayetteville was at the head of navigation on the river, it developed early as a port and center of commerce. Attempts had been made to build a railroad from Fayetteville to Raleigh as early as 1833, but none had been successful until the Raleigh and Southport arrived in Fayetteville in 1906. By that time, however, Fayetteville was an important station on the Atlantic Coast Line main line from Richmond to Florida. Throughout the late 18th and early 19th centuries, Fayetteville, which had been named for the Marquis de Lafayette in 1783, vied with New Bern for the honors of being the state's largest city and its capital. By 1906, both those cities had lost both honors to Charlotte and Raleigh, respectively, and both Fayetteville and Southport were surpassed as port cities by Wilmington, about halfway between them. Fayetteville continued to grow and prosper as a center of commerce, however.

The R&S had been built largely through the efforts of Mr. John A. Mills, a lumberman of Raleigh, mainly to serve his lumber company. It was a common carrier, however, and was a reasonably successful one. Only two weeks before the announcement of its sale to the NS, the *News and Observer* speculated that Mr. Mills planned to buy the Durham and Charlotte road himself and connect it to the R&S. It also predicted that he would connect his lines to the Elkin and Allegheny Railroad, which he was building in the northwest part of the state. Then it anticipated that he would build into Virginia to connect with the Norfolk and Western. Of

REMOVING AND LOADING COAL into railroad cars at Egypt Coal Mine, Cumnock.

The coal mine at Egypt, NC. This mine was owned at one time by Samuel Henszey, who built the Egypt Railway to serve it in 1890. It came under Norfolk Southern ownership in 1911 along with John Lennig's Sanford and Troy Railroad, which had taken over the Egypt Railway. The coal produced by this mine was of very poor quality with high clay content. NS logically tried to burn this readily available coal in its steam locomotives, but soon gave this up in favor of importing better quality coal from offline. The mine finally closed in 1928. (S. David Carriker collection)

course, the NS purchase of the R&S ended this speculation. The Elkin and Allegheny did not turn out to be a very successful line and was abandoned in the 1930s.

The Durham and Charlotte Railroad obviously was intended to connect the two cities of its name. If it had fulfilled this objective, it would have provided all but twenty miles of a route from Raleigh to Charlotte, which the RC&S was trying to complete. Unfortunately, by November 1911, the D&C was far short of either planned end point. It then ran from Colon, NC, 40 miles southwest of Raleigh, to Troy, NC, about 60 miles east of Charlotte. The D&C was a finan-

cially shaky road, even by NS standards, and the chances of its completing its expansion plan on its own were not very bright. The eight-mile line from Colon to Cumnock was technically a separate railroad, the Sanford and Troy Railroad, but was owned by the owners of the D&C and was operated as part of that road. (Sanford is a few miles from Colon)

Although it seems hard to believe today, predecessor companies of the D&C and the S&T had once engaged in a railroad war to see which would get the business of shipping coal out of the North Carolina coalfields in the vicinity of the Deep River. The S&T was successor to the Egypt Railway, which had been begun by Samuel Henszey and associates in 1890. Henszey owned a coal mine at Egypt, which was then a small town adjacent to Cumnock but is now nearly deserted. The mine had been served by the Western Railroad, which later became the Cape Fear and Yadkin Valley Railroad, since 1861. Apparently Henszey was dissatisfied with the rates he had to pay the CF&YV to ship the coal, and formed the Egypt Railway to connect with the Raleigh and Augusta Air-Line Railroad, which would later become the Seaboard Air Line, at Colon, NC, eight miles from Egypt. Henszey's railway also connected with the CF&YV at Egypt, so he could force the CF&YV and the RAA-L to compete with each other for his business.

In 1891, a year after the Egypt Railway was chartered, John Lennig of Philadelphia and associates chartered the Glendon and Gulf Mining and Manufacturing Company. This company planned to build a railroad between the two towns of its name, and as the name implied, to engage in mining and manufacturing activities as well. Gulf, the proposed eastern end of the railroad, is about three miles west of Cumnock (or Egypt), and was on the main line of the Cape Fear and Yadkin Valley Railroad. This portion of the CF&YVRR later became the Atlantic and Yadkin Railroad, a Southern Railway subsidiary. The Glendon and Gulf proposed to make a connection at Gulf to ship out coal from mines to be established near Glendon.

As soon as Samuel Henszey of the Egypt Railway heard of the plans of the Glendon and Gulf, he announced formation of the Raleigh and Western Railway, ostensibly to extend the Egypt Railway to Asheboro. He immediately began to build the extension, but his real purpose became clear when he went out of his way to locate the new line across the path of the Glendon and Gulf, and began laying track not at the end of existing track at Egypt, but just west of Gulf, where the G&G would have to go to reach the CF&YV. He then took Lennig and the Glendon and Gulf to court in an attempt to block them from crossing his new line. The courts sided with the G&G, however, and that road was permitted to build into Gulf.

Work stopped on the Asheboro extension of the Raleigh and Western after this, but the R&W did continue to operate the Egypt Railway and the Egypt coal mine for several years. The operation was a money-loser, however. As an example, the financial statement for the year ending June 30, 1901 showed gross earnings of $2,277, but a net deficit of $9,598. By 1908, the accumulated deficit had reached $112,042 and operation was suspended. By this time, John Lennig had changed the name of the Glendon and Gulf to Durham and Charlotte Railroad, and announced plans to extend it to those cities. In 1909, he formed the Sanford and

Troy Railroad to buy out his old rival Henszey's Raleigh and Western.

The Sanford and Troy was extended from Egypt to Gulf along the right-of-way of the Raleigh and Western which had never had rails laid on it. The Durham and Charlotte had been extended from Glendon to Troy, about thirty miles on its way to Charlotte, by this time. Mr. Lennig also planned to extend his line from Colon to Sanford, a growing town where a connection could be made with the Atlantic Coast Line. This would have made the name Sanford and Troy accurate, but that extension was never built. The S&T became part of the NS along with the D&C.

Above: An early view of Aberdeen and Asheboro 4-6-0 number 10 at the company shops in Biscoe. Number 10 later became number 85 of the Norfolk Southern, and was sold to the Bennetsville and Cheraw Railroad in 1923.
(S. David Carriker collection)

Left: Aberdeen and Asheboro 4-4-0 number 4, shown at an unknown date and place. Information is contradictory on the history of this locomotive but apparently it was built for the Aberdeen and West End Railroad, a predecessor of the A&A, by Richmond Locomotive Works in 1895, and later became Norfolk Southern third number 18, then was scrapped in 1925.
(D. P. McDonald collection)

Aberdeen and Asheboro 4-4-0 number 8 at Pinehurst, NC about 1900. This locomotive was built by Richmond Locomotive Works in 1898, but apparently it never entered the roster of the Norfolk Southern.
(Harold K. Vollrath collection)

The Sanford and Troy acquired the coal mine at Egypt along with the Raleigh and Western, and passed it along to the NS. It was only natural for the NS to use coal from its own mine in its steam locomotives, but eventually it decided that this coal was of such poor quality that it was better to bring in coal from off-line. It hardly needs to be said that other customers had little use for this coal either. Today, the only visible evidence that coal was ever mined in this region is a highway historical marker near Cumnock.

The Norfolk Southern Annual Report for 1943 reported that a state survey had estimated that 38 million tons of coal were still available in the area, and optimistically stated that "if the drilling confirms the estimate of the amount of coal available, it should result in considerable industrial activity . . . , and this devel-

A view of Steeds depot on the Asheboro and Montgomery Railroad, which became the northern end of the Aberdeen and Asheboro Railroad. A&A 2-6-0 number 3, shown by the depot, was disposed of before the NS took over the A&A.
(Joe D. Steed collection)

opment should be of great benefit to your company." Don't expect to see unit coal trains rolling out of this area any time soon, however. The Carolina Power and Light Company power plant at Brickhaven, only a few miles from these coal fields, still imports coal from out of state, demonstrating the undesirability of burning coal from this region.

By the time of its merger into the NS, the Durham and Charlotte was making money, but not much. For its last year, gross earnings were $46,693, and net earnings were $4,159. Obviously, nobody was likely to get rich hauling coal from the North Carolina mines.

Just one day after the *Raleigh News and Observer* announced the purchase of the Raleigh and Southport and the Durham and Charlotte by the NS, it had another front page announcement. The NS had also bought the Aberdeen and Asheboro Railroad. This line had been started as a logging road called the Aberdeen and West End Railroad by the Page family of Aberdeen, NC, and first extended 2 fi miles northwestward into the woods out of Aberdeen. By 1911, this had grown into a common carrier railroad with main line from Aberdeen to Asheboro, and branches to Mount Gilead, Jackson Springs, Ellerbe, and Carthage.

The A&A was the biggest and most successful of the new roads purchased by the NS. It had a good freight business, mainly in forest and agricultural products. In particular, the Ellerbe Branch served a big peach-growing region which provided considerable revenue for the railroad. Unlike the other new roads, the A&A had a significant passenger business. For its last full year, receipts from passenger traffic were almost $50,000, more than the combined passenger and freight

Asheboro, NC was the north end of the Aberdeen and Asheboro Railroad, and continued to be served by the Norfolk Southern after its takeover of the A&A. A 500 class 2-8-0 is shown here on trackage in Asheboro. (Marvin Black collection)

income of the Durham and Charlotte. Much of this was due to the tourist trade to such destinations as Pinehurst and Jackson Springs.

Pinehurst was then, as now, a major golfing center and the A&A, in conjunction with the Seaboard Air Line, operated regular Pullman service direct from New York to Pinehurst. This business continued to furnish revenue to the NS until World War II. In 1929, Seaboard inaugurated an all-Pullman train, the "Carolina Golfer," exclusively for Pinehurst service, the last six miles operating over the NS. Unfortunately, this was a most inopportune time to start a new luxury vacation train, and it lasted only until the following spring. In subsequent years, the Pinehurst Pullmans were hauled to Aberdeen in Seaboard's Florida trains, then turned over to the NS.

There was some question at the time as to Norfolk Southern's intent in purchasing the A&A. Its main line was more or less perpendicular to the Durham and Charlotte's line, which it crossed at Star, NC. And neither Aberdeen nor Asheboro was any closer to Charlotte than Troy was. *The Raleigh News and Observer* speculated that the NS would probably extend the A&A main line from Asheboro to High Point and Winston-Salem. But in fact it seems that the NS mostly wanted the last thirteen miles of the A&A's Mount Gilead Branch, which would become an extension of the D&C line from Troy to Mount Gilead. A connection already existed between the roads at Troy. The first nine miles of the branch from Biscoe to Troy were of no use to the NS and this portion was abandoned.

The Aberdeen and Asheboro built a four-mile branch line from West End, NC to Jackson Springs, a resort town, in 1900. Technically, it was originally a separate company called the Jackson Springs Railroad, but it was soon merged into the A&A. The Jackson Springs depot is at the distant right in this view. Norfolk Southern abandoned this line in 1938 because the resort was no longer generating much rail traffic, but the depot is still in existence. (Williams photo, S. David Carriker collection)

The NS merged the railroads it purchased in November 1911, into the Raleigh, Charlotte, and Southern as a first step in fulfilling the charter of that road. This left three gaps for the RC&S to close in order to create a complete line from Raleigh to Charlotte. The first of these was at Raleigh. Both the NS and the Raleigh and Southport ran passenger trains to and from Raleigh Union Station, but both got there by trackage rights, NS from the north (over the Seaboard Air Line) and R&S from the south (over Southern Railway). The gap was closed by construction of a new line. This was only about two miles long, but was expensive construction as it passed through the heart of downtown Raleigh. Several highway overpasses and underpasses had to be built to avoid having grade crossings disrupt downtown auto traffic. A crossing of the busy joint trackage of the Southern Railway and Seaboard Air Line at what became Boylan Tower was also necessary.

The second gap was between Varina on the Raleigh and Southport main line and the end of Sanford and Troy track at Colon, 22 miles. This line was completed by June 22, 1913, at which time a special train carrying Mr. E. Carl Duncan made the first run from Mount Gilead to Raleigh. Regular service between these two points began on July 1, 1913. After this, the former R&S main line from Varina to Fayetteville became a branch.

The final segment of new track needed was by far the longest, 53 miles from Mount Gilead to Charlotte. This construction took considerable time, and service was gradually extended to various intermediate points. On October 1, 1913, for example, the first train ran into Aquadale, a new town which served as a station for Rocky River Springs, site of a small resort hotel.

Finally, by early November 1913, the line was completed. The first train left the Charlotte station site for Raleigh the morning of Saturday, November 15, 1913. The station building itself had not yet been completed. This train was a special inspection train for company officials, including President C. H. Hix and Chairman of the Board Marsden J. Perry. Regular service began on December 1, 1913, with Raleigh newspapermen riding the first train to Charlotte, and at the same time Charlotte newspapermen riding the first train to Raleigh.

Opening of the road to Charlotte was greeted with enthusiasm in most quarters, but not all. In particular, the residents of Pittsboro, Siler City, Ramseur, and Albemarle were disappointed by the fact that the new line bypassed their towns. The people of Asheboro were also unhappy that their town was not on the main line, but at least the former A&A main line to Asheboro was still an active branch. No doubt the original shareholders of the Raleigh, Charlotte, and Southern kicked themselves often for selling the charter to Mr. Duncan instead of building the road themselves along its first projected route through their home towns.

A special passenger train is arriving at Pinehurst, pulled by Aberdeen and Asheboro 4-6-0 number 32 and an unidentified additional locomotive. This photo gives an indication of the substantial amount of passenger traffic Pinehurst generated for the A&A, and later for the NS. A&A number 32 was formerly number 10, and later became number 85 of the NS.
(S. David Carriker collection)

The citizens of Concord, North Carolina were also unhappy as they had pushed hard to have the proposed line between Albemarle and Charlotte routed through their city. Concord was on the Southern Railway main line, but residents probably thought they would get better shipping rates if there were a competing line. But Concord was not close to a direct line between Mount Gilead and Charlotte, so the NS was not interested in going through there.

First passenger schedules between Raleigh and Charlotte featured through trains numbers 30 and 31, which left early in the morning and arrived about six and one-half hours later, making six stops along the way. This gave an average speed of only about 25 miles

Opposite top: A Norfolk Southern passenger train at the Pinehurst station, October 1916. Pinehurst was already an important golfing resort by the time the Norfolk Southern took over the Aberdeen and Asheboro in 1911. This brought the railroad considerable passenger business. NS Ten-Wheeler number 91, shown in the photo, was no stranger to the area, having been on the A&A roster as number 33. Prior to that, it had been number 57 of the Buffalo, Pittsburgh, and Western, built by Baldwin in 1883. (Harold K. Vollrath collection)

Opposite bottom: A view of the construction of the Norfolk Southern line through Raleigh connecting to the Raleigh and Southport. The view looks south toward Varina and Charlotte from approximately the location of the future Boylan interlocking tower. The two tracks already in place are the Southern Railway and Seaboard Air Line main lines. The near track was owned by the Seaboard, and runs from Richmond, to the left, to Hamlet, to the right. The far track was owned by the North Carolina Railroad and leased to the Southern, running from Goldsboro, to the left, to Greensboro, to the right. The two tracks have been operated jointly as double track by both railroads for many years. (North Carolina Division of Archives and History)

Below: This photo shows how the crossing at Boylan looked after completion of the NS line through the area. The interlocking tower is in the center of the photo. The NS main line northward curves to the left into the background under Boylan Avenue. The three tracks crossing the photo from left to right in front of the tower are, from front to back: a Southern Railway siding, the Southern Railway main track, used jointly with Seaboard Air Line as the northbound track, and the Seaboard Air Line main track, the joint SAL-SR southbound main. The curved track from the foreground to the right side of the photo is the Norfolk Southern connection to Raleigh Union Station, out of the photo to the right. (John W. Barriger III photo, Barriger Railroad Collection, St. Louis Mercantile Library)

One of the biggest obstacles to the completion of the Norfolk Southern extension to Charlotte was crossing the Pee Dee River at Hydro, NC. Here the construction crew proudly poses on the bridge as construction is completed. Locomotive is NS 4-4-0 number 41.
(S. David Carriker collection)

an hour, but this was still a little better than the best times available via the longer Southern Railway or Seaboard Air Line routes between Raleigh and Charlotte. There were also accommodation trains between Charlotte and Star, and between Raleigh and Star, but these were scheduled mainly to be connections for Aberdeen and Asheboro trains at Star, and did not make convenient connections with each other for through travel.

Train number 31 made excellent connections with number 3, the Midnight Express, from Norfolk, so that travelers could board a Norfolk-to-Raleigh Pullman at 8:30 P.M., change trains in Raleigh at 7:15 the next morning, and be in Charlotte by 2:00 P.M. Charlotte-to-Norfolk passengers were not so well off. They left Charlotte on number 30 at 7:25 A.M. and arrived at Raleigh at 2:00 P.M., but then had to wait until 9:30 P.M. for the Midnight Express, train number 4, for Norfolk, arriving there more than 24 hours after leaving Charlotte. Train number 18 left Raleigh for the north soon after number 30 arrived, but went only as far as Washington.

Newspaper articles discussing the new schedules suggested that they were slow because the roadbed was new, and would probably soon be speeded up, and also that more through trains were expected to be added shortly. This turned out to be grossly overoptimistic. The reality was that business was disappointing, and before long numbers 30 and 31 were the only passenger

trains on the line. They then had to stop at all 29 intermediate stations between Charlotte and Raleigh, so that schedules were slowed down rather than speeded up. Although the straight line distance Mr. Mann had seen on his map was forty miles shorter than the SR and SAL routes, the line as actually built was only twenty miles shorter. This was not enough of a saving to divert much traffic from the other routes. This applied to freight traffic as well as to passenger traffic.

Although the NS never scheduled a through passenger train between Norfolk and Charlotte, it did schedule through freight trains between those points. (A hog can ride between Charlotte and Norfolk without changing cars, but you can't?). Train numbers 63 and 64 were the chief through freight trains covering the entire main line for most of the history of the railroad. There were also switchers which worked at the bigger towns along the way, and several local freights covering parts of the main line. Of course, each branch line also had freight service, usually provided by a mixed train in the teens and twenties. Additional information on freight operations will be found in Chapter 10.

Completion of the line to Raleigh fulfilled the objective of the Raleigh, Charlotte, and Southern, so on January 1, 1914, that company was absorbed into the Norfolk Southern Railroad Company.

Even before this happened, there was considerable speculation that expansion of the NS would continue. On Saturday, October 19, 1912, Dow Jones and

Company, publishers of the *Wall Street Journal*, released a news bulletin which stated:

"Recent entrance of such representative men as W. E. Corey, R. R. Colgate, F. A. Vanderlip, Joseph W. Harriman, A. W. Krech and R. H. Swartwout, to the board of the Norfolk Southern Railway promises not only the strongest kind of financial backing for this new southern property, but forecasts from now on an aggressive policy of extension and development.

"Within the past year the company through purchase of several small railroads has extended its lines further south, and it is not improbable that before long further extensions will be made either through acquisition of existing lines or construction of new ones. Eventually it is expected the Norfolk Southern will reach out into Georgia, Alabama and Florida and become an active competitor with the Coast Line, Seaboard and Southern railways for the east coast and Panama business.

"Norfolk Southern's traffic for the past five years has been increasing in larger proportion that that of any of the other established lines. In 1912, gross earnings per mile of line increased $543, or in excess of 11% over 1911, while Southern Railway's per mile gross increased only 5.2%, the Coast Line's only 6%, and the Seaboard's 5.2%. In five years from 1908 to 1912, inclusive, Norfolk Southern's gross, per mile, has

increased 50.5%, that of the Southern Railway 27.6%, Seaboard 25.7% and Coast Line 25%. A summary of these increases in 1912 over 1911 and in 1912 over 1908 show as follows:

	1912	1911	Inc .	%Inc.
Norfolk Southern	$5,412	$4,869	$543	11.10%
Southern	9,020	8,574	446	5.20%
Coast Line	7,452	7,030	422	6.00%
Seaboard	7,547	7,172	375	5.20%

	1912	1908	Inc.	%Inc.
Southern	9,020	7,069	1951	27.60%
Norfolk Southern	5,412	3,596	1816	50.50%
Seaboard	7,547	6,004	1543	25.70%
Coast Line	7,452	5,963	1489	25.00%

"At this rate of increase it is only a question of a few years until Norfolk Southern's total gross per mile of line reaches a volume which will compare favorably with that of the old established lines. It is now some $2,000 per mile under the Coast Line's and Seaboard's, but its increase per mile last year was $121 larger than the Coast Line's; $168 larger than the Seaboard's; and $97 per mile larger than the Southern Railway's."

Unfortunately, these predictions were inaccurate. The NS never caught up with the other systems named in gross per mile of line, and in fact its percentage growth soon fell behind that of the others. This will be quantified in the following chapter. And the NS never came close to Georgia, Alabama, or Florida. The days of major extensions were now over.

The first Norfolk Southern passenger train to leave Charlotte for Raleigh is ready to depart on the morning of November 15, 1913. The locomotive cannot be positively identified, but appears to be 4-4-0 number 32. This is an inspection train for company officials, including President C. H. Hix and Chairman of the Board Marsden J. Perry. The first public passenger train left Charlotte on the morning of December 1, 1913. The location is at Sixth and A Streets near the center of Charlotte. The steeple of Charlotte City Hall shows in the background. NS had built a building intended to be a freight depot at this site, but delayed building a passenger depot because a new Charlotte Union Station had been proposed, which would serve the NS as well as the Southern Railway, the Seaboard Air Line, and the Piedmont and Northern. A temporary ticket office was opened in the freight depot to serve the first passengers. Nothing came of the Union Station idea, so NS expanded the freight depot into a combination passenger and freight depot. (CharlotteObserver)

Above: Fort Story at Cape Henry did not provide a large volume of traffic for the NS, but it did result in some unusual shipments, starting in 1915 when the fort was established. Here a 16-inch railway gun which had come in over the NS is shown at the fort about 1942. Its purpose was to protect the entrance of Chesapeake Bay during World War II. The NS had also brought in guns for this purpose in the early days of World War I, although not as large as this one.
(U. S. Army Transportation Museum, Fort Eustis, VA.)

Opposite page: Lease of the Durham and South Carolina Railroad gave Norfolk Southern access to the important manufacturing city of Durham, NC. The most important business for the NS was provided by the American Tobacco Company plant, shown here in April 1937. Close examination of the photo will show the old NS scroll herald on some of the boxcars.
(John W. Barriger III photo, Barriger Railroad Collection, St. Louis Mercantile Library)

Chapter 5

Boom (?) And Bust (!)

With the assimilation of the Raleigh, Charlotte, and Southern into the parent Norfolk Southern, the company ended its active pursuit of southward expansion. It is likely that, in their more optimistic moments, the owners continued to dream of building on to Atlanta, Charleston, Wilmington, or Knoxville, or perhaps all of them. But as they examined the reality of the somewhat disappointing traffic statistics, these dreams must have seemed unattainable.

Operations changed little in the years 1914-1917. On December 28, 1917, operations were taken over by the federal government, along with the country's other railroads. This lasted until March 1, 1920. The effects of government control were largely financial, as the government was more interested in keeping trains running at all costs to move war material than in producing a profit for stockholders. Operating revenues rose steadily, but operating expenses rose much more rapidly, so that the company operated at a deficit of more than half a million dollars in 1920.

The World War I era did result in some new trackage being added to the NS to aid in the war effort. Shortly before the war began, the Commonwealth of Virginia had built a rifle range for training of national guardsmen at a location about one mile south of the old

Princess Anne Hotel site in Virginia Beach. The NS built a spur to this location, which later became known as Camp Pendleton. NS continued to operate special trains on the spur for guardsmen traveling to the camp until the track was removed, along with the oceanfront trackage, in 1950. Also just before World War I, Fort Story was opened at Cape Henry on the North Beach Route. NS built tracks into the Fort, and obtained some business in supplying and staffing it. The supplies brought in included some of the heaviest loads ever carried by the NS in the form of sixteen inch coast artillery guns to protect the entrance to Hampton Roads harbor.

On May 27, 1920, Norfolk Southern leased the Durham and South Carolina Railroad. This road should not be confused with the Durham and Southern Railroad, another short line which ran out of Durham parallel to the D&SC, and eventually became part of what is now CSX Transportation. The D&SC, like so many of the NS predecessors, had its origin as a logging road, and was owned by the Chatham Lumber Company. It had been opened from Durham to a connection with the Seaboard Air Line at Bonsal, NC, in 1905.

Just before the NS bought the Raleigh and Southport Railroad, the D&SC had announced plans to build a line to Rawls, North Carolina, south of Fuquay Springs, to connect with the R&S. This fueled speculation that the NS would buy the D&SC as well as the R&S, but this did not occur at that time. The NS eventually did buy the line, but not until 1957, after leasing it for almost forty years.

The D&SC continued with its proposed extension after the NS took over

the R&S, but before it could be completed, the NS line between Varina and Colon was finished. So, instead of crossing the NS and building on to Rawls, a connection was made where the D&SC extension met the new NS line. This spot was called Duncan, honoring both Julius A. Duncan, General Manager of the D&SC, and E. Carl Duncan, who as we know was the driving force behind the development of the NS Charlotte extension. Apparently, the two Duncans were not related.

Addition of the leased D&SC line to the NS system increased the route mileage operated by the NS

Above: A view of the New Holland, Higginsport, and Mount Vernon Railroad, probably at New Holland in the 1920s. Locomotive number 32, a 2-6-2, had been obtained from the John L. Roper Lumber Company. It had been built as number 32 of that company by Baldwin in 1914 (Serial number 41292). The small locomotive on the flat car is an 0-4-4T which cannot be identified, but is probably another ex-John L. Roper Lumber Company engine, as they had several similar to this. The Roper Company had extensive logging operations in the area served by the NHH&MtV, but these were winding down by that time, so the locomotive is probably being shipped to a new owner or to scrap. (Philip P. Coulter, Sr. photo, Philip P. Coulter, Jr. collection)

Above left: A view of NHH&MtV 2-6-2 number 32, probably at New Holland in the 1920s. The man on the running board is not identified. (Philip P. Coulter, Sr. photo, Philip P. Coulter, Jr. collection)

Below left: This railbus provided passenger service for the New Holland, Higginsport, and Mount Vernon Railroad. This photo is probably at New Holland in the 1920s. As you would guess, the road's passenger traffic was not large. What passengers there were could transfer to Norfolk Southern trains at Wenona, a small station on the former Albemarle and Pantego Railroad fifteen miles south of Mackeys. (Philip P. Coulter, Sr. photo, Philip P. Coulter, Jr. collection)

to 942, the highest it ever attained. It also provided the NS with important new business, as Durham was one of the leading manufacturing cities in the state. The American Tobacco Company was a particularly valuable customer.

In 1920, when the NS leased the D&SC, Ernest Williams of Lynchburg, VA, president of the D&SC, joined the NS board of directors. In 1925, he replaced Marsden J. Perry as chairman of that board. Since

Williams had been closely associated with the Duke family tobacco interests while he led the D&SC, this led to speculation that the NS would merge with the railroads controlled by the Dukes, including the Durham and Southern, the Piedmont and Northern, and the Georgia and Florida. This never happened, however.

In 1920 an agreement was reached with Southern Railway for the establishment of through rates and divisions via Charlotte. This was of great value to the NS as it could now solicit overhead traffic in the north and northeast, and in the territory south of

Charlotte.

Also in 1920, construction was begun on the New Holland, Higginbotham, and Mount Vernon Railroad Company from New Holland, North Carolina, to a connection with the NS at Wenona, North Carolina, a small town on the Mackey's Ferry-Belhaven Branch. (The name Higginbotham was soon changed to Higginsport.) This 34-mile line never became a part of the NS, but was considered by NS management to be of sufficient importance that its inception was noted in the NS 1920 Annual Report. The report stated that "The operation of this line and the development of the territory served by it should be of increasing value to your property." The road was shown for several years in NS timetable maps by a heavier line than other connecting railroads, indicating that management continued to consider it an important connection.

The NHH&MtV was built as part of an ambitious plan to drain Lake Mattamuskeet to produce new farmland. Lake Mattamuskeet is a shallow lake covering about 40,000 acres located east of Belhaven and just north of Pamlico Sound. Promoters of the plan built a large pumphouse on the south shore of the lake, at a point they called New Holland, showing that they had been inspired in their project by the draining of land in Holland. The pumps had a combined pumping capacity said to be the largest of any installation in the world at the time. They were powered by steam engines and coal-fired steam boilers. NS would haul coal for the boilers to the NHH&MtV connection. Shops for the New Holland Railroad were also located at New Holland.

Draining the lake exposed very fertile soil, and for a few years good crops were produced on the drained land. In 1932, however, one of the tropical storms that are an ongoing threat to eastern North Carolina filled the lake bed faster than the drainage pumps could empty it, destroying the entire crop. This convinced the promoters of the plan that it was not practical, and the idea was abandoned.

The New Holland Railroad proved to be even less successful than the drainage plan, and it ceased to operate sometime in the late twenties. The railroad lay dormant for years, but the rails were finally taken up in 1933, using equipment borrowed from the NS. Earlier, NS was asked to appraise locomotive number 100 of the New Holland Railroad for resale. NS appraised it at $7,000, but did not buy it. A portion of the embankment of the line can still be seen rising out of Lake Mattamuskeet, and the massive building that housed the drainage pumps remains intact but unused at New Holland, which is now little more than a ghost town. It is said that some of the railroad's equipment still lies at the bottom of the lake.

In its early years, the NHH&MtV was promoted aggressively. Its listing in the 1922 issues of The Official Guide of the Railways covered an entire page for its one train each way daily, and included schedules of connecting service to Cincinnati and Columbus, Ohio, and Jacksonville, Florida, starting with the NS Belhaven Branch trains. The listing also stated that "This road traverses the 'Mattamuskeet Eden' of North Carolina, a territory unexcelled for agricultural pursuits."

As we have said, the lease of the D&SC brought the mileage operated by the NS up to its maximum of 942. This maximum lasted less than two years. On January 20, 1922, operation of the twelve-mile long Carthage Branch was discontinued. That branch, which connected with the Aberdeen Branch at Pinehurst, had been built in 1907 as the Carthage and Pinehurst Railroad by the Page family, builders of the Aberdeen and Asheboro, and immediately had been leased to that line for operation. The lease passed to the NS with the purchase of the A&A. The branch never contributed much income to the NS, and by 1921 it was only a drain on scarce resources, so the NS had applied in that year for permission to abandon.

Throughout the 1920s, NS business grew steadily, although not as fast as its owners hoped. In 1926, operating revenues topped 10 million dollars for the first time, led by a 14 percent increase in freight tonnage over 1925. In 1916, operating revenues had been less than five million dollars. Even with this growth, NS business was slow compared with other Class I railroads. The following table of traffic statistics for 1925 shows how NS trailed its major competitors in the region. In particular, the line of percentage increase of gross revenue per mile of road from 1912, shows that NS was losing ground to the other systems instead of catching up with them as predicted by Dow Jones and Company in 1912 (see table on page 68).

The biggest contribution to the increase in NS freight business came from hauling stone, sand, and other like materials, as North Carolina began an extensive highway-building program. Shipment of these materials more than tripled between 1917 and 1926. Agricultural products showed a healthy increase, as the NS promotion of its territory as a prime farming area began to bear fruit (and vegetables). Tobacco and cot-

The Aberdeen and Asheboro station at Carthage, NC. This was the terminus of the Carthage Branch of the A&A, which became the branch of the same name of the NS. The branch was not as profitable as the road had hoped, and as a result became the first NS branch to be abandoned, in 1922. The A&A locomotive to the right of the station cannot be indentified. (Winstead collection)

ton produced sizeable revenue also. Manufactured goods furnished a growing percentage of the freight handled, although the optimistic predictions of the railroad's promoters for this business were never achieved.

Express and LCL (less-than-car-load) freight were also important in this period. Now that trucks have taken most of this traffic away from the rails, it is easy to forget how important this was to even the smallest towns in the twenties. A Norfolk Southern Shippers Guide of 1926 lists more than 2,700 individual shippers and receivers of shipments at 86 stations. Most of these were small local businesses such as grocery stores, drug stores, bakeries, and banks. A few of these listings give an idea of the diversity of businesses that used rail transportation in those days:

S. M. Woodley, hotel and cafe, Mackeys, NC
Chadwick Theaters, motion pictures, Suffolk, VA
Duffy Drug Co., proprietary medicine manufacturer, New Bern, NC
Seashore Summer School, Inc., teacher training school, Oriental, NC
Mrs. Lucy Stobaugh, hatmaker, Newport, NC
John Flanagan Buggy Co., vehicle manufacturer, Greenville, NC
Easymake Pudding Co., hotel supplies, Charlotte, NC

As freight business grew in the twenties, the bottom dropped out of the passenger business. Passenger revenue, which had reached 1.7 million dollars in 1920, was down to 0.8 million in 1926. Management recognized the cause of the problem. Better roads were causing people to switch to highway transportation. Ironically, NS was contributing to this problem by supplying cheap transportation of road-building materials, as we have already noted.

Of course, NS was not alone among railroads in finding that the automobile was making inroads into its passenger business, but NS was particularly vulnerable. The first class service from Norfolk to Raleigh and New Bern looked impressive in the timetables, but few people used it. Large numbers of people used the

Comparative Analysis of Revenue and Freight Traffic in 1925

	Norfolk Southern	Southern Railway	Seaboard Air Line	Atlantic Coast Line
gross revenue per mile of road ($)	$9,809	$21,987	$16,004	$19,885
percent increase from 1912, gross per mile	81%	144%	112%	167%
freight train miles per mile of road	970	2,651	1,649	2,034
revenue ton-miles per miles of road (000)	489	1,204	871	908

Virginia Beach lines and the Pinehurst service in season, but the distances involved were too short to generate much revenue, and "in season" was much too short to please the railroad. As we have already noted, most through passenger traffic between the biggest cities was subject to strong competition. Even in 1920, when passenger business was relatively good, the average distance traveled per passenger on the steam lines was only 33 miles, showing that most trips were very local in nature. Average number of passengers per train mile was only 45. By 1926, there were only 26 passengers per train mile, and the average distance was down to 24 miles. Trips that short were certainly very vulnerable to highway competition.

The first NS reaction to the declining passenger income was to convert passenger runs to mixed trains. This began during the carmen's strike of 1922, when the railroad claimed it could not keep all passenger and freight equipment serviced with only supervisory personnel. However, the 20/20 vision of hindsight leads us to the opinion that this was a convenient excuse to take action the railroad wanted to pursue anyway. There was certainly no rush to resume full passenger trains when the strike was over.

The switch began with branches on the sparsely populated west end of the railroad. Aberdeen-Asheboro train numbers 70 and 71 became mixed in 1922, soon followed by the Fayetteville Branch trains. By 1924, even Raleigh-Charlotte main line passenger train numbers 30 and 31 were converted to mixed trains. The same thing happened to trains on the north end branches to Oriental, Suffolk, Belhaven, and Columbia in quick succession.

A form of highway transport that competed significantly for NS passenger business in those days, but which is now almost forgotten, was the jitney. Jitneys were more or less intermediate between a small bus line and a taxi, and were generally one-man, one-vehicle operations covering short trips. For example, longtime residents of Columbia, NC, recall the local jitney operators taking considerable business from the NS Columbia Branch in the twenties. The jitneys would meet the main line passenger trains from Norfolk and Raleigh at Mackeys, then take the passengers directly to Columbia for a dollar. They would arrive in Columbia long before the connecting NS branch line train, which was a mixed train subject to considerable delays at intermediate stations. Again recall that most local businesses such as the Bank of Creswell would be getting frequent express and LCL freight shipments by this train.

Before 1926 was over, NS management had an idea to combat highway competition. Practicing the old principle of "if you can't beat 'em, join 'em," they formed the Norfolk Southern Bus Corporation, a wholly owned subsidiary. This company first operated a bus route between Norfolk and Virginia Beach via Cape Henry. The rail bridge over Lynnhaven Inlet was given a solid deck to permit the buses to run over it. The bus line became a competitor to the NS electric North Route line, which seems self-defeating, but NS owners realized that if they didn't provide competing bus service, somebody else would. In fact, the Virginia Beach Bus Line already ran between Norfolk and Virginia Beach paralleling the NS South Route.

By 1934, the Virginia Beach Bus Line had

Norfolk Southern Bus Corporation bus number 152 at an unknown date and place. This was an Aerocoach model P-37 bus purchased in 1945. The bus company purchased new buses numbers 151-185 in the years immediately following World War II to modernize its fleet. Most of these were transferred to the Carolina Coach Company when it took over the Norfolk Southern Bus Company in 1954. The NS bus color scheme was green and cream, similar to the railbuses and the larger electric cars. (W. R. Newton collection)

A Norfolk Southern railbus, probably number 102, the Sir Walter Raleigh, approaches a grade crossing at Zebulon, NC, on October 10, 1937. The Sir Walter Raleigh was assigned to a new service between Raleigh and Washington when it was received in 1935, and continued to be the regular equipment on that schedule until the major reduction in NS passenger service in 1938. (North Carolina Division of Archives and History)

acquired other lines offering competition to NS steam lines in northeastern North Carolina. In November of that year, the NS Bus Corporation bought out the competing company. In 1941, the NS Bus Corp. purchased the Virginia-Carolina Transportation Company, which not only operated bus lines in NS Railroad territory, but also operated trucking service in the same area. Expansion of these services continued throughout the forties, so that by the end of that decade, NS buses and trucks went almost everywhere in northeastern North Carolina and southeastern Virginia that NS trains did, as well as to some towns off NS rails. By this time, the NS Bus Corp. had a fleet of sixty buses. NS also began to operate trucking lines parallel to the Aberdeen, Asheboro, and Ellerbe Branches. The NS continued in the bus and trucking business until February 1954, when the bus company was sold to the Carolina Coach Co.

In 1929, the Pennsylvania Railroad, which by this time operated the New York, Philadelphia, and Norfolk Railroad by lease, completed a new terminal for its Chesapeake Bay ferry operation at Little Creek, on the south shore of the bay at the northern edge of the city of Norfolk. The PRR built a line from Little Creek to a connection with the Norfolk Southern's North Route to Virginia Beach at Camden Heights, then obtained trackage rights from there to North Junction, where the NS connection to the South Route left the old Chesapeake Transit Company line. The PRR established a new yard and freight house at St. Julian Avenue, adjacent to this point, near the Norfolk and Western line into their Lamberts Point Yard. This permitted the PRR to reduce the length of their slow and costly ferry operation.

The NS North Beach route was far from adequate to handle the heavy traffic the PRR expected, so the PRR built a second track alongside the existing NS track between Camden Heights and North Junction.

Norfolk Southern railbus number 103, the Cavalier, and Norfolk Southern Bus Corporation highway bus number 29 at the Park Avenue station in Norfolk. This is most likely a publicity photo taken at or soon after the first run of the railbus to Virginia Beach in 1935. (Tal Carey collection)

The two tracks were then used jointly as double track. At about the same time, NS obtained trackage rights over the Virginian Railway from Tidewater Junction to Coleman Place, another crossing point of the two roads. This provided NS with a double track line all the way from Camden Heights to Carolina Junction, a considerable improvement over the old single track line from North Junction to South Junction, which ran in a city street.

By January 1929, business had improved enough that the directors declared and paid a dividend of $2.25 per share. This was the first dividend paid since 1914. The company had increased its bonded

director of the Seaboard Air Line, and was familiar with the NS since he was also president of the Cavalier Hotel Corporation. In October 1933, Mr. Loyall resigned as receiver and was replaced by Morris S. Hawkins, who had been his assistant and secretary of the NS prior to the receivership.

Operations of the company were not materially altered by the depression at first, but as business conditions continued to deteriorate, changes became inevitable. Passenger service was an obvious target for cost reduction, since patronage was declining rapidly even before the depression. The night trains between Norfolk and Raleigh were discontinued in 1932, ending

Atlantic and North Carolina Railroad 0-6-0 number 4, shown here at Goldsboro, NC in August 1941, was given to the A&NC by the NS when the latter road ceased to operate the former in 1935. It had kept its last number 4 from NS days. It originally was number 14 of the Norfolk and Southern, built by Schenectady in 1900. By the date of the photo, the Atlantic and North Carolina had become the Atlantic and East Carolina, but the locomotive had not yet been relettered. (Harold K. Vollrath collection)

indebtedness considerably in extending the line to Charlotte, and interest payments on the debt were absorbing most of the operating profit so that dividends had been stopped. Another dividend of $1.25 per share was paid on July 3, 1929, but then President George Loyall reported to the stockholders that "No action was taken on the dividend which, if declared, would have been payable January 3, 1930. Your Board felt the business outlook was such that a declaration of this dividend would not be to the best interest of your Company." This turned out to be a classic understatement.

The depression of the 1930s turned NS operating profits into deficits. It is hardly a surprise that the company was soon forced into receivership. This occurred on July 28, 1932, and would last almost ten years. Railroad President Loyall was appointed a receiver, with Louis H. Windholz a co-receiver. Mr. Windholz was knowledgeable about railroads, being a

Pullman service between these cities and to New Bern. The parlor car service to New Bern was also ended. Passenger service on the Currituck Branch to Munden had been replaced by NS Bus Company service some years before. Interline Pullman service to Virginia Beach and Pinehurst continued, but the only all-passenger runs to Pinehurst were one Sunday-only trip each way, when there was no freight to be handled in the weekday mixed train.

As traffic levels continued to be depressed throughout the thirties, other changes in service became necessary, but NS management did not merely eliminate existing service. In 1935, they actually tried to increase business by introducing new passenger service. Not only was the service new, but also the equipment. Two railbuses were purchased from ACF-Brill, and named *Carolinian* and *Sir Walter Raleigh*. They were delivered in December 1934, and, after being exhibited at several cities on the railroad, began regular service January 6, 1935. The first was put on a new Beaufort-Goldsboro run, and the other on a new Raleigh-Washington, NC run. The NS had experimented with a McKeen car on the Norfolk-Munden line in 1907, but that car had proved to be unreliable and had been converted to electric operation. The gasoline-powered railbuses which the ACF-Brill combine introduced in 1933 were a big improvement over the McKeen car, however.

The new runs in North Carolina did not attract much business and did not last long, but the railbuses themselves were a success. Two additional railbuses, named *Cavalier* and *Princess Anne*, were purchased for the Virginia Beach lines in 1935, and were an immediate success, providing more passenger comfort and lower costs compared to the now aged electric cars. The two railbuses withdrawn from the North Carolina runs were moved to the Virginia Beach lines. In 1942, the NS was able to acquire two additional ACF-Brill railbuses secondhand from the Seaboard Air Line, which were added to the Virginia Beach operations. These two units were slightly larger than the four original NS machines, but were mechanically similar. When the railbuses took over passenger service to Virginia Beach, the electric operation was discontinued and steam power took over the freight service.

It might be supposed that the depression would have resulted in widespread abandonments of unprofitable branch lines. There were some abandonments, but not as many as might have occurred. A major reduction in NS trackage did take place on November 16, 1935, when the lease of the Atlantic and North Carolina Railroad was canceled and operation of that road reverted to its original owners (still mainly the state of North Carolina). The NS found that income from operation of the line was now far short of the lease payments.

The state-controlled Atlantic and North Carolina Railroad Company struggled along with operation of its line for a few years, but was soon looking to lease it to a private operating company again. On April 29, 1939, the road was leased to the Atlantic and East Carolina Company headed by Mr. H. P. Edwards, who had been General Manager of the Atlantic and Western Railroad, a short line running from Sanford to Lillington, NC. The A&EC lease of the A&NC was taken over by Southern Railway in 1957. So, when Southern Railway took over the NS in 1974, the former A&NC and NS once again came under common management. Operations remained separate for several years, but in July 1981, the employees of the Norfolk Southern and the Atlantic and East Carolina agreed to merge into a single seniority district. So now the Albemarle Seniority District covers all the former NS lines plus the A&EC in common operation. The two are still separate companies on paper, however.

Termination of the NS lease of the A&NC left the NS with a disconnected three-mile branch from Morehead City to Beaufort. Although this line had been built as an extension of the A&NC, it was never owned by the state-owned company, so was not taken over by that company when the lease was terminated. The NS did not want the line and immediately applied for permission to abandon it, but local investors formed the Beaufort and Morehead Railroad to purchase the line.

An Atlantic and East Carolina passenger train at the Morehead City station in June 1944. Locomotive number 102 was one of three Ten Wheelers the Atlantic and North Carolina had bought secondhand from the Atlantic Coast Line in 1936 to replace the tired motive power it inherited from the NS. These locomotives were called "copperheads" because they were built with copper caps on their smokestacks. By this time, the caps were gone but the nickname remained. Number 102 retains its A&NC lettering in this photo, seven years after the A&NC became the A&EC. Barely visible on the tender is the A&NC herald of a jumping fish inside a circle, with the words "The Old Mullet Road" around the outside of the circle. A&EC passenger service ended March 31, 1950. (Harold K. Vollrath collection)

First day of operation of the BMH was August 1, 1937. A shaky operation in its early days, the BMH received a big boost when a jet fuel terminal was built on its line, resulting in the slogan, "Route of the Jets," being adopted. Today, most of the line has been abandoned. The North Carolina Port Authority operates the remainder, from Morehead City to Radio Island, about halfway to downtown Beaufort, as part of the Morehead City port trackage. In May 1997, however, shipments of jet fuel to Radio Island ceased, so little traffic remains on the line.

In 1937, NS began a program to reduce highway grade crossing hazards

Above: In 1946 the Atlantic and East Carolina dieselized its operations by purchasing two F2 model units from EMD, numbering them 400 and 401. F units like these were rare on short lines. This photo, taken August 16, 1948, shows locomotive number 400 with passenger train number 5 ready to leave Morehead City for Goldsboro. Note the tobacco leaf herald and the slogan, "The Tobacco Belt Route". The passenger depot, which appears at the right, is still in existence although no longer used for railroad purposes. Passenger service on the A&EC ended on March 31, 1950. (John Treen photo, Ed Fielding collection)

Below: A passenger train of the Beaufort and Morehead Railroad at Beaufort, NC in 1944. Locomotive number 3 is an 0-6-0, lettered B&M but actually leased from the Atlantic and East Carolina. It had been built for the Atlantic and North Carolina as number 30 by Baldwin in 1905, before the N&S leased the A&NC. It was renumbered 3 by the N&S and kept that number after being returned to the A&NC in 1935. (John Treen photo, Ed Fielding collection)

by building several overpasses and underpasses, and by installing protection devices such as gates, bells, and warning lights. This was made possible largely as a result of a loan from the Reconstruction Finance Corporation. At the time, John W. Barriger III was head of the RFC's Railroad Division. Mr. Barriger later went on to a long and distinguished career as a railroad executive, including terms as president of the Monon, the Pittsburgh and Lake Erie, the Katy, and the Boston and Maine Railroads. As part of his duties with the RFC, he took an inspection trip over the entire NS main line and most of its branches in April 1937, making a detailed photographic record of the railroad. Several of his photographs are used to illustrate this book.

In March 1938, the Norfolk Southern shocked everyone, including the North Carolina Utilities Commission, when it applied to discontinue all passenger service with the exception of trains numbers 1 and 2 between Norfolk and Raleigh. This was the largest such request the Utilities Commission had ever received, and would make the NS almost totally

a freight carrier. There was an initial storm of opposition from cities along the routes that were to lose service. Most of this died down after the NS showed that they were also being served by bus service and hardly anyone was riding the trains.

Raleigh persisted in its opposition a little longer than most places as it was in competition with

Above: The Beaufort and Morehead was always noted for its small locomotives. This 4-2, number 4, was obtained secondhand from the Warrenton Railroad in Warrenton, NC. I had been built by Baldwin in 1922. Note that has gotten a new headlight at some point in life, apparently from Atlantic and East Carolina number 797, a 2-8-0 which had the number from its early days on the Delaware, Lackawanna, and Western Railroad. (Roy Eubanks photo, James D. Curtin, III collectio

Above left: Another small locomotive which appeared on the BMH roster was 2-6-2 numb 7, which had been obtained from the Tavera and Gulf Railroad. It had been built by the Alco Schenectady plant in 1922. Here it is pushing cars from Beaufort to Morehead City for the A&EC connection. (John Treen photo, Ed Fielding collection)

Below left: The BMH was only three miles long, but much of that consisted of two long wood pile trestles, so its pile driver was kept busy. Here the pile driver is working on one of the trestles with General Electric 44-Tonner number 7410, an ex-Norfolk Navy Yard unit. (John Treen photo, Ed Fielding collection)

Below: In later years, the BMH became a haven for Whitcomb diesels such as number 8 shown here at Beaufort, near a new engine house. This was an 80-ton unit, the biggest of the four Whitcombs on the road's roster. This scene is typical of the Beaufort vicinity, with i many waterways. (David Burnette photo)

several other North Carolina cities to have a large Veterans Administration hospital located there. The US government was considering availability of public transportation as one of the factors in deciding the location, and Raleigh didn't want to lose any

during the selection process. In July 1938, Fayetteville was selected for the hospital (in spite of the fact that it would shortly lose its NS passenger service), and Raleigh dropped its opposition to the passenger service cutback.

With all opposition now placated, the Utilities Commission approved the request. By the end of 1938, NS passenger service was down to a single daily train between Norfolk and Raleigh, the railbus service to Virginia Beach, and the through Pullman runs to Virginia Beach and Pinehurst. These Pullman runs carried no local passengers, however. There was no longer any passenger service between Raleigh and Charlotte, or to Fayetteville, Asheboro, Aberdeen, Oriental, Columbia, New Bern, Suffolk, or Belhaven. All the service discontinued had consisted of mixed trains by this time.

As an example of how the passenger service was losing money, in their latter days trains numbers 30 and 31 were taking in $3.92 daily gross revenue from passengers, while the expense of operating passenger cars in these mixed trains averaged $45.01 per day.

In 1939 the roundhouse and coal chute at Glenwood Yard burned to the ground in a spectacular fire. The blaze started when a pressurized oil hose in the roundhouse burst, spraying oil onto a forge. There were three 500 class engines in the roundhouse at the time, two of which had their steam up. NS employees made a valiant effort to get these engines out, but were beaten back by the rapidly spreading fire.

Being prudent as usual, the NS had insurance on everything. A new roundhouse and coal chute were erected and the NS shop forces rebuilt all three engines and returned them to service.

Two short branches were abandoned in the late thirties, the Jackson Springs Branch of the old

John W. Barriger III, head of the Railroad Division of the Reconstruction Finance Corporation, took this photo on the occasion of his inspection trip over the NS in April 1937. The people in the photo, from left to right, are F. L. Nicholson, NS chief engineer; L. P. Kennedy, NS general superintendent, steam lines; Morris S. Hawkins, NS receiver; C. P. Dugan, NS transportation assistant to the receiver; Mr. Hamilton, RFC; L. A. Beck, NS chief purchasing and mechanical officer; Mr. Wright, RFC; and J. F. Dalton, NS chief traffic officer. The office car Virginia, in which the RFC officers made their trip, is behind them.
(John W. Barriger III photo, Barriger Railroad Collection, St. Louis Mercantile Library)

Aberdeen and Asheboro Railroad, and the line from Mackeys (formerly Mackey's Ferry) to Bishop Cross, which was most of the old Albemarle and Pantego Railroad. The portion of the A&P between Bishop Cross and Belhaven remained in service, connected to the main line at Pinetown. Rails were retained on nine miles of the former A&P track from Mackeys through Roper for several years for car storage.

In 1940, a much bigger abandonment took place when the tracks from Suffolk to both Edenton and Elizabeth City were taken up. By this time, Suffolk had a surfeit of railroads, with no less than five lines other than the NS running through the city. All these other lines offered shorter routes to Norfolk, and there was little traffic between Suffolk and the two southern end-

By March 1942, when this photo near Aberdeen, NC was taken, the NS Aberdeen Branch was essentially freight only, but look at the "freight" being hauled in this run! The railroad still handled daily New York-to-Pinehurst Pullmans from the Seaboard connection at Aberdeen to Pinehurst during the peak golfing months of October through May. Here three Pullmans are included in the daily freight train. The employees' timetable of the era showed a Sunday-only passenger train, which handled these Pullmans when the weekday freight did not run.
(Robert W. Richardson photo)

A view of Suffolk, VA about 1918. Tracks leading out of the right side of the photo are NS tracks leading to downtown Suffolk and the Nansemond River. Track proceeds to Edenton in the center background, with the Elizabeth City line leading off to the left twenty-five miles down the track. The NS track in the photo was sold to the Virginian Railway in 1940 when the branch was abandoned, and is still in existence as part of today's Norfolk Southern Corporation. The track in the center foreground is the Atlantic and Danville Railroad leading to Portsmouth, VA, with its line to Danville curving out of the picture in the right distance. Trackage on the left belongs to the Atlantic Coast Line, also heading for Portsmouth in the foreground and for Rocky Mount, NC in the distance. At the time of the photo, Southern Railway operated the A&D by lease, and also had trackage rights into Portsmouth over the ACL. This view shows only half of the rail lines in Suffolk, as the Norfolk and Western, the Seaboard Air Line, and the Virginian all ran roughly parallel to the bottom of the photo behind the photographer. Norfolk Southern used the N&W station as its passenger terminal. (Virginia Department of Agriculture and Consumer Affairs)

Corporation also provided bus connections between Park Avenue station and the Union Bus Terminal in downtown Norfolk, stopping at Terminal Station on the way. NS corporate offices remained in Terminal Station until plans were announced to tear it down in 1961.

As the 1930s ended, Norfolk Southern business began to pick up as a result of preparations for World War II. NS traffic benefitted more than some other roads because of the large volume of exports through Hampton Roads. Also, there were many military establishments in NS territory, especially in the Norfolk vicinity, which generated additional traffic.

NS management decided that new motive power was essential to handle efficiently the increased freight traffic. The last new locomotives the NS had purchased had been three 2-8-0's from Baldwin in 1927. To modernize its steam roster, the NS ordered

points. Most of the trackage in Suffolk itself was still useful to local businesses, and this was sold to the Virginian Railway. A small part of this remains in service today, now owned by Norfolk Southern Corporation.

The track on the Suffolk branch had already been out of service for several years, and had been used for storage of refrigerator cars out of the harvest season. It is said that on one occasion when the railroad attempted to move a group of cars out, they found that the brass journal bearings had been stolen out of them.

In May 1940, the NS decided it was paying more money to the Norfolk Terminal Railway Company for use of the Norfolk Terminal Station than the sparse traffic could justify, so operation of trains numbers 1 and 2 to and from that station was discontinued. A new passenger platform was built in Berkley, and this became the end point for these runs. By this time, most of the railbus runs to Virginia Beach, instead of using Terminal Station, originated and terminated at the Park Avenue station, 0.6 miles east. A few railbus runs used Terminal Station after this, mostly to provide convenient connections for travelers on Norfolk and Western passenger trains. Norfolk Southern Bus

In 1940, the NS stopped using Norfolk Terminal Station for their passenger trains because the sparse traffic could not pay for the expense of using the station. A new platform, visible at the left of the train in this photo, was built at Main Street in Berkley to serve as the Norfolk terminal for the steam trains. The Norfolk Southern Bus Corporation operated connecting service from downtown Norfolk. Ten-Wheeler number 133 and two cars make up the train on this occasion, for which the date is unknown. (H. Reid photo, Tal Carey collection)

five new 2-8-4's from Baldwin, which were delivered beginning in February 1940. These locomotives had many features unique to the NS roster, which will be discussed in the chapter on steam locomotives.

With the improvement in business, NS finances improved to the point where an end of the long receivership could be foreseen. A plan and agreement of reorganization was issued on June 15, 1940, but considerable time was required before all details of the reorganization were worked out. Finally, the actual transfer of the property of the old Norfolk Southern Railroad Company to the new Norfolk Southern Railway Company took place on January 21, 1942.

Former NS RR Receivers Louis H. Windholz and Morris S. Hawkins became Chairman of the Board and President, respectively, of the new NS Ry. Most of the other officers of the new company were men who had been associated with the NS for many years, including Vice President-Traffic J. F. Dalton, Secretary J. R. Pritchard, Treasurer J. F. George, General Auditor G. C. Reveille, Chief Engineer F. L. Nicholson, Chief Purchasing and Mechanical Officer L. A. Beck, General Superintendent Steam Lines L. P. Kennedy, and General Superintendent Electric Lines L. B. Wickersham. (Note that the latter title was still used even though electric operation had ended years earlier.)

Mr. Windholz did not have long to enjoy the advantages of administering a solvent company, as he died on July 24, 1942. He was replaced as Chairman by Carroll M. Shanks of Newark, NJ. Mr. Hawkins also suffered an untimely end to his term on March 14, 1946, when he died as a result of a gunshot wound. It has been speculated that the shooting was accidental, but the identity of the gunman and his intent were never discovered. Mr. Hawkins was succeeded as President by Louis A. Beck. Mr. Hawkins had served the railroad for more than thirty-six years.

The new NS Railway took over all the property of the old NS Railroad, including such subsidiaries as the NS Bus Corporation, with one notable exception. The John L. Roper Lumber Company finally ceased to be owned by the railroad. Stock of that company was distributed among the stockholders of the NS Ry. The Roper Company continued in business as an owner of timberlands, and even briefly resumed lumber manufacture by buying a small sawmill in Roper, NC, once the site of one of the company's largest mills. The new mill furnished wood for a casket manufacturing plant in Elizabeth City, but this business did not last long. The Roper Lumber Company finally went out of business in the 1950s.

By the time the new Norfolk Southern Railway was officially in business, the United States was fully involved in World War II, and the NS, along with all other U. S. railroads, worked at top speed to provide the transportation required to meet wartime needs. Freight volumes continued the increase of the late 1930s, and even passsenger traffic rose considerably, most related to the military activity in NS territory. The war accelerated the switch from water transport to rail transport because many ships formerly used for coastwise and river traffic were taken over by the government for military uses, and also because in the early days of the war, the threat of German submarine activity off the U. S. east coast discouraged coastwise shipping.

As the war wound down to its close in 1945, NS managers found it necessary to consult their crystal balls to determine what changes the postwar era would bring. We will examine their resulting decisions in the next chapter.

In February and March of 1940, Norfolk Southern took delivery of by far its most modern steam power in the form of five 2-8-4s manufactured by Baldwin. Number 600, the first of these, is shown here at Carolina Junction, still new enough that the drivers and pilot truck wheels still have white rims. Just before number 600's delivery, the newest steam locomotive on the road was 2-8-0 number 545, already thirteen years old. (Richard E. Prince photo, Frank E. Ardrey, Jr. collection)

Above: The last passenger trains on the NS were operated on January 31, 1948. This view shows southbound train number 1 approaching the Norfolk and Western Railway crossing at Berkley Junction (now known as NS Junction) on that damp and dreary winter day. The roof of the interlocking tower is in the lower right corner of the photo. (James A. Ramsey photo)

Below: Another view of the last run of NS passenger train number 1 on January 31, 1948, just after crossing the N&W at Berkley Junction. The train is approaching Carolina Junction and Yard in this view. (James A. Ramsey photo)

Chapter 6

The Later Years

The first major decision NS management had to face for the postwar years was the future course of its motive power roster. The five new 2-8-4s did an admirable job throughout the war, but there were only enough of them to handle the most important trains. The remaining steam motive power was now getting quite old and showed the effects of heavy wartime usage. By 1945, the NS had not sampled diesel motive power as most Class I roads had, but reports from the roads that had done so indicated that diesels offered operating advantages that could not be ignored. NS managers briefly considered buying five more 2-8-4s, but soon decided that dieselization was the way to go. One factor influencing the decision was the knowledge that they literally could not afford the luxury of buying more steam power and then changing their minds later. So in 1946, five diesel switchers and ten road freight diesel locomotives were ordered from Baldwin. Shortly afterward, three General Electric 70-ton diesels were ordered for passenger service. The chapter on diesel locomotives will give more information on these orders.

It was also important for NS management to try to predict the future of its passenger business. There was little room for optimism. We have noted that war-related traffic boosted passenger revenue temporarily, but a rapid decline began as soon as the war ended. Some railroads ordered new passenger equipment after the war to try to encourage peacetime rail travel, but the NS waited to see what traffic levels might develop before ordering any new equipment. It became apparent that the levels would be about as high as the track elevation above sea level at Albemarle Sound. Not surprisingly, no new passenger cars were ordered. On November 8, 1947, operation of the railbuses to Virginia Beach was discontinued. Not long after, the railbuses were shipped to Cuba.

Passenger service between Norfolk and Raleigh did not last much longer. On January 31, 1948, the last runs were made. This made NS one of the first Class I railroads to eliminate all passenger service. Trains numbers 1 and 2 continued to run as mail and express trains between Norfolk and Raleigh, powered by the 70-tonners, for a few years, however.

In late 1951, the mail contract was lost and the railroad immediately stopped running trains numbers 1 and 2 on October 31 of that year. As it turned out, they were discontinued too soon as the North Carolina State Utilities Commission had not authorized the discontinuance. NS was forced to resume their operation on

In December 1946, Norfolk Southern took delivery of its first diesel locomotive, Baldwin model DS-4-4-660 number 661. This photo appears to have been taken at the request of NS management to publicize this important event. The names of the individuals in the photograph were not recorded, but a consensus of railroad employees from that era indicate that the man on the left is Mr. L. P. Kennedy, who was general superintendent of the NS steam lines at the time. The man on the right is recognized to be Mr. J. C. Poe, who succeeded Mr. Kennedy as general superintendent of the steam lines when he was promoted to vice-president. Opinions are divided as to the identity of the three men in the middle. One or more of these may be Baldwin employees. The location of the photo is Glenwood Yard in Raleigh.
(H. A. Stewart, Jr. photo, Tal Carey collection)

November 5, 1951, but the railroad immediately applied for the necessary permission to abandon them. Taking into account the railroad's promise to provide truck express service in their place, the Utilities Commission gave its permission and the true last runs took place on December 12, 1951.

As an interesting sidelight to the discontinuance of the express and mail trains numbers 1 and 2, we note that correspondence indicates that management in late summer of 1951 considered converting these trains from diesel power back to steam. One letter said the 70-ton locomotives were hard on track and caused exces-

sive maintenance expense. This claim seems strange considering that these locomotives for many years after were the only power allowed on the lightest branch on the railroad, the Bayboro Branch. Another letter says steam power would be needed to heat the cars for crew comfort in the coming winter. This statement also sounds strange, since stoves had been put in these cars when the 70-ton locomotives began to pull them. It has been said that the real reason for considering a return to steam power was to increase operating expense, making it easier to justify discontinuing these trains. No one remembers steam power being used on these trains on

An aerial view of Columbia, NC taken shortly before the railroad was abandoned in 1950. The station is the gable-roofed building just to the left of the top of the steel tower beside the end of the railroad bridge. The trestle across the Scuppernong River was approximately 2150 feet long at this time, but had once been over a mile long. Nearly all the land in the lower left corner of the photo was fill placed to reduce the length of the trestle. The trestle had also included a swing span to permit navigation at one time. (Collon Snell photo)

a regular basis at this time, and as we have noted, service ended soon after this. It seems unlikely that the full story will ever be known, but it makes for entertaining speculation.

While NS management quickly lost interest in passenger service after World War II, it felt that the future of its freight service was promising. In order to encourage this development, two new freight trains were added to the schedule. These trains, numbers 98 and 99,

Above: A NS train at the Oriental, NC station shortly before the abandonment of operations into that town in 1950. Locomotive is unidentified but is probably a 2-8-0. The depot shown in the photo is still in existence today as a private residence, more than fifty years after it ceased serving the function for which it was built. (Richard W. Walker photo)

Below: 2-8-0 number 544, one of the last six steam locomotives owned by the NS, is shown here working at Asheboro. Photo is undated but it appears to be shortly before the abandonment of track into Asheboro by the NS in 1952. Number 544 would be gone as well by February 1954. The track it is on remains in place to this day, however, as it was turned over to Southern Railway subsidiary High Point, Randleman, Asheboro and Southern Railway after NS discontinued service. In 1974, this trackage again became part of the Norfolk Southern when the new company of that name was formed as a combination of the old NS with the Carolina and Northwestern, which had included the HPRA&S. Operation of the track was not combined with the former NS operations, however. (Marvin Black collection)

were inaugurated on October 6, 1946. Initially, train number 99 was scheduled from Norfolk to Charlotte in 19 hours, and by 1955, this time was reduced to 16 hours 20 minutes. We will discuss these trains further in Chapter 10.

NS soon began to investigate the possibility of providing trailer on flat car, or "piggyback", freight service on these fast freight trains. In June of 1949, the Mechanical Department was asked to draw up plans for the conversion of some of Norfolk Southern's flats to TOFC flats for this service. Having no experience with this type of equipment, the Mechanical Department turned to the New York, New Haven, and Hartford Railroad for assistance. The New Haven had considerable experience with piggyback service, having started its program in 1938. With this technical help, the NS developed a set of blueprints for the car which they designated FC-1. Suppliers were contacted for price quotes on the various components needed for the conversion, but that was as far as the program progressed, and the cars were never built.

Early in 1947, an important change in NS management took place. A group headed by Patrick B. McGinnis took control, with McGinnis becoming chairman of

the board and "Major" Joseph T. Kingsley becoming president. Nearly the entire board of directors was replaced by McGinnis' associates.

At first, stockholders found much to like about the new management. The financial structure of the company was improved, expenses were cut, and dividends were increased. McGinnis and Kingsley also pushed aggressively for total dieselization, discontinuance of passenger service, and abandonment of unprofitable branches.

Before long, however, some of the stockholders began to have second thoughts. Not all the actions of the new management met with their approval. An inordinate amount was expended on entertaining shippers, such as annual special trains to the Kentucky Derby. Salaries, expense accounts, and other "perks" for the executive officers were increased greatly. For example, a luxurious penthouse apartment was rented by the railroad near the Virginia Beach oceanfront for use by top executives when they left their New York offices to visit the railroad. Also, rumors began to circulate that the officers were pocketing some of the proceeds from sale of surplus equipment such as the deactivated steam locomotives.

In 1952, a group of stockholders led by brothers Perry and Harry Selheimer and longtime employee J. Raymond Pritchard, by this time vice-president of the road, mounted a proxy fight to take over management and reverse some of the undesirable practices of the

The NS Asheboro Branch survived long enough to see diesels for a time. In this photo, AS416 number 1601 is switching near the Asheboro depot. The NS tracks shown here are still operated by today's Norfolk Southern Corporation, as is all other Asheboro trackage illustrated in this book. (Marvin Black collection)

McGinnis group. At about the same time, the Interstate Commerce Commission began an investigation of these NS management practices.

As part of the ICC investigation of the NS, the state of North Carolina presented a witness, Consulting Engineer T. A. Cox, Jr., of Asheville, NC, who testified that the railroad was not maintaining the major trestles in a safe condition. He said of the Albemarle Sound trestle, "I considered the trestle extremely dangerous the way it gave down and rocked with the weight of the train." The railroad presented witnesses who rebutted this testimony. Unfortunately, Mr. Cox's allegations were proved tragically correct a few years later when the trestle collapsed under the weight of a train, killing two crewmen.

McGinnis, Kingsley, and their associates emerged victorious in a stockholders meeting held on June 28, 1952, but the fight and the ICC investigation did not end there. Soon afterward, however, Patrick McGinnis withdrew from the chairmanship of the NS and moved on to other railroads, including the Central of Georgia, the New Haven, and the Boston and Maine. You will probably recall that his management style attracted much unfavorable publicity when applied to these better known roads. Eventually he was sent to prison for illegally enriching himself at the expense of these companies.

Major Kingsley continued to battle the insurgent stockholders for a short time, but without McGinnis' support he was soon voted out of office. Management of the company was taken over by a group made up largely of the pre-McGinnis managers. Cecil M. Self became president in 1953, and was succeeded by J. Raymond Pritchard, a NS employee since 1906, a year later.

Although the McGinnis years were ones of considerable turmoil and unfavorable publicity for the railroad, some benefits resulted from his actions. Funded debt was reduced considerably, so that excessive interest obligations were lowered. Elimination of passenger service did not appeal to the public, but too few people actually rode the trains to make them economically viable. Conversion to diesel power, which advanced considerably in the McGinnis years, was disappointing to railfans, but hindsight shows us

Norfolk Southern's Currituck Branch to Munden, VA had been built by the Norfolk, Virginia Beach, and Southern Railroad in 1898, shortly before the NS absorbed that line. It connected with the Virginia Beach South Route at Clapham Junction (Euclid station), but was never electrified. This drawing shows the way Munden appeared between 1914 and 1923, when McKeen car number 90 operated regularly on the branch. In earlier years, one of the NS Railroad's steamboat lines operated from the pier in the background down the North Landing River to Currituck Sound and Poplar Branch, NC. This was a popular vacation destination for hunters of wildfowl. (John H. Kelly, Jr. drawing, Mrs. John H. Kelly, Jr. collection)

that it was inevitable and essential to the survival of the railroad.

Abandonment of no longer profitable branch lines also was important in lowering costs of operation. Abandonments in the McGinnis era included the entire Columbia Branch, the Bayboro-Oriental portion of the Oriental Branch, and the Star-to-Asheboro portion of the old Aberdeen and Asheboro main line. Also, with the cessation of railbus operations on the Virginia Beach lines, the oceanfront rail line from Cape Henry south to Lake station, where the South Route turned west to Norfolk, had little traffic and was torn up. A new station, called Virginia Beach station, was built at the end of track just west of the old Lake station. The connecting track between steam and electric lines from Euclid to Providence Junction was also abandoned.

We have already mentioned that the Suffolk and Jackson Springs branches had been abandoned before 1941. During World War II, the Currituck branch had been cut back five miles from Munden to Back Bay, and the remainder was abandoned in 1949. So, by the time of Patrick McGinnis' departure from the NS, the track mileage operated was down to 620. Further reductions took place soon after, as the Ellerbe Branch was abandoned, and the Virginia Beach North Route was cut back again, with eight miles of track removed from Cape Henry station to Shelton station.

By early 1954, shortly after the departure of McGinnis and Kingsley, dieselization of the railroad had progressed to the degree that the last remaining steam locomotives could be stricken from the roster. At this time, only six remained on the property: D6 class 4-6-0 number 133, E2 class 2-8-0s numbers 205 and 215, and E3 class 2-8-0s numbers 538, 542, and 544. The last operation of a steam locomotive on the Norfolk Southern of which a record remains occurred on January 12, 1954, when number 538 was assigned to the morning yard job at Glenwood Yard, Raleigh. The six remaining steamers were officially removed from the roster on January 29, 1954, and were hauled out of Carolina Yard on February 5, 1954.

The departure of McGinnis and Kingsley from the NS did not end the management controversy. In

A three-car electric train stands at the Cape Henry station in the mid 1930s. The original lighthouse, built in 1791, is seen above the second car. The second lighthouse, built in 1881, appears above the first car. The depot is just out of the picture to the left. It is still in existence, now being used by the U. S. Army as part of the Fort Story facilities. Russell Simmons, long a conductor on the Virginia Beach lines, stands on the car step.
(Mrs. Jane Simmons Adkins collection)

New Baldwin AS-416 number 1611 prepares to leave Carolina Yard with a funeral train of the last six NS steam locomotives on February 5, 1954. The locomotives included D6 class 4-6-0 number 133, E2 class 2-8-0s numbers 205 and 215, and E3 class 2-8-0s numbers 538, 542, and 544 (their order in the photo is unknown). NS management was pleased to use this photograph in their 1954 annual report as an indication of its modernization of the railroad, but many railfans would have preferred to ignore it. (H. A. Stewart, Jr. photo, Tal Carey collection)

chairman of the board, had joined the NS along with Patrick McGinnis, but fortunately for the railroad, he did not subscribe fully to McGinnis' ideas. Clearly he did not share the "get rich quick and get out" philosophy, as he remained president until he retired sixteen years later. It was a period in which he and his associates were presented with many challenges in keeping the railroad running, as we will see. Henry Bruns of New York replaced Mr. Oetjen as chairman of the board in 1957.

1956, another proxy fight resulted in the Selheimer brothers losing control to a group headed by Frank Mauran III and Henry Oetjen. Frank Mauran's family, of Providence, Rhode Island, had owned a large block of stock for many years. At about this time, President Pritchard and Executive Vice-President L. P. Kennedy, both longtime employees of the company, retired. Other longtime officers who retired around this time included Assistant Executive Vice-President J. S. Cox, Treasurer J. F. George, Assistant Comptroller C. C. Spencer, Chief Mechanical Officer J. H. Wilson, and General Superintendent J. C. Poe.

Henry Oetjen, who became president and

The first major challenge occurred at 12:02 A.M. July 5, 1957, when a section of the Albemarle Sound trestle collapsed under the weight of the locomotives of a northbound freight train. Engineer William Munden and Conductor S. R. Bray lost their lives in this accident, and three other crewmen, Road Foreman J. G. Lowery, Brakeman C. E. Jones, and fireman Burt Rankin, were rescued after escaping from the locomotives, which plunged into twenty feet of water. Fireman Rankin spent several hours in the Sound before he was found clinging to one of the timbers which had broken off the trestle. Locomotive numbers 1605 and 1610 were later lifted out of the Sound, rebuilt, and returned to service. The ICC report attributed the accident to decayed timbers. NS management suggested that the trestle may have been damaged by a runaway barge, as

Henry Oetjen, president of the Norfolk Southern from 1956 to 1972, on the right, and J. R. Roughton, president of Roughton Pontiac Corporation of Norfolk, examine a newly purchased 1956 Pontiac station wagon, which NS converted to be a highway-railroad vehicle. Location is Norfolk Terminal Station, at the time still the NS headquarters building although no longer served by regular NS train service.
(H. A. Stewart photo, W. R. Newton collection)

Above: NS diesel number 1610 being lifted out of Albemarle Sound after the trestle collapse of July 5, 1957. A large floating crane belonging to Merritt-Chapman-Scott Corporation is doing the lifting. The drawspan of the bridge can be seen in the background of this view, which looks south along the bridge.

Above right: Diesel number 1605 was the other locomotive involved in the Albemarle Sound bridge collapse, and is here being lifted out of the sound. Note the higher placement of the headlight in number 1605's short hood, compared to that of number 1610 in the previous photo.

Right: The NS pile driver had a rush job to do in July 1957, the rebuilding of the Albemarle Sound bridge. The bridge remained out of service for ten days.
(Three photos Fred Curling)

the bridge tender reported observing unusual barge and tugboat activity near the bridge the night of the accident, but this was never confirmed. During the ten-day period required to repair the trestle, NS through freight trains were detoured over the Atlantic Coast Line between Norfolk and Plymouth.

This tragic affirmation of the earlier comments of Consulting Engineer Cox convinced management that a thorough renovation of the trestle was necessary. For several years, the NS had been practicing a less expensive but less effective method of maintaining the trestle. The portions of the trestle above the waterline were frequently damaged by the coastal storms that plague this region. The underwater portions of the pilings were usually not damaged at these times. When this happened, the NS often cut the damaged pilings off at the waterline and built a new timber framework on top of the submerged part of the old pilings. This was much cheaper than driving new pilings into the bottom of the sound, but it resulted in a weaker structure. After the collapse, it was decided that all the portions of the trestle which had been repaired in this way needed to be rebuilt with full length pilings.

Realizing that rebuilding the trestle would be desirable was one thing, but finding a way to pay for it was another. The problem was finally solved after many months of negotiations by obtaining a two million dollar loan from the federal government.

The details of this loan had barely been finalized on September 12, 1960, when another disaster hit the Sound trestle in the form of Hurricane Donna. This destroyed much of the portion of the trestle which had not already been rebuilt. The drawspan was not destroyed, but the destruction on both sides isolated it,

83

Above: Hurricane Donna did extensive damage to the Albemarle Sound trestle in September 1960, taking it out of service for more than three months. This view shows the first train at Edenton station heading south toward the bridge after the repairs were completed. Superintendent S. Clyde Cherry is passing orders to conductor Dick Pinner on the caboose. The date is December 29, 1960. The Edenton Peanut Company plant is prominent in the background. Mr. Pinner was making his last trip before retirement. (Harry Bundy photo)

Below right: Another view on December 29, 1960 of the first train across Albemarle Sound after Hurricane Donna. Reportedly, railroad president Henry Oetjen is one of the men on the pilot of the lead locomotive in this photo. Note the boat, which contains other railroad employees keeping a watchful eye on the progress of the train. (W. R. Newton collection)

so that the bridge tender had to sit through the storm until he could be rescued by boat. When he was finally rescued, he told the rescuers that if anybody ever needed his fingerprints, they were indelibly engraved into the desktop in the control shanty.

While the hurricane did not cost the lives of any NS railroaders, it caused considerably greater expense to the railroad than the earlier collapse had. Not only did the railroad have to rush the rebuilding of the trestle to make it suitable for resumption of service, but in the meantime a repetition of the detour over the Atlantic Coast Line was necessary. This time the detour lasted more than three months, ending on December 29, 1960. During that time, the NS had to pay $175,000 in fees for use of the ACL track. Complete reconstruction of the trestle took until 1963, at which time it was named the William F. Knorr bridge for a member of the company Board of Directors.

It is interesting to note that while the rebuilding of the bridge strengthened it considerably, it did not completely eliminate the "giving down and rocking" noted by Consulting Engineer Cox. It was not possible to drive piling to a solid footing in the soft bottom of Albemarle Sound. The pile driver would place the weight on a pile and force it down to a specified depth, then hold it until it became "set." This has been likened to pushing a match stick into moist chewing gem.

Another major challenge during these days and even earlier was the change in the nature of freight traffic. As we have noted, in its earliest years, the railroad had counted logs and lumber as major sources of traffic. Much of this was now gone, although pulpwood and woodchips continued to be a significant source of revenue. Agricultural products had replaced these items as the timberlands had been converted into farmland, but this business was now changing. Trucks were taking over the perishable fruit and vegetable business.

Potatoes and peaches, long major items of rail traffic, were now essentially lost to the NS. Cotton had ceased to be an important source of revenue several years earlier. Tobacco was still important but was not a growing market. The only agricultural category which was increasing was grain, mainly corn and soybeans. Sand, gravel, and other construction materials were now the biggest source of freight traffic. Coal moved over NS rails, but all originated off-line and traveled only short distances on the NS, so this business was not nearly as profitable as for many of the other eastern railroads.

Manufactured products were considered a very desirable source of revenue, and NS had always worked to attract this business, but it had never grown as fast as management would have liked. In the 1950s, with most agricultural traffic declining, NS pushed even harder to encourage manufacturing along its lines. Some success was noted in this effort in the next few years, notably the construction of a large new Weyerhauser pulp mill at a new location called Weyco, on the New Bern Branch near Vanceboro, and a large Kelly-Springfield tire plant on the Fayetteville Branch.

In the postwar years, less than car load (LCL) freight traffic declined rapidly on all U. S. Railroads as trucks took over this business. In an attempt to retain some of it, NS inaugurated a new LCL service on trains 98 and 99 in September 1959. This service was given the name "Tarwheel Service," and four boxcars were assigned to it. These cars, numbers NS 25045, NS 25212, NS 25242, and NS 25394, each received a special paint job with "Norfolk Southern Tarwheel" and "Overnite Merchandise Service between Charlotte and Norfolk" emblazoned on the sides. Merchandise deliv-

As the sign says, construction was under way on the NS Lee Creek Branch when this photo was made in November 1965. NS employees Garland Speight, George Comer, and Bennie Pierce(left to right) examine the construction. Note that concrete ties are being installed. The right-of-way at this point was formerly the route of Atlantic Coast Line subsidiary Washington and Vandemere Railroad, abandoned in 1952. (Harry Bundy photo)

ered to the NS Monday through Friday at Norfolk or Charlotte prior to the cut off time would be transported to the opposite end of the railroad overnight. There was also an option of pickup or delivery service available at both ends of the road. Unfortunately, the newly painted boxcars failed to halt the decline in LCL traffic.

In 1962, NS managers reconsidered the idea of beginning piggyback service, and this time decided in favor of doing so. They chose to get flat cars for the service from the Trailer Train pool instead of converting their own flat cars. The construction of ramps for circus style loading began near the end of the year and continued on into 1963. Ramps were located at Norfolk,

Seaboard Coast Line obtained trackage rights over Southern Railway to operate into the Lee Creek plant of Texas Gulf Sulphur in 1977, and Seaboard successor CSX Transportation continues to exercise those rights. This view shows the daily CSX train running on NS rails from Lee Creek to Greenville, NC, where it will return to CSX rails, on June 21, 1997. The location is the small town of Blount's Creek, and at this location, the rails are on the roadbed once occupied by the Washington and Vandemere Railroad, owned by CSX predecessor Atlantic Coast Line. Note the mixture of original concrete ties and replacement wooden ties.
(Robert C. Reisweber photo)

Virginia Beach, Shelton, Elizabeth City, Wilson, Raleigh, Durham, and Charlotte. Trailers for this service were leased from REALCO, a subsidiary of Railway Express Agency. They were standard double axle 40-foot trailers with the reporting marks RNSZ.

By this time, trains 98 and 99 had been discontinued. With no dedicated fast freight train, short route hauls, and the expense of contracting with a trucking company at each ramp location for the loading and unloading of trailers, Norfolk Southern's TOFC program faced long odds for success. While some piggyback traffic did move on the NS, much of it was freight that had previously been hauled in boxcars by the railroad instead of new business. Within a few years the TOFC program was terminated and the leased equipment returned to its owner.

The most promising development for new business for the NS was the news in 1957 that serious consideration was being given to the mining of phosphates in the area near Aurora, North Carolina. Aurora is only about thirty miles from Chocowinity, and NS quickly began to plan a new branch to the area.

Another major challenge arose in connection with this development. This was created by the Atlantic Coast Line. That railroad had operated a subsidiary company, the Washington and Vandemere, between the two North Carolina towns of its name. The line went through Aurora and skirted the edge of the area of the phosphate deposits. It must have been a considerable shock to ACL managers to hear that a major source of rail traffic was about to open up in the area, because they had abandoned the W&V just a few years earlier. They immediately challenged the right of the NS to build a line into the area, even though they had relinquished their own rights to operate there. The ICC ruled in favor of the NS, but the ACL then appealed the decision to the United States District Court in Richmond. The court reaffirmed the ICC decision and opened the way for NS construction of the new line, but this decision did not become final until 1965.

The new line was called the Lee Creek Branch. It left the main line at Phosphate Junction, two miles north of Chocowinity, and extended to Lee Creek, a small stream which empties into the Pamlico River near Aurora. At this point, Texas Gulf Sulphur Company built a large chemical complex to process the phosphates being mined in the vicinity. The branch was built with 100-pound rail, and was one of the earliest applications of prestressed concrete ties. It is also notable that a large portion of the new line was built directly on the abandoned roadbed of the Washington and Vandemere. As a supreme irony, in 1977 Seaboard Coast Line, successor to the ACL, obtained trackage rights to run to the Texas Gulf complex over the roadbed they had abandoned twenty-five years earlier.

Service on the new line began in 1966, even before it was 100 percent complete. Texas Gulf Sulphur had a pressing need for shipments of heavy mining machinery before construction could be completed. As a temporary measure, track laying was speeded up by spacing ties twice as far apart as usual in some locations, with the remaining ties installed as time permitted later on. Since the concrete ties were spaced more widely than wood ties anyway, railroad officials must have had a few anxious moments when the first train ran.

The concrete ties were not a complete success in this application, as they deteriorated more rapidly than had been expected. It is probable that the wider than normal spacing, combined with the leaving out of every other tie at some locations in the early days of operation had something to do with this. Today most of the concrete ties have been replaced by conventional wood ties on the branch. The railroad has not allowed the concrete ties to be completely wasted, however. Worn out ties have been used to build retaining walls between the tracks and adjacent waters at some locations.

In 1961, NS was notified that its lease of office space in the Norfolk Terminal Station building would soon be canceled as the building was about to be torn down. NS was forced to develop plans for a new headquarters location. The decision was made to build a new office building in Raleigh on what is now known as Capital Boulevard, adjacent to the main line near Crabtree Creek, north of Glenwood Yard. At the same time, a feasibility study was done to determine if it would be cost effective to build a new shop and yard complex along the main line just north of the new office building, to replace cramped Glenwood Yard. It was concluded that the cost of these new facilities would be too great to be practical, but the new office building was built and became home to NS corporate offices until the merger with Southern Railway. The building is still in existence today, although no longer used by the railroad.

A small but useful addition to the trackage operated occurred in 1965, when the Norfolk Southern began to operate some of the trackage in Farmville, NC, formerly belonging to the East Carolina Railroad, an

GP18 number 15 works by the blimp hangar at Weeksville, NC. This building, called Dock Number One, had been built in 1940, and was used to house airships which patrolled the east coast for German submarines during World War II. It is 960 feet long and 300 feet high, covered with metal with curved "clamshell" folding doors at each end. An even larger hangar, Dock Number Two, built largely of wood, stood nearby until destroyed by a spectacular fire in 1995. NS delivered shipments of helium here to fill the blimps. (Fred Elkins photo, Robert C. Reisweber collection)

Atlantic Coast Line subsidiary. The East Carolina, which crossed and connected with the NS at Farmville, was abandoned in that year. Farmville, although a small city, generated a significant amount of rail traffic. Appropriately enough, most of this was farm related, particularly tobacco.

In 1966, NS added more trackage to its lines. This was the 7 fi mile long Weeksville spur out of Elizabeth City. The spur had originally been built and operated by the U. S. Government. It served a Coast Guard Air Station, but the main business was an unusual one, an airship base built by the U. S. Navy. This had been built in 1940 to house blimps used during World War II to search for German submarines off the east coast. The base received shipments of helium over the NS. These shipments were novel in that charges were based not on weight but on lack of weight. That is, how much more the empty car weighed than the loaded car. Fortunately, no car ever came in overloaded to the point that it floated away!

In 1969, 19 miles of the track of the NS Durham Branch had to be relocated in connection with construction of a flood control dam on the New Hope River. The construction was paid for by the federal government and called for replacement in kind. This presented somewhat of a problem, as in this case, "in kind" meant 70-pound rail, and no steel company was rolling 70-pound rail at this date. The Corps of Engineers offered to supply 100-pound relay rail, but the NS declined this. As a result, a special order of 70-pound rail was obtained. The line relocation was completed and opened for business in 1973. Ironically, developments were by then under way which would make the entire Durham Branch redundant.

During the 1960s, a wave of mergers of railroad companies was gathering momentum. The idea that there were too many competing companies in the railroad industry was not new. Soon after World War I, the Interstate Commerce Commission began to develop plans to combine the numerous independent companies then existing into a few much larger companies. This effort did not make much progress as most of the companies involved found something to dislike in each plan as soon as it was announced. In December 1929, the Commission announced a nationwide plan to form 21 systems to include nearly all the existing companies. This plan assigned the Norfolk Southern to a system based on the Southern Railway. Two other big southeastern railroads were proposed, one based on the Atlantic Coast Line and Louisville and Nashville, the other on the Seaboard Air Line, which was to include the Norfolk and Western, the Wabash, the Lehigh Valley, and several others. You are no doubt aware that this plan was never implemented, although some of the recommended combinations did come to pass later.

The merger mania beginning in the 1960s and still going on was not a part of any comprehensive plan, but simply the result of various individual companies negotiating with each other. The first merger to have an important effect on the NS was that of the Atlantic Coast Line and Seaboard Air Line. This finally took place on July 1, 1967, after several years of discussions. The NS had recognized as soon as the preliminary negotiations between these companies started that this merger would increase competitive pressure on its own business. As a result, NS requested that the new Seaboard Coast Line open certain new traffic areas to it, which request was granted by the ICC. The ICC also

On June 20, 1972, Norfolk Southern hosted an inspection train of officials of future merger partner Southern Railway over the railroad. This view, taken from the locomotive cab just north of the Albemarle Sound bridge, shows the train as it is about to cross the sound. (Fred Elkins photo, Bennie Pierce collection)

NS even though passenger and perishable freight traffic had not used the connection for a long time. The Pennsylvania Railroad had long since lost most of its interest in the route and had reduced maintenance on it. The bankrupt Penn Central, of course, had even less interest in spending any of its scarce funds on upkeep of this line. As a result, the NS lost considerable traffic, and also found itself owed money by Penn Central that it could not collect. Fortunately, the NS was able to stay out of the bankruptcy courts, however.

By the early 1970s, NS business was picking up due to the new industrial developments along its lines that we have already mentioned, but NS management was still plagued by its longtime problem of a lack of sufficient funds to modernize the line to maximize the growth potential. Heavier rail was being laid, wooden trestles were being replaced with fills and steel and concrete bridges, and new special purpose freight cars were being bought as fast as finances permitted, but this was not fast enough. Management decided that

placed an unusual condition on the merger, namely that Norfolk Southern and eight other southeastern roads be included in the merged company if they so chose within in the next five years. However, NS management stated at the time that it was not planning to do this, and was not discussing a merger with any other railroad.

Another merger which had impact on the Norfolk Southern was that of the Pennsylvania Railroad and the New York Central Railroad into Penn Central in 1968. Much has been written about that merger and the bankruptcy of the new company only two years later. You are probably already aware that the Penn Central bankruptcy created a domino effect on most northeastern railroads, as debts due to them from the Penn Central became uncollectible, driving these already financially weak companies into bankruptcy also. It is not nearly as well known, but Norfolk Southern was also affected. The connection with Penn Central, successor to the Pennsylvania Railroad subsidiary New York, Philadelphia, and Norfolk, was still important to the

It is January 27, 1974, and Norfolk Southern and Southern Railway have started to combine operations in Raleigh. NS AS416 number 1612 works by the Southern Railway depot in this view. Number 1612 and all the other NS Baldwins would be out of service within days. This depot saw no passenger service in 1974, but became the Amtrak depot for Raleigh when Amtrak trains were rerouted over the former Southern Railway line from Raleigh to Selma, NC in 1986. (Robert Graham photo)

By May 1974, Norfolk Southern units were being seen throughout the Southern Railway system. In this view, a solid lashup of NS GP18s handles a Southern train through Greensboro. Rebuilding and repainting of the NS units to conform to SR standards was under way, but these three units had not yet gotten their turn. (Tom Sink photo)

merger with a larger and better financed system offered the best possibility for upgrading the line.

In 1972 it was announced that merger talks with Southern Railway were under way. The announcement did not produce much adverse reaction, and was quickly approved by the stockholders of both NS and Southern, and by the ICC. The merger actually took place on January 1, 1974. By this time, Henry Oetjen had retired as NS president and had been replaced by Dominic A. Flammia, Jr., who had previously been vice-president-marketing. Henry Bruns remained as chairman of the board until the end.

Southern Railway was not being charitable in agreeing to absorb the NS. It recognized that it would get significant benefit from the merger. Most important was a line of its own into the Hampton Roads port area. Southern had handled a significant amount of freight to that port almost from the time it was organized in 1894, but it needed 155 miles of trackage rights over the Atlantic Coast Line from Selma, NC to Portsmouth, VA to get there. The money paid for the rights was an undesirable expense, particularly as the line had become redundant to the new Seaboard Coast Line, which preferred the parallel route of the Seaboard Air Line into Portsmouth. Absorption of the NS would allow Southern Railway to put its traffic on NS rails and discontinue paying for trackage rights. The ultimate result of this is that most of the old ACL line into Portsmouth has now been abandoned.

Southern Railway began to make changes as soon as the merger became official. The most obvious of the early changes was to Norfolk Southern motive power. The EMD locomotives were rebuilt with high short hoods replacing the original low short hoods, to conform to Southern Railway standards of the time. They also received the Southern black, gray, and gold color scheme and the large Southern name on the long hood. They were renumbered to group them with other Southern units of like model. The GE 70-ton diesels also got Southern paint, but the Baldwin locomotives were not wanted by Southern and were out of service and waiting to go to scrap within weeks of the merger.

The repainting of diesels in the Southern color scheme with the prominent Southern name was symbolic of the disappearance of Norfolk Southern, but that disappearance was not complete, and the paint jobs were symbolic of that as well. NS, instead of being merged into Southern Railway Company proper, was absorbed into a wholly-owned subsidiary, the Carolina and Northwestern Railway Company. That company

In 1974, Southern Railway was still operating the Piedmont as a secondary Washington-Atlanta passenger train on their main line. The train was a money-loser, and the railroad tried to cut its losses by using it in as many ways as it could find, such as by ferrying freight locomotives. On March 23, 1974, the northbound Piedmont arrives in Salisbury with two former Norfolk Southern locomotives on the point. GP18 number 2 is getting some practice at running long hood first, as will be normal after rebuilding, although at the time of the photo, the control stand was still set up for running with short hood first. (Curt Tillotson photo)

On March 5, 1974, Southern Railway operated this funeral train of the remaining former Norfolk Southern Baldwin AS416s on their way to be scrapped. In this photo the train is passing through Burlington, NC., over track already used by traffic formerly routed over the Norfolk Southern Western District. (Robert Drake photo, Robert C. Reisweber collection)

was originally a narrow-gauge railroad running from Chester, SC, to Lenoir, NC, but was widened to standard gauge in 1902. By 1974, the company had absorbed several other short lines such as the Danville and Western, the Blue Ridge Railway, and the High Point, Randleman, Asheboro, and Southern. (The latter line had taken over a short portion of the NS Asheboro branch in that city when it was abandoned, incidentally.) Another component was the Yadkin Railroad, which had run from the Southern Railway main line at Salisbury, NC to a connection with the NS at Norwood until twelve miles of the southern end of the line were

abandoned in 1938. At the time the NS was merged into the Carolina and Northwestern, the latter company's name was changed to the Norfolk Southern Railway Company, so that name did not disappear with the merger. The new paint scheme on the former NS locomotives showed this by small "NS" initials below the numbers on the cab sides.

Since the Norfolk-to-Raleigh line of the Norfolk Southern was to become a main line of Southern Railway, that company soon invested in an upgrade program to that line which the old NS management had always wanted but could never afford. Continuous welded rail was installed, and many trestles, notably including the Albemarle Sound trestle, were upgraded with steel pipes and precast concrete caps replacing the wood pilings and caps. Several of the branch lines also benefitted from increased maintenance expenditures.

Although Southern Railway had big plans for the Norfolk-to-Raleigh end of the main line, it had no such plans for the Raleigh-to-Charlotte end. Through freight was diverted to the long-established Southern Railway line between those points via Greensboro. So the dream of the founders of the Raleigh, Charlotte, and Southern to take business away from that line finally expired. The NS line remained largely intact, but became essentially a branch line. The last few miles in Charlotte were removed, as Southern installed a new connection from the NS main line just north (by timetable, east by compass) of the Charlotte Yard to its own adjacent Charlotte Yard. The NS yard and the tracks to the Seaboard interchange and the old NS downtown station site were removed. This made

Even before the merger of Norfolk Southern and Southern Railway became official on January 1, 1974, Southern had begun to invest in upgrading the NS track. Here, the Southern Railway rail train is carrying rail to upgrade the Fayetteville Branch on November 3, 1973. (Wharton Separk III photo)

Southern the possessor of valuable land in downtown Charlotte which it no longer needed and could sell for other development.

With Southern Railway operating its Norfolk-bound trains over the NS, Carolina Yard became the main yard for Southern in the Norfolk area. The old Southern Railway yard at Pinner's Point, beside the ACL yard, where Southern had maintained several wharves in olden days, declined in importance. A new intermodal facility was installed at Carolina Yard, but the former NS locomotive backshop was closed and maintenance of former NS locomotives was transferred to other Southern facilities.

Another line for which Southern Railway had little use was the newly reconstructed Durham branch. Durham was an important point on the Southern Raleigh-to-Greensboro line, which could easily handle the traffic. The portion of the Durham Branch from Duncan to Bonsal was immediately removed from service. The part from Durham to Bonsal continued to be

It is December 23, 1976, and Southern Railway has strengthened this trestle south of Glenwood Yard in Raleigh by replacing the wood trestle components with steel. Number 8259 is one of the aging GP7s that Southern assigned to former NS lines in the years immediately after the merger. (Curt Tillotson photo)

operated for several years to serve a pulpwood yard located at Bonsal and to carry equipment and construction materials to the site of the Harris Power Plant of the Carolina Power and Light Company, then under construction. Norfolk Southern crews would be called at Glenwood Yard on an as-needed basis to run over Southern rails to Durham where they would access the former NS Durham Branch to go to Bonsal. This operation ended in 1982, at which time the remaining trackage of the branch was abandoned except for four miles out of Bonsal. This was sold to the East Carolina Chapter of the National Railway Historical Society, which uses it for a museum and excursion railroad called the New Hope Valley Railroad. The latter name duplicates the original name of the Durham and South Carolina Railroad which built the line.

Not long after the Southern Railway took over the NS, news came out which promised an increase of business over the old NS lines. The newly formed U. S. Railroad Administration was hard at work trying to make a workable rail system out of the mess that was Penn Central and the other bankrupt northeastern roads. They decided to create a new Consolidated Rail Corporation (Conrail)

Southern Railway began to route through freight from Raleigh to Charlotte via its own line through Greensboro soon after the merger. In this view, a train out of Glenwood Yard with NS GP18 Number 1 on the point has negotiated trackage rights over the Seaboard Coast Line to get to the SR main line headed toward Greensboro. A train on NS track waits to pass through Boylan interlocking headed north to Glenwood after the Greensboro-bound train passes. (Wharton Separk III photo)

By December 5, 1986, the date of this photo, the days of the Albemarle Sound bridge were numbered. Southbound freight trains ran out of Norfolk on Mondays, Wednesdays, and Fridays, laying over for the night in Plymouth, then returning northbound the following day. There was still enough traffic on this Friday to make a good sized train. On January 6, 1987, the bridge would be closed and was soon removed. (Kurt Reisweber photo)

out of the most economically viable parts of those roads. This did not include the southern end of the old Penn Central Delmarva Division (the former New York, Philadelphia, and Norfolk), so they solicited offers from other railroads to take it over. Southern Railway offered to take over the former Penn Central trackage from Wilmington, Delaware, south. If this had happened, Southern would no doubt have upgraded the very badly deteriorated track, which would have made the Norfolk connection to the old NS better able to compete for business with other routes. Unfortunately, the deal fell through. Conrail operated the line in the first year of its existence. ("Operate" should be considered a euphemism for what went on there at that time). After that, the line from Pocomoke City, MD, south, was purchased by the Accomack- Northampton District Transportation Authority, an agency of those two Virginia counties. It was first operated under contract by the Virginia and Maryland Railroad, and is currently operated by the Bay Coast Railroad, which still operates a car ferry across Chesapeake Bay, but with traffic level much reduced from the best days of long ago.

The merger with Southern was a big boon to the Norfolk-to-Raleigh line. Only eight years later, however, an event occurred which negated that effect.

This was the merger of Southern Railway with the Norfolk and Western Railway to produce the new Norfolk Southern Corporation. The name sounded familiar, but there was little other resemblance between this huge new corporation and the old Norfolk Southern. And it was no surprise to anyone that one of the results of this merger was the diversion of most of the Southern Railway traffic to Norfolk onto the highly-developed double-track N&W line into Norfolk. The upgrading of the original NS line was then halted. The small amount of traffic that continued to cross the Albemarle Sound trestle was not enough to pay for its maintenance. Before long, through freight runs between Norfolk and Raleigh were discontinued. A thrice-weekly run from Norfolk to Plymouth, returning the following day, handled the few remaining cars that needed to cross the sound. At Plymouth, connection was made with the daily Chocowinity-Plymouth local, which connected in turn with a daily Raleigh-Chocowinity run. This was not a very expeditious way to get a shipment from Norfolk to Raleigh. Finally, in January 1987, the Albemarle Sound bridge was taken out of service and was soon torn down.

At this point, it is necessary to provide some additional information on the structure of today's

The thrice-weekly freight train between Norfolk and Plymouth heads north across the Albemarle Sound bridge on the morning of January 3, 1987. Lead unit, number 1309, is the first of twenty GP35s in the last order for this model placed by Norfolk and Western, still in N&W paint. Neither photographer Terry nor the train crew knew it at the time, but this would be the last revenue run across the bridge. (Dennis Terry photo)

Norfolk Southern Corporation and its relation to the Norfolk Southern name. This is rather dry and confusing material, but without it confusion may occur as to which Norfolk Southern is being talked about. The Norfolk Southern Corporation which was formed in 1982 was essentially a holding company owning the Southern Railway and Norfolk and Western Railway, which were technically still separate companies. But remember that Southern Railway still had a subsidiary company named Norfolk Southern Railway Company, which operated the original NS and the lines which had made up the Carolina and Northwestern. To reduce the confusion, that NS Ry Co. was then renamed the Carolina and Northwestern Railway Company. The former NS diesels that had gotten the small initials "NS" on the cab then had those initials replaced by "CRN" to indicate the new name. Incidentally, Southern Railway between 1974 and 1982 bought a few new locomotives in the name of the Norfolk Southern Railway. These also got the NS initials on the cab, and they also were relettered CRN for the new company. One of these was an SD40-2, a monster vastly different from any motive power ever bought by the original NS.

In 1991, another financial restructuring took place. At that time, the Southern Railway Company was renamed the Norfolk Southern Railway Company, and this company became the owner of the Norfolk and Western Railway Company. So the 1883 Norfolk Southern Railroad Company name has progressed to the 1991 Norfolk Southern Railway Company name, but obviously it would be facetious to suggest that nothing had changed but a little orderly growth.

It is ironic that the merger which made the Norfolk Southern name apply to one of the largest U. S. Railroads also ended the usefulness of the original Norfolk Southern as a through route. It might be thought that this would result in the original Norfolk Southern quickly withering away and disappearing. But in fact, a surprising amount of original NS trackage remains active today. More than 500 miles of the peak mileage of 942 is still in service. Today's Norfolk Southern Corporation operates the 196 miles of main line from Mackeys to Gulf, the three miles from Carolina Junction to Berkley, the Lee Creek, New Bern, and Fayetteville Branches, the Virginia Beach South Route as far as Oldfield station, milepost 15.2, and the former Atlantic and North Carolina Railroad from Goldsboro to Morehead City.

The latter line is now owned by the North Carolina Railroad Company, which absorbed the Atlantic and North Carolina Railroad Company in 1989. Both these companies had been owned mainly by the state of North Carolina, which has now assumed total ownership of the North Carolina Railroad Company. The NCRR and the A&NC connected at Goldsboro, forming a continuous line from Charlotte through Greensboro and Raleigh to Morehead City. The line is now operated by today's Norfolk Southern Corporation by trackage rights. The state elected to give trackage rights to NS instead of renewing the lease so that it would have more control over the future development of the route, possibly including expanded passenger service.

In addition, NSC has turned over operation of additional trackage to several short lines under its Thoroughbred Short Line program. In this program, marginally profitable lines were sold or leased for operation by short lines with minimum overhead expenses. This included 70 miles of main line between Carolina Junction and Edenton to the Chesapeake and Albemarle Railroad, 104 miles of main line between Gulf and

Carolina Coastal Railway now operates the former Norfolk Southern Belhaven Branch under the Norfolk Southern Thoroughbred Short Line Program. Here their Baldwin S12m unit number 127 is hauling cars loaded with grain, their primary commodity, past Wilkinson station toward Pinetown on August 28, 1993. The large house on the left is one of the plantation houses built by the Wilkinson family, which was the driving force behind the development of Belhaven as a port in the 1890s. John Wilkinson was vice-president of the John L. Roper Lumber Company. Number 127, a former Missouri-Kansas-Texas Railroad (Katy) unit, was the last Baldwin locomotive (albeit re-engined by EMD) to operate regularly on the NS lines. It was removed from service in 1998, and was cut up at Pinetown in 2001. (Robert C. Reisweber photo)

Charlotte and the Aberdeen branch to the Aberdeen, Carolina, and Western Railway, the Belhaven Branch to the Carolina Coastal Railway, and the remaining portion of the Virginia Beach North Route (which now ends at Diamond Springs, milepost 7.8) to the Bay Coast Railroad. The only important trackage which has been abandoned completely since the SR-N&W merger is the nineteen miles of track from Edenton to Plymouth, including the Albemarle Sound bridge, most of the Virginia Beach South Route and the Beaufort and Morehead Railroad, and the remainder of the Oriental Branch to Bayboro, which the original NS wanted to abandon before the SR merger but was denied permission to do so.

So while at first glance, it appears that the old NS has been completely obliterated by the huge new Norfolk Southern Railway, beneath the surface significant reminders of the old NS remain. Trains still rumble over the long trestles across the Neuse and Pamlico Rivers, and children in such places as Raleigh, New Bern, Wilson, and Fayetteville wave at crews on black-and-white diesels as their fathers did to crews on red, yellow, and black diesels or 2-8-0 and 2-8-4 steam locomotives. Some of the crewmen they

wave to are the same original NS crewmen their fathers waved to, although time is taking its inevitable toll. It is fruitless to try to predict how long these vestiges of the original Norfolk Southern Railroad will continue to exist, but we hope that these pages will preserve their memory.

Early in 1997, Eastern Shore Railroad, which then operated the Chesapeake Bay car ferry service and the connecting trackage formerly owned by the Pennsylvania Railroad, took over operation of what remained of the former Norfolk Southern North Route to Virginia Beach. Here, ESHR GP10 number 8096 spots a car at Gordon Paper Company, the only remaining customer on the line, at Diamond Springs, current end of active track. The date is May 1, 1997. The Bay Coast Railroad now operates this track. (Robert C. Reisweber photo)

Locomotive number 6, an 0-4-0, was the first switcher purchased by the Norfolk Southern. It was built by Baldwin in 1886, was renumbered as second number 1 in 1906, and sold to the John L. Roper Lumber Company (by then a NS subsidiary) in 1907. It had 49 inch drivers, 130 pounds steam pressure, weighed 53,900 pounds, and exerted 11,156 pounds tractive effort. Note the link-and-pin coupler pocket on the pilot beam. (Railroad Museum of Pennsylvania, Pennsylvania Historical and Museum Commission)

Chapter 7

Steam Locomotives

In 1881, the infant Elizabeth City and Norfolk Railroad opened its motive power roster with three locomotives. The three were numbered 1 through 3, logically enough, and in conformance to common practice of the day, were also given names. Number 1 was named *W. B. Dominick* after the Treasurer of the Corporation. Numbers 2 and 3 were named *William Underwood* and *Graham King,* respectively. The significance of these two names has been lost to time, but it is likely that they were prominent investors in the venture. As we have noted earlier, corporate President William B. Philips had to be content with seeing his name on the company's first tugboat. A photo of locomotive number 1 appears in chapter 1 of this book.

All these locomotives had a 4-4-0 wheel arrangement, scarcely unusual for the 1880s, and were purchased from the Baldwin Locomotive Works. This was not unusual either, as Baldwin was by far the biggest of the U. S. locomotive builders in the nineteenth century, but it established a pattern to which EC&N successor Norfolk Southern would hold with unusual consistency in the years to come. In fact, until Baldwin withdrew from the locomotive manufacturing business in 1956, NS ordered no more than five new locomotives from any other builder. It did buy a few products of other builders secondhand, and inherited others from railroads it absorbed, but most of these soon left the roster.

During its early years, NS's locomotive numbering scheme was simple. Each new locomotive obtained was given the next higher number, regard-less of type, size or origin. Most were 4-4-0s, but there were also a few 2-6-0s and two switchers, an 0-4-0 and an 0-6-0. The first of the non-Baldwin locomotives was another 4-4-0 built by the Manchester Locomotive Works, and numbered 4. Little record remains of this locomotive, but it had left the roster by 1906. It is not even known for certain that number 4 was not a secondhand locomotive. The 0-6-0, numbered 14, was bought from Schenectady Locomotive Works in 1900. It would be 1948 before another non-Baldwin would be purchased. We will have to wait for the chapter on diesel locomotives to learn more about that purchase. Apparently it was not dissatisfaction with number 14's performance that led NS to avoid other builders, since it stayed on the NS roster for 35 years.

0-6-0 number 14 is shown at Berkley, probably not long after delivery by Schenectady Locomotive Works in 1900. This was the last steam locomotive the NS ordered from any manufacturer other than Baldwin. It was renumbered 3 in 1906 and renumbered again to 4 a year later. It was turned over to the Atlantic and North Carolina when the lease of that road ended in 1935, and is shown elsewhere in this book as A&NC number 4.
(Harold K. Vollrath collection)

When the NS began to take over other railroads and add their locomotives to its roster, the simple numbering scheme became awkward. The added locomotives were already numbered, and often in conflict with existing NS numbers. In 1906, when the big merger occurred which brought the A&NC, the V&CC, the PO&W, and the R&PS into the fold, it was decided that a systematic numbering scheme and classification should be adopted. The classification scheme adopted was the common one of giving each different wheel arrangement a separate class signified by a letter of the alphabet. Under each class, though, the N&S (as it had now become) adopted a novel subclassification scheme. Each subclass contained locomotives with the same cylinder diameter, and was represented by a number following the letter. Most railroads used numbered subclasses, but they did not usually represent cylinder diameters. Although the classification was officially established by management, train crews usually referred to locomotives by road number series instead.

The N&S subclassification scheme gave a rough idea of the size and power of the locomotive, as these usually increased with increasing cylinder size. It also gave a clue about the age of the locomotive, as newer locomotives were usually bigger and had larger cylinders. However, it had the disadvantage that locomotives that had nothing in common but wheel arrangement and cylinder diameter sometimes were put into the same class.

Establishing a logical classification system was easy, but the N&S soon found that implementing it was easier said than done. No sooner would they get the locomotives classified and numbered than new locomotives were obtained which should logically fit in the

Number 9, shown here in service at Glenwood yard, Raleigh, July 9, 1936, was the third of three 0-6-0 switchers built for the NS by Baldwin in 1920. The other two, numbers 7 and 8, spent most of their time at Carolina Yard and at Wilson. All three were scrapped shortly after the diesel switchers began to arrive on the property. (William Monypenny photo, Frank Ardrey, Jr. collection)

0-6-0 number 7 is at Carolina Yard in May 1946. Tommy Coates is at the pilot step. (Harold Vollrath collection)

middle of the already determined classes and numbers. It was not until some time after the assimilation of the Raleigh, Charlotte, and Southern locomotives into the roster that the plan was completely implemented, and even then some inconsistencies remained, as we will see. Meanwhile, several locomotives were renumbered, some more than once. In most cases, we will only refer to a locomotive's final number and class in this book. Information on earlier numbers can be found in Richard E. Prince's book, *Norfolk Southern Railroad, Old Dominion Line, and Connections.*

Class A

The N&S put all its switchers into class A. This created a brief exception to the unique wheel arrangement-class relation, as in early years the road owned switchers with both four and six driving wheel arrangements. This did not last long, however, as the four drivered switchers were off the roster by 1912. Originally there were four subclasses. Class A1 was an 0-4-4T locomotive which had been PO&W number 1. Class A2 was an 0-4-0 which had been V&CC number 18. Classes A3 and A4 were 0-6-0s with 17 and 18 inch diameter cylinders, respectively. There was only one locomotive in A3 class, number 3, which had been A&NC number 30, while A4 class included three locomotives. One, the oddball Schenectady product formerly Number 14 but now number 4, was considerably older and lighter than the other two.

After the switchers with four drivers left the roster, the 0-6-0 subclasses A3 and A4 became new subclasses A1 and A2. In 1920, three new 0-6-0s were purchased from Baldwin, and were given a new A3 class as they had 19 inch diameter cylinders.

Road numbers 1-19 were originally set aside for switchers, but the numbers never went over 9 as this

Left: This photo of Norfolk and Southern 4-4-0 number 21 was apparently taken about 1900. That would make it the first of three locomotives to carry N&S number 21 and the former number 1 of the Norfolk, Virginia Beach, and Southern. The location is unidentified but the surroundings are typical of the N&S Virginia Beach lines. This locomotive became N&S number 27 in 1907 and was sold to the John L. Roper Lumber Company in 1910. It was classified B3, having 16 inch diameter cylinders. (Norfolk Public Library)

covered all the steam switchers the road ever owned. The 0-4-4T and 0-4-0 were numbers 1 and 2 respectively, and the seven 0-6-0s had numbers 3-9, increasing with increasing subclass number.

In 1935, the four oldest 0-6-0s, numbers 3-6, were turned over to the newly independent Atlantic and North Carolina Railroad. The remaining three 0-6-0s, numbers 7-9, continued to serve the railroad as yard switchers until diesel switchers began to appear on the property in 1946.

Above: 4-4-0 number 47 is shown here at Norfolk in August 1918. It had been built for the Suffolk and Carolina Railroad as number 12 by Baldwin in 1904. It was classified B5 in 1907, then reclassified B4 in 1911 when the last of the original B2 class locomotives was retired and the class numbers were shifted down. In later years, number 47 was often used on the Columbia Branch mixed train. It was retired in 1934.(Thomas T. Taber photo, Railroad Museum of Pennsylvania, Pennsylvania Historical and Museum Commission)

Class B

Class B consisted of locomotives of the 4-4-0 wheel arrangement. This was a very popular wheel arrangement on the N&S as it was on most roads in their early years. By the time the class system was set up, the three original EC&N 4-4-0s had left the roster along with the mysterious Manchester number 4, but the N&S had bought several more and added other 4-4-0s from most of the roads it absorbed. From the time of the first classification, 45 locomotives of this wheel arrangement entered the roster. Some of these were quite elderly, such as two former A&NC engines which dated back to the U. S. Military Railroad of the Civil War era.

There were originally six subclasses, with cylinder diameters increasing from 14 inches to 19 inches with increasing subclass number. The six subclasses were reduced to five in 1911 when number 21, the only B2 class locomotive, was retired. Subclasses B3 through B6 then became B2 through B5, respectively. A year later, the B5 class disappeared when its only two locomotives, numbers 58 and 59, were sold.

Road numbers 20-99 were set aside for this wheel arrangement, but 59 was the highest number used. Some newly acquired locomotives of this wheel arrangement took numbers of earlier engines stricken from the roster. Some locomotives were renumbered to keep the road numbers consistent with the subclass

Below: Engineer William Butt poses in the cab of NS 4-4-0 number 56. Location is not known, but it appears to be the original passenger station in Edenton, near the ferry dock. Number 56 was one of seven identical 4-4-0s built by Baldwin in 1907 to handle the expanded N&S passenger service to New Bern and Raleigh, and the photo was probably taken soon after that to show off the new power. (Edward Harris collection)

As an illustration of the hodgepodge created by the subclassification by cylinder diameter, subclass B3 (formerly B4) included eleven locomotives, coming to the N&S from six different roads, with no more than three of them being built to any single design. Only the wheel arrangement and 17 by 24 inch cylinder size were common to all.

Class C

Class C included locomotives of the 2-6-0 wheel arrangement, known as the Mogul type. This type first came to NS rails in 1890, and became the heavy mainline freight hauler on the line for the next several years. Later, they were replaced in this service by heavier locomotives of 4-6-0 and 2-8-0 wheel arrangement, and became mainly branch line freight and mixed train engines. Since their reign as the premier freight locomotives was fairly short, only fourteen locomotives of this wheel arrangement ever entered the roster.

There were three subclasses of Moguls, with 17, 18, and 19 inch diameter cylinders, respectively. Road numbers from 100 up were set aside for these locomotives. Class C1 locomotives were numbered 100-103 and Class C2 contained numbers 104-107. The four C3 class engines were numbered 116-119, following eight Ten-Wheelers which had originally been classified C2. We will say more about that in the next section.

The four C3 class engines had been ordered by

number. This also resulted in road numbers 17-19 being removed from the group set aside for class A, and being applied to small B1 class 4-4-0s acquired in 1912 from the Raleigh and Southport and the Aberdeen and Asheboro.

The class B locomotives were the primary main line passenger power on the N&S in the early years, and also were used on branch line passenger and mixed trains. They were replaced by Ten-Wheelers on main line passenger trains in the 1920s, but continued on branch line trains.

The most important group of 4-4-0 locomotives were the seven class B4 locomotives, earlier classified as B5, numbered 51 through 57. These were built new for the N&S (by Baldwin, of course) in 1907 to handle the expanded passenger service following the merger of 1906. Although downrated to branch line service, all seven continued on the roster until the 1930s. Number 52 was the last to be retired, in December 1937.

A view of Mogul number 104 on a trestle, perhaps the Albemarle Sound trestle under construction in 1908 or 1909. (DeGolyer Library, Southern Methodist University, Dallas, TX, collection)

the Virginia and Carolina Coast Railroad from the American Locomotive Company Richmond Works just before joining the N&S, but were not delivered until after the merger. They were the heaviest and most powerful of the 2-6-0s on the NS, and lasted the longest, not being retired until the early 1940s. All the others were gone by 1936.

Two of the C1 class Moguls were different in that they had been built as Vauclain Compounds, but had been rebuilt as simple engines. A third Vauclain Compound, originally N&S 2-6-0 number 10, had also been rebuilt simple, but in 1902 was further rebuilt to a 4-4-0 type, so became B5 class engine number 43 when the classification was made. Apparently the rebuilding did not produce a very satisfactory engine as it was scrapped in 1910.

An additional 2-6-0 locomotive was obtained from the Kinston Carolina Railroad in 1924. The KC was a NS subsidiary at that time. It was given road number 102, in place of the Cl class locomotive of that number which had been retired. There is no record of its classification, but it should have been C3 as it had 19 inch diameter cylinders. It was scrapped in 1933.

Class D

In 1907, the N&S purchased eight new locomotives of the 4-6-0 Ten-Wheeler type

Above: A view of 2-6-0 number 107. Date and location are not identified, but the location appears to be Belhaven. Date is probably after 1910, since the scroll herald on the tender says Norfolk Southern rather than Norfolk & Southern. The N&S bought number 107 in 1904 and the NS scrapped it in 1936. (Railroad Museum of Pennsylvania, PHMC)

Right: Number 117 was the second of four 2-6-0 Moguls which had been ordered from Richmond Locomotive Works by the Virginia and Carolina Coast Railroad just before it became part of the N&S in 1906. This view is at New Bern on August 31, 1936. (Philip P. Coulter, Jr. collection)

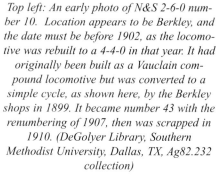

Top left: An early photo of N&S 2-6-0 number 10. Location appears to be Berkley, and the date must be before 1902, as the locomotive was rebuilt to a 4-4-0 in that year. It had originally been built as a Vauclain compound locomotive but was converted to a simple cycle, as shown here, by the Berkley shops in 1899. It became number 43 with the renumbering of 1907, then was scrapped in 1910. (DeGolyer Library, Southern Methodist University, Dallas, TX, Ag82.232 collection)

Middle left: Ten-Wheeler number 113 was one of eight of that wheel arrangement (eventually numbered 108-115) that were built new for the N&S in 1907 to handle the expanded freight service resulting from the extensions to Raleigh and New Bern. Location and date of this photo is unknown but it is probably no later than 1910, as the ampersand appears between the words Norfolk Southern on the tender. Later, number 113 was rebuilt with piston valves, Walschaerts valve gear, and larger drivers, similar to number 110 shown later. These engines, plus similar number 114, then became the road's main passenger power until the end of that service in 1948. (DeGolyer Library, Southern Methodist University, Dallas, TX, Ag82.232 collection)

Lower Left: 4-6-0 number 111 at Norfolk Terminal Station in May 1932. Numbers 108, 109, 111, and 112 were the group first converted from freight service to passenger service by the replacement of the 57 inch drivers with 62 inch, and the replacement of Stephenson valve gear with Southern valve gear. As shown, the cylinders were not altered. This rebuilding was done starting in 1919, but the order in which they were done is not known. These four locomotives then became the main passenger locomotives on the line, but decreasing passenger service and the availability of the more recently converted numbers 110, 113, and 114 made them superfluous in the 1930s. Number 111 was scrapped in 1939. (Harold K. Vollrath collection)

intended for freight service. At first they were placed in the C2 class as they shared the eighteen-inch cylinder diameter with the 2-6-0s of that class. Apparently at the time, the N&S felt that all freight locomotives with six drivers should go into the C class. Also, all freight locomotives were then given consecutive numbers beginning with 100, regardless of wheel arrangement. Later on, these Ten-Wheelers were reclassified D4, as the D

class was then set up to contain that wheel arrangement. The numbers of these eight locomotives remained 108-115 until they were retired, however, placing them in the middle of the C class numbers.

Another group of five Ten-Wheelers was bought from Baldwin in 1911, and soon afterward, an assortment of fourteen more 4-6-0s joined the roster from the Aberdeen and Asheboro, the Raleigh and

Southport, and the Durham and Charlotte. The D class was then established for the Ten-Wheelers, with six subclasses. Road numbers 85 through 98 were borrowed from the group set aside for 4-4-0s to be given to the smallest Ten-Wheelers from the merged roads. Road numbers for Ten-Wheelers eventually got up to 138, but note that all the Moguls retained their numbers in this sequence.

Although the Ten-Wheelers were mainly freight and mixed train locomotives in their early years, it was not long before the first 2-8-0 Consolidation types were purchased and soon became favorites for freight trains. At the same time, NS management began to think that heavier power for the passenger trains would be desirable. As a result, a program was begun to rebuild some of the Ten-Wheelers to make them suit-

Top Right: 4-6-0 number 110 makes the station stop at Edenton with train number 1 in August 1937. This photo shows the result of the rebuilding of this engine for passenger service, with piston valves and Walschaerts valve gear. Driver diameter was also increased from 57 inches to 62 inches for higher speed, although this is not obvious from the photograph. Engines numbers 113 and 114 were similarly rebuilt. These three engines then became the primary power for passenger trains numbers 1 and 2 until they were discontinued on January 31, 1948. (Roy Legg photo, Harry Bundy collection)

Middle Right: Number 133, shown riding the turntable at Carolina Yard, was the third of the four later D6 class Ten-Wheelers, built by Baldwin in 1913. These were the largest, most powerful, and most modern passenger locomotives owned by the NS. They were not the regular power for passenger trains numbers 1 and 2 in later years, but were very useful for pulling Pullmans to Virginia Beach and Pinehurst, for heavy troop and excursion trains, and branch line freight trains. They remained in service until almost the end of steam, and number 133 was one of the last six NS steamers to go to the scrappers. Engineer Bill Munden, who lost his life handling the diesel powered train involved in the Albemarle Sound wreck, is the man in the cab in this photo. (James A. Ramsey photo)

Lower right: A left side view of D6 Ten-Wheeler number 131, taken at Norfolk in August 1916. The locomotive was then only three years old, but it looked little different thirty years later, when its useful life was coming to an end. (Thomas T. Taber photo, Railroad Museum of Pennsylvania, PHMC)

Number 130, shown here at Aberdeen in 1937, is an example of the early D6 class 4-6-0s, which were numbered 126-130. These locomotives were built (by Baldwin, of course), in 1911 with slide valves and Baker valve gear, and used saturated steam. They were very useful in their early years on passenger and mixed trains on the hilly western end of the railroad, but with the end of all that service in 1938, they lost much of their utility to the railroad. Number 130 was the only one of the five to remain in service through World War II, being scrapped in May 1948.
(Harry Bundy collection)

able for passenger service. The locomotives selected were the road's first eight Ten-Wheelers, numbers 108-115.

The first conversion was applied to locomotives numbers 108, 109, 111, and 112. They were all given larger diameter driving wheels to increase their speed capability, but their new 62-inch drivers hardly qualified them to challenge New York Central Hudsons to a race. They were easily fast enough to maintain the 22 mile per hour average scheduled speed of NS passenger trains, however. Their old driver diameter had been 57 inches. The conversion also included applying Southern valve gear in place of the Stephenson valve gear originally supplied. The locomotives' tractive effort dropped to 20,788 pounds from 22,612 pounds because of the increased driver diameter, still adequate for the short NS passenger trains.

Records are incomplete as to the dates of these conversions. It is known that two were converted in 1919, but the dates for the other two are not available. Which two of the four were done in 1919 is also unknown.

At some unknown later date, a more extensive rebuilding was performed on locomotives numbers 110, 113, and 114 of the same group. This involved not only the replacement of drivers, again with new ones of 62-inch diameter, but also the replacement of the original slide valve cylinders with new piston valve cylinders. They also received new valve gear, but Walschaerts was used instead of Southern on these engines. These three engines then became the favored engines for the scheduled passenger trains until dieselization. No 113 was scrapped in 1946, but the other two lasted until 1948.

Since all passenger service other than Norfolk-to-Raleigh trains numbers 1 and 2 ended by 1938, the four earlier rebuilt locomotives were no longer needed for passenger service after that, and all were scrapped by 1940. Number 115, the last of the class D4 Ten-Wheelers, which was never rebuilt, was also gone by then.

The heaviest and most modern Ten-Wheelers on the road were the four D6 class engines, numbers 131-134, which were built in 1913. They were built superheated with piston valve cylinders and Baker valve gear, and exerted 31,800 pounds tractive effort. These locomotives were not regularly used on train numbers 1 and 2, but often powered the Pullman runs to Virginia Beach and Pinehurst, and troop trains, which were usually heavier than the regular passenger trains. They were also used on freight, mixed, and special excursion trains. Number 133 was one of the last six steam locomotives on the road, not going to scrap until 1954, while its three sisters lasted almost as long.

Class D6 also included the five Ten-Wheelers, numbers 126-130, which were built in 1911. They were not nearly as modern as numbers 131-134, having slide valves, and not being superheated. They were all scrapped by 1948.

Class D also included two secondhand Ten-Wheelers purchased from the New York Central in 1920, numbered 135 and 136, and classified D5. Also in 1920, two more Ten-Wheelers joined the roster as a result of the lease of their former owner, the Durham and South Carolina Railroad. These were numbered 137 and 138 and classified D4, since they had 18 inch diameter pistons. All four of these locomotives were scrapped by 1940, as were all the former A&A, R&S, and D&C Ten-Wheelers.

Left: Number 128 was one of the early D6 class Ten-Wheelers, built in 1911 with slide valve cylinders, and using saturated steam. (B. E. Lewis photo, Thomas King/C. K. Marsh collection)

Right: 4-6-0 number 138 was one of two Ten-Wheelers that joined the NS roster in 1920 with the lease of the Durham and South Carolina Railroad. It had been number 101 on that road. The other, formerly number 100, became NS number 137. D&SC number 100 had been built by Baldwin in 1906, and was very similar to NS Ten-Wheelers numbers 108-115 as originally built. D&SC number 101 was built by Baldwin in 1911, apparently to the same design as number 100. They served between Duncan and Durham before the NS lease of the D&SC, but afterward they were mainly assigned to the NS Suffolk Branch. This view shows number 138 at Edenton, the south end of that branch. It was retired in November 1939, by which time the Suffolk Branch was inactive although not yet officially abandoned. (Harold K. Vollrath collection)

Class E

Class E included 2-8-0 Consolidation type locomotives. The first order of these arrived on the road in 1910, and were initially numbered 120-122, the next numbers in the freight locomotive series, but were later renumbered 204-206 as it was decided that the Consolidations should be put into the 200 series. These locomotives originally were not superheated and had slide valve cylinders, but in 1929 and 1930, numbers 205 and 206 were rebuilt superheated with piston valve cylinders. Number 204 would probably have gotten the same treatment if the depression had not forced a reduction in expenditures.

NS was impressed with the performance of these locomotives on freight trains, and was soon looking for more Consolidations. Three more of this type were purchased secondhand from the Norfolk and Western. These were first numbered 123-125, but became 200-202 later on. Having 20 by 24 inch cylinders, they then were placed in class E1, while numbers 204-206, with 21 by 28 inch cylinders, became class E2. Numbers 200-202 were more than 20 years old when bought by the NS, and they lasted only until 1926.

Another E1 class Consolidation came to the NS along with the Raleigh and Southport Railroad. This was first given road number 99, but soon became number 203. This locomotive proved to be the longest lived of all NS steam locomotives, as it was sold to the Atlantic and Western in 1948. When it was retired from that road in 1952, it was placed on public display in downtown Sanford, NC, where it remains today, the only surviving example of original Norfolk Southern steam power.

In 1913, the NS bought five more E2 class Consolidations from Baldwin, which were numbered 207-211. These were built superheated with piston valves, and were slightly more powerful than numbers

es. All these locomotives were still active after World War II.

In 1922, the NS was ready for more new freight locomotives. By this time, most railroads were ordering 2-8-2 Mikado type locomotives, but NS decided to buy more Consolidations. The NS was not the only class I railroad to order new Consolidations in this era, but the others, such as Western Maryland and Reading, were ordering them for heavy, slow speed coal drag service. NS freight trains were not nearly as heavy, but NS construction did not allow nearly as much locomotive weight. So the new NS Consolidations were much

204-206 as they had 200 psi steam pressure rather than 190. Then in 1916, six more E2s were purchased and numbered 212-217. These had the same tractive effort as numbers 207-211 but were slightly heavier

In 1920, the NS bought nine Consolidations secondhand from the New York Central System. These were also classed E2 as they shared the 21-inch cylinder diameter with numbers 204-217. They were numbered 218-226. They were considerably older than the NS's own E2s, and all were disposed of in the early 1930s. These were called "bohunks" on the NS, and were not popular with the crews because they did not steam well.

An amusing incident is told about one of these engines. On the night of May 24, 1924, the crew of southbound through freight number 61 had "bohunk" number 226 on the head end. They decided to impress the crew of a northbound train they were to meet at Chapanoke by having the 226 "pop off" when they passed. The head end brakeman passed coal up to the fireman so that he could build up the fire faster. At Suffolk Junction, eight stay bolts blew and the head end crew joined the birds. The locomotive coasted up the track until it stopped. One crewman was injured as a result of his jump, but otherwise only embarrassment resulted.

The NS's original E2s proved to be very useful. Even after they were replaced by heavier power on mainline through freights, they handled freight on branches which were too light for the heavier power, which included most branch-

Above: Number 205 was the second of the E2 class 2-8-0s, which had 21 by 28 inch cylinders. It was one of three of the class built by Baldwin in 1910, and was originally numbered 122. All three of these first used saturated steam and had slide valve cylinders, but numbers 205 and 206 were rebuilt later with piston valves, as shown, and were superheated. Number 204, the first of the three, never got this treatment. This photo shows number 205 at Durham on July 9, 1936. It stayed on the roster until the last of steam, January 29, 1954. (William Monypenny photo, Frank E. Ardrey, Jr. collection)

Below: 2-8-0 Number 203, shown here in service at Glenwood Yard at Raleigh in the late 1930s, was originally number 10 of the Raleigh and Southport Railroad, which was built by Baldwin in 1911, shortly before the R&S became part of the NS. It was a one-of-a-kind locomotive on the NS roster and the lightest consolidation on the road after 1926, but must have been quite satisfactory as the NS kept it until 1948. At that time it was sold to the Atlantic and Western Railroad in Sanford, NC. It is now on public display in downtown Sanford lettered as Atlantic and Western number 12, the only remaining example of NS steam power. (H. L. Kitchen photo, Harry Bundy collection)

lighter than those of the other roads mentioned, but they shared the characteristic that a high percentage of their weight was on their drivers.

The five new Consolidations the NS ordered in 1922 were bigger than the E2 class. They had 22 inch diameter cylinders, so they were classified E3. At first, they were numbered 227-231, but later were renumbered 527-531. Apparently management thought they were enough larger and more modern than the 200 class 2-8-0s that they rated a new number series. The 300 and 400 series numbers were not used because they were occupied by cabooses and work equipment, respectively. The 500s were an immediate success, and three more batches of the same design were ordered over the next five years, making a total of nineteen locomotives. This was the largest number of locomotives of a single design ever to enter the NS roster.

All the E3 class locomotives remained on the roster through World War II. After the first road diesels arrived, the need for them decreased, so seven were sold in 1948 and entered service on the National Railway of Mexico. The remaining twelve lasted into the 1950s. Numbers 538, 542, and 544 were among the last six steamers to leave the property on February 5, 1954. Number 538 apparently was the last of the NS steam locomotives to actually run under steam. It was assigned to work the 7:00 A.M. yard job at Glenwood

Topo Right: Number 217, shown here at Star, was the newest of the E2 class Consolidations, having been built by Baldwin in 1916. It was the last of a batch of six built in that year, all of which were slightly heavier than the eight earlier E2 class engines built for the NS. Note the three air pumps. All NS Consolidations originally had two air pumps, but many had a third pump added later. The E2 class locomotives became the primary NS main line freight engines when they were delivered, but were later displaced from this duty by the heavier E3 class. They remained very useful on some branch lines which could not support the weight of the E3 class, however. (Marvin Black collection)

Middle Right: E3 class 2-8-0 number 537 at a coal chute on August 3, 1945. Location is uncertain but appears to be Raleigh. Note that by this time, number 537 had three air pumps instead of the two it had when built. (William Nixon collection)

Bottom Right: E3 class Consolidation number 541 is shown at the coal chute in Raleigh in 1936. NS eventually placed nineteen locomotives of this class on the roster, and they were the primary main line freight engines until the 2-8-4s were delivered in 1940. The E3 engines were six tons heavier than the E2s and exerted 13 percent greater tractive effort. (B. E. Lewis photo, C. K. Marsh, Jr. collection)

Left: 2-8-0 number 538 is shown at the coal chute in Charlotte on June 8, 1940. Number 538 was one of the last six steam locomotives on the NS roster. On January 12, 1954, it worked the 7:00A.M. yard job at Glenwood Yard in Raleigh. According to best available records, this was the last actual operation of steam power on the NS lines. (P. E. Parrish photo, D. Wallace Johnson collection)

Right: This photo of E3 class Consolidation number 540 shows an unusually good view of tender details. By the time of this photo, all remaining NS Consolidations and Ten-Wheelers had tenders similar to this, featuring the rounded extensions to the tank top, the built up coal bunker, and a multitude of wood planks between tank and frame. Note the back-up light and the radio antenna. The engineer is believed to be J. P. Harris. Also note the wide spacing between the words Norfolk and Southern on the tender. With the railroad about to be reorganized and ready to emerge from receivership in the early 1940s, management decided that all relettering jobs on the tenders should receive this wide spacing, leaving room for an ampersand or the word "and" in case the new corporation should return to the name Norfolk and Southern Railroad. This turned out to be unnecessary, as the new name came out Norfolk Southern Railway, but the large gap was simply left in place. (D. P. McDonald collection)

Below:2-8-0 number 541 is on the turntable at Carolina Yard in February 1951. (H. Reid photo, Bennie Pierce collection)

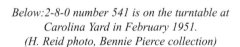

Yard on January 12, 1954. No record of any later operation of a steam locomotive on Norfolk Southern has been found.

Class F

As NS business began to pick up in the late 1930s, management realized that new motive power would be needed to handle it. The newest locomotive on the line was more than ten years old. Many locomotives had gone to scrap during the decade, and several others might as well have, considering their age and condition. New power was discussed with both Baldwin and the American Locomotive Company (Alco). Alco suggested that NS buy 2-10-0s, which would have been a logical step up from the 2-8-0s. Baldwin, on the other hand, suggested 2-8-4s, which appealed to NS management. Five of these locomotives were ordered and delivered in the spring of

Right: Number 600, the first of the NS 2-8-4's, has just received a fresh coat of paint in this photo at Carolina Yard. Its appearance has changed little since it was new, as only the shield over the headlight and the lack of white paint on the tires are different from the photo taken shortly after delivery, shown in chapter 5. The shield over the headlight was added to prevent oil from dripping from the bell ringer mechanism onto the headlight lens. (H. A. Stewart, Jr. photo, Tal Carey collection)

Below: 2-8-4 number 602, shown at Carolina Yard on July 4, 1948. By this time, it was eight years old and would serve the NS for less than three more years. (D. Wallace Johnson photo)

1940. They were placed in class F and numbered 600-604.

While the 2-8-4 wheel arrangement had gained considerable popularity on U. S. Railroads by this time, the NS locomotives were unique in that they were the lightest of this wheel arrangement ever built. This, of course, was due to the light construction of the railroad. NS had been upgrading the line with heavier rail and stronger bridges as finances permitted, but the resources available placed severe restrictions on the amount of improvement achieved.

Although the new locomotives were lighter than others being built at the time, they were furnished with many features applied to larger locomotives of the day. This included a stoker, front-end throttle, roller bearings on the leading truck, six wheel tender trucks, and a booster on the trailing truck. All these features were making their first appearance on the NS. In fact, not only was this the first use of a trailing truck booster on the NS, it was the first use of a trailing truck of any kind. Other features of the design were a one-piece cast steel locomotive bed with integral cylinders and a cast-steel water-bottom frame tender called a Hichen tender. Also included was a lateral motion driving box cushioning device on the first set of drivers that reduced the rigid wheelbase in order to negotiate sharp curves on the Western District.

The F class locomotives exerted 60,400 pounds of tractive force including 11,100 pounds from the booster. This was much greater than the 40,400 pounds of the E3 class Consolidations. As a result, each 2-8-4 was rated at 1550 tons load in the hilly country from Gulf to Mount Gilead, compared to 1000 tons for the E3s. With 63-inch drivers compared to 57-inch on the E3s and a large firebox for generation of plenty of steam, they were not only capable of hauling heavier loads, but could do so at higher speeds.

The new locomotives were highly successful on the NS, and were very important in meeting the challenge of expediting the World War II freight traffic. At the end of the war, however, additional new motive power was needed as the older steam power was now badly worn out. As we noted earlier, management briefly considered ordering five more of the F class 2-8-4s, but finally settled on diesels instead. Since the new diesels took over the through freight trains, and the 2-8-4s were not suitable for local and branch line freights, the latter had little to do after the arrival of the diesels. In late 1950, all five were sold, eventually winding up in service on the National Railway of Mexico along with the seven E3 class Consolidations mentioned earlier

This view of 2-8-4 number 602, made at Raleigh in 1942, shows the left side of the locomotive. Note that the shield over the headlight had not yet been applied at this date. The piping under the rear of the running board leads to the Elesco exhaust steam injector and the trailing truck booster engine.(Wiley M. Bryan photo, Thomas King/C. K. Marsh, Jr. collection)

Steam Locomotive Roster 1914-1954

We have elected to cover in this roster Norfolk Southern steam motive power only in the years from 1914 on, because in earlier years there were many renumberings as the railroad took over motive power from its predecessor lines. These renumberings can be confusing. For a complete all-time roster of NS steam power, see *Norfolk Southern Railroad, Old Dominion Line, and Connections*, by Richard E. Prince.

Road no.	Builder	Const. Date	Const. no.	Driver dia., in	Steam press., psi	Weight, pounds	Tractive effort,pounds	Disposition date	Notes
Class A1, 0-6-0, 17" x 24" cylinders									
3	Baldwin	1905	26855	50	170	92,000	20,045	1935	2
Class A2, 0-6-0, 18" x 24" cylinders									
4	Schenectady	1900	5633	50	180	99,000	23,794	1935	3
5	Baldwin	1907	30520	50	180	104,300	23,794	1935	4
6	Baldwin	1907	30589	50	180	104,300	23,794	1935	4

Class A3, 0-6-0, 19" x 28" cylinders

7	Baldwin	1920	52998	51	190	144,280	32,000	1948	1
8	Baldwin	1920	52999	51	190	144,280	32,000	1948	1
9	Baldwin	1920	53000	51	190	144,280	32,000	1946	1

Class B1, 4-4-0, 14" x 20" cylinders

17	Richmond	1898	2748	48	145	61,000	10,062	1925	1,5
18	Richmond	1895	2510	48	145	56,000	10,062	1925	1,6
19	Richmond	1897	2639	48	145	56,000	10,062	1919	7

Class B2, 4-4-0, 16" x 24" cylinders

22	Richmond	1891	2172	60	145	90,700	12,621	1925	1,8
23	Richmond	1891	2173	60	145	90,700	12,621	1925	1,8
24	Richmond	1895	2456	68	145	94,600	11,136	1925	1,8
25	Richmond	1895	2457	68	145	94,600	11,136	1925	1,8
28	Baldwin	1897	15461	62	160	74,000	13,477	1925	1,9
29	Baldwin	1898	15585	62	160	74,000	13,477	1925	1,9

Class B3, 4-4-0, 17" x 24" cylinders

31	Baldwin	1889	9717	55	130	77,680	13,935	1925	1,10
32	Baldwin	1898	15940	62	160	90,000	15,214	1927	1,11
33	Richmond	1906	40184	62	180	110,500	17,116	1935	1,12
34	Richmond	1906	40185	62	180	110,500	17,116	1932	1,12
35	Richmond	1906	40186	62	180	110,500	17,116	1932	1,12
36	Baldwin	1889	9990	62	140	90,000	13,313	1925	1,13
37	Baldwin	1898	16273	60	145	95,000	14,248	1932?	1,14
38	Pittsburgh	1899	1530	60	145	90,800	14,248	1932	1,15
39	Pittsburgh	1900	1567	60	145	90,800	14,248	1932	1,15
40	Baldwin	1901	18675	60	145	95,000	14,248	1932	1,15
41	Baldwin	1901	18676	60	145	95,000	14,248	1932	1,15

Class B4, 4-4-0, 18" x 24" cylinders

44	Rogers	1882	3143	68	140	94,500	13,608	1925	1,16
46	Baldwin	1904	23885	68	155	98,000	15,066	1926	1,17
47	Baldwin	1904	23487	66	185	115,000	18,527	1934	1,17
49	Baldwin	1904	23901	68	155	98,000	15,066	1932?	1,17,14
50	Pittsburgh	1900	1637	63	165	104,400	16,524	1935	18
51	Baldwin	1907	30522	66	180	110,100	18,017	1932	1
52	Baldwin	1907	30532	66	180	110,100	18,017	1937	1
53	Baldwin	1907	30570	66	180	110,100	18,017	1935	19
54	Baldwin	1907	30571	66	180	110,100	18,017	1935	19
55	Baldwin	1907	30491	66	180	110,100	18,017	1932	1,20
56	Baldwin	1907	30508	66	180	110,100	18,017	1935	19,20
57	Baldwin	1907	30521	66	180	110,100	18,017	1935	19,20

Class C1, 2-6-0, 17" x 24" cylinders

100	Baldwin	1901	18925	62	180	101,200	17,112	1936	1
101	Baldwin	1902	20147	62	180	101,200	17,112	1936	1
103	Baldwin	1896	14742	56	180	105,000	18,950	1926	1

Class C2, 2-6-0, 18" x 24" cylinders

104	Baldwin	1890	11149	56	160	94,000	18,888	1932	1
105	Baldwin	1890	11150	56	160	94,000	18,888	1933	1
106	Baldwin	1904	23850	62	180	110,000	19,186	1934	1
107	Baldwin	1904	23923	62	180	110,000	19,186	1936	1

Class C3, 2-6-0, 19" x 24" cylinders

102	Baldwin	1884	7449	53fi	190	94,700	26,200	1933	1,12
116	Richmond	1906	40180	57	180	131,000	23,528	1941	1,12
117	Richmond	1906	40181	57	180	131,000	23,528	1940	1,12
118	Richmond	1906	40182	57	180	131,000	23,528	1940	1,12
119	Richmond	1906	40183	57	180	131,000	23,528	1940	1,12

Class D1, 4-6-0, 15" x 24" cylinders

| 85 | Baldwin | 1900 | 18424 | 48 | 160 | 85,625 | 15,300 | 1923 | 22 |

Class D2, 4-6-0, 16" x 24" cylinders

| 86 | Baldwin | 1904 | 24229 | 56 | 180 | 96,100 | 16,320 | 1914 | 23 |

Class D3, 4-6-0, 17" x 24" cylinders

87	Lima	1908	1052	56	200	112,000	18,950	1926	1,24
88	Baldwin	1907	31902	56	180	111,250	18,616	1932	1,24
89	Baldwin	1908	33095	56	180	111,250	18,616	1934	1,24
90	Baldwin	1911	36042	56	180	111,250	18,616	1932	1,24
91	Baldwin	1883	6793	49fi	160	96,000	19,056	1932	1,25
92	Baldwin	1907	32059	55	180	103,000	19,294	1937	1,26
93	Brooks	1897	2857	50	170	108,000	18,866	1934	1,27

Class D4, 4-6-0, 18" x 26" cylinders

94	Pittsburgh	1889	1097	44	160	105,900	20,035	1926	1,28,33
95	Rogers	1880	2595	50	140	92,000	18,507	1920	29,33
96	?	?	?	44	140	84,800	21,031	1919	1,30
97	Baldwin	1881	5538	49	130	90,000	17,536	1925	1,31,33
108	Baldwin	1907	30391	62	180	143,800	20,788	1936	1,32,34,36

109	Baldwin	1907	30392	62	180	143,800	20,788	1939	1,32,34,36
110	Baldwin	1907	30390	62	180	143,800	20,788	1948	1,32,35,36
111	Baldwin	1907	30384	62	180	143,800	20,788	1939	1,32,34,36
112	Baldwin	1907	30302	62	180	143,800	20,788	1932	1,32,34
113	Baldwin	1907	30303	62	180	143,800	20,788	1947	1,32,35
114	Baldwin	1907	30317	62	180	143,800	20,788	1948	1,32,35
115	Baldwin	1907	30318	57	180	133,050	22,612	1937	1,32
137	Baldwin	1906	30128	57	180	116,500	22,680	1940	1,37
138	Baldwin	1911	37420	57	180	116,500	22,680	1939	1,37

Class D5, 4-6-0, 19" x 26" cylinders

98	Baldwin	1889	10101	54	130	114,000	15,912	1926	1,38
135	Pittsburgh	1900	2035	63	190	153,100	24,130	1932	1,39
136	Pittsburgh	1900	2040	63	190	153,100	24,130	1937	1,39

Class D6, 4-6-0, 20" x 28" cylinders

126	Baldwin	1911	37300	60	190	165,000	30,210	1940	1
127	Baldwin	1911	37301	60	190	165,000	30,210	1941	1
128	Baldwin	1911	37302	60	190	165,000	30,210	1944	1
129	Baldwin	1911	37328	60	190	165,000	30,210	1940	1
130	Baldwin	1911	37329	60	190	165,000	30,210	1948	1
131	Baldwin	1913	40101	60	200	172,250	31,800	1953	1
132	Baldwin	1913	40102	60	200	172,250	31,800	1952	1
133	Baldwin	1913	40103	60	200	172,250	31,800	1954	1
134	Baldwin	1913	40104	60	200	172,250	31,800	1952	1

Class E1, 2-8-0, 20" x 24" cylinders

200	Roanoke Mach	1889	83	50	135	120,565	24,608	1926	1,40
201	Roanoke Mach	1890	84	50	135	120,565	24,608	1926	1,40
202	Rogers	1891	4554	50	135	120,565	24,608	1926	1,40
203	Baldwin	1911	37161	50	200	144,000	32,600	1948	41

Class E2, 2-8-0, 21" x 28" cylinders

204	Baldwin	1910	34683	57	190	162,000	34,986	1946	1,42
205	Baldwin	1910	34684	57	190	172,525	34,986	1954	1,42
206	Baldwin	1910	34682	57	190	172,525	34,986	1953	1,42
207	Baldwin	1913	40096	57	200	172,525	36,800	1951	1
208	Baldwin	1913	40097	57	200	172,525	36,800	1951	1
209	Baldwin	1913	40098	57	200	172,525	36,800	1953	1
210	Baldwin	1913	40099	57	200	172,525	36,800	1952	1
211	Baldwin	1913	40100	57	200	172,525	36,800	1948	1
212	Baldwin	1916	42925	57	200	179,350	36,800	1952	1
213	Baldwin	1916	42926	57	200	179,350	36,800	1948	1
214	Baldwin	1916	42927	57	200	179,350	36,800	1948	1

215	Baldwin	1916	42928	57	200	179,350	36,800	1954	1
216	Baldwin	1916	42929	57	200	179,350	36,800	1952	1
217	Baldwin	1916	42930	57	200	179,350	36,800	1948	1
218	Brooks	1899	3386	63	200	168,000	35,700	1932	1,43
219	Brooks	1899	3394	63	200	168,000	35,700	1934	1,43
220	Brooks	1900	3407	63	200	168,000	35,700	1933	1,43
221	Brooks	1900	3612	63	200	174,000	35,700	1933	1,43
222	Brooks	1900	3613	63	200	174,000	35,700	1933	1,43
223	Brooks	1900	3617	63	200	174,000	35,700	1935	43,44
224	Brooks	1900	3620	63	200	174,000	35,700	1932	1,43
225	Brooks	1900	3629	63	200	174,000	35,700	1933	1,43
226	Brooks	1900	3634	63	200	174,000	35,700	1932	1,43

Class E3, 2-8-0, 22" x 28" cylinders

527	Baldwin	1922	55557	57	200	191,370	40,400	1951	1,45
528	Baldwin	1922	55558	57	200	191,370	40,400	1952	1,45
529	Baldwin	1922	55559	57	200	191,370	40,400	1953	1,45
530	Baldwin	1922	55560	57	200	191,370	40,400	1952	1,45
531	Baldwin	1922	55561	57	200	191,370	40,400	1948	45,46
532	Baldwin	1923	56855	57	200	191,370	40,400	1948	46
533	Baldwin	1923	56856	57	200	191,370	40,400	1952	1
534	Baldwin	1923	56857	57	200	191,370	40,400	1948	46
535	Baldwin	1923	56858	57	200	191,370	40,400	1948	46
536	Baldwin	1923	56859	57	200	191,370	40,400	1948	46
537	Baldwin	1923	56860	57	200	191,370	40,400	1948	46
538	Baldwin	1926	59065	57	200	191,370	40,400	1954	1
539	Baldwin	1926	59066	57	200	191,370	40,400	1952	47
540	Baldwin	1926	59067	57	200	191,370	40,400	1948	46
541	Baldwin	1926	59068	57	200	191,370	40,400	1952	1
542	Baldwin	1926	59069	57	200	191,370	40,400	1954	1
543	Baldwin	1927	59822	57	200	191,370	40,400	1951	1
544	Baldwin	1927	59823	57	200	191,370	40,400	1954	1
545	Baldwin	1927	59824	57	200	191,370	40,400	1953	1

Class F1, 2-8-4, 23 fi" x 30" cylinders

600	Baldwin	1940	62322	63	250	335,400	49,300	1950	48
601	Baldwin	1940	62323	63	250	335,400	49,300	1950	48
602	Baldwin	1940	62324	63	250	335,400	49,300	1950	48
603	Baldwin	1940	62325	63	250	335,400	49,300	1950	48
604	Baldwin	1940	62326	63	250	335,400	49,300	1950	48

Notes

1 — Scrapped.
2 — Originally Atlantic and North Carolina no. 30. Returned to A&NC as no. 3 in 1935.
3 — Originally Norfolk and Southern no. 14. Sold to Atlantic and North Carolina as no. 4 in 1935.
4 — Nos. 5 and 6 sold to Atlantic and North Carolina as nos. 5 and 6, respectively, in 1935.
5 — Originally Raleigh and Cape Fear no. 1.
6 — Originally Aberdeen and West End no. 4, later Aberdeen and Asheboro no. 21.
7 — Originally Aberdeen and West End no. 5, later Aberdeen and Asheboro no. 22, sold to Manatee

Lumber Co. in 1919.

 8 — Nos. 22-25 were originally Atlantic and North Carolina nos. 10-13, respectively.

 9 — Nos. 28,29 were originally Norfolk, Virginia Beach, and Southern nos. 2,3, respectively.

10 — Originally Carolina Central no. 32, later Aberdeen and Asheboro no. 27.

11 — Originally Norfolk, Virginia Beach, and Southern no. 5.

12 — Nos. 33-35 ordered by Virginia and Carolina Coast but delivered to N&S.

13 — Originally Coudersport and Port Allegany no. 1.

14 — Originally Atlantic and North Carolina no. 14. Some sources say this locomotive and NS no. 49 exchanged numbers in 1927, although this would make the new numbers inconsistent with others of their respective classes.

15 — Nos. 38-41 were originally Atlantic and North Carolina nos. 15,16,18,19, respectively.

16 — Originally New York, West Shore, and Buffalo no. 67.

17 — Nos. 46,47,49 were originally Suffolk and Carolina nos. 16,12,17, respectively.

18 — Originally Atlantic and North Carolina no. 17. Returned to A&NC as no. 17 in 1935.

19 — Sold to N. Block, 1935.

20 — Nos. 55-57 were originally nos. 48-50, respectively.

21 — Originally New Orleans and Northeastern no. 229, acquired from Kinston Carolina in 1924.

22 — Originally Aberdeen and Asheboro no. 10. Sold to Bennettsville and Cheraw.

23 — Originally Raleigh and Cape Fear no. 4. Sold to Kinston Carolina.

24 — Nos. 87-90 were originally Raleigh and Southport nos. 5,7,8,9, respectively.

25 — Originally Buffalo, Pittsburgh, and Western no. 57, later Aberdeen and Asheboro no. 33.

26 — Originally Aberdeen and Asheboro no. 35.

27 — Originally Lake Shore and Michigan Southern no. 244, later Aberdeen and Asheboro no. 36.

28 — Originally Pittsburgh and Western no. 112, later Aberdeen and Asheboro no. 34.

29 — Originally Nashville, Chattanooga, and St. Louis no. 14, later Aberdeen and Asheboro no. 37. Sold to Bennettsville and Cheraw.

30 — Originally Durham and Charlotte no. 4. Had 18" x 22" cylinders.

31 — Originally Norfolk and Western no. 46, later Durham and Charlotte no. 5.

32 — Originally had Stephenson valve gear, slide valve cylinders, and 57-inch drivers.

33 — Had 18" x 24" cylinders.

34 — Rebuilt with Southern valve gear.

35 — Rebuilt with Walschaerts valve gear and piston valve cylinders.

36 — Nos. 108-111 were originally nos. 118,119,117,116, respectively.

37 — Nos. 137,138 were originally Durham and South Carolina nos. 100,101, respectively.

38 —Originally Western New York and Pennsylvania no. 117, later Aberdeen and Asheboro no. 38. had 19" x 24" cylinders.

39 — Nos. 135,136 were originally Indiana, Illinois, and Iowa nos. 26,31, respectively. Purchased from New York Central System in 1920.

40 — Nos. 200-202 were originally Norfolk and Western nos. 221,222,290, respectively. First NS numbers were 123-125, respectively.

41 -- Originally Raleigh and Southport no. 10. First NS number was 99. Sold to Atlantic and Western as no. 12. On public display in Sanford, NC.

42 -- Nos. 204-206 were originally NS nos. 121,122,120, respectively.

43 -- Nos. 218-226 were originally Lake Shore and Michigan Southern nos. 703,711,722,727,728,731,734,742,746, respectively. Bought from New York Central in 1920. Had 21" by 30" cylinders.

44 -- Sold to Rowland Lumber Company, New Bern, NC.

45 -- Nos. 527-531 were originally numbered 227-231, respectively.

46 -- Nos. 531,532,534-537, 540 became Ferrocarriles Nacionales de Mexico nos. 1655,1656,1650,1651,1652,1653,1654, respectively.

47 -- Sold to Pan-American Engineering.

48 -- Nos. 600-604 became Ferrocarriles Nacionales de Mexico nos. 3350-3354, respectively. Trailer truck booster increased tractive effort to 60,400 lbs.

Above: Number 1601 was the first of NS's Baldwin model AS416 roadswitchers. This model was the successor to the DRS-6-4-1500. NS received number 1601 in 1951, and eventually rostered seventeen units of this model. Note that the bell on the AS416s was mounted at the top of the long hood, the front of the unit, on this model on the NS. The 1500 series locomotives had their bells mounted under the frame. The unit behind number 1601 is DRS-6-4-1500 number 1503. A quick way to distinguish between the two models on the NS was by the placement of the grilles on the long hood. As you can see here, they were halfway up the hood on the AS416s, but at the bottom of the hood on the DRS-6-4-1500s. This difference cannot be used to distinguish between Baldwin roadswitchers of 1500 and 1600 horsepower on other railroads, however. Number 1601 still has its original paint scheme, with the yellow stripe and black numbers within it on the cab sides, in this view made in Star, NC in June 1957. (Harold K. Vollrath collection)

Below: Baldwin DS-4-4-1000 number 1002 is at Carolina Yard in this undated photo. It has its original paint scheme with the road numbers in the yellow stripe on the cab side. Later, it received the "chevy" herald, but sister number 1001 retained this livery until it was traded in to EMD in 1966.(James A. Ramsey photo)

Chapter 8

Diesel Locomotives

As we have already noted, at the end of World War II, Norfolk Southern management decided to dieselize. The first diesel order placed was for five switchers. These were ordered from longtime favorite NS supplier Baldwin, and included three 660 horsepower locomotives of model DS-4-4-660, and two 1000 horsepower model DS-4-4-1000 units. These were given road numbers 661, 662, 663, 1001, and 1002, respectively. This provided a correspondence between road numbers and horsepower. They were delivered in an attractive paint scheme of vermilion red, Dupont number 83-2622, with a single wide full length yellow stripe and three narrower black stripes on the front end. Cab and hood tops and undercarriage were black. The road name was spelled out in black letters in the yellow stripe on the hood, and the road number appeared in black in the yellow stripe on the cab sides. These units were delivered between December 1946 and May 1947, and immediately took over most yard switching assignments from steam switchers numbers 7-9.

The 1001 and 1002 spent most of their time around Norfolk, working at Carolina Yard, on interchange runs, and in their early days on Virginia Beach freight runs. Eventually they were withdrawn from the Virginia Beach lines, apparently due to their weight. These units were not permitted to cross the Albemarle Sound trestle, again because of their weight. They were quite popular with crews because of their pulling power. Their tractive effort rating, 72,831 pounds, was the highest of any locomotive the road ever owned.

Locomotive numbers 661 through 663 were light enough to be permitted to cross the sound trestle, so they were seen at many points around the system, particularly at Glenwood Yard in Raleigh. Number 662 went to Durham Yard when it was first delivered. This was to honor a commitment made to the Durham Chamber of Commerce in September 1946. The chamber had asked the four Class I railroads in Durham to replace their steam switchers with diesels to help improve air quality by elimination of smoke in the business district and nearby residential areas. NS, Southern and Seaboard agreed to supply diesels, but Norfolk and Western suggested using smoke control devices on their steam engines as they were not yet dieselized.at this time.

All five of the switcher diesels remained in service until the 1960s, at which time newer power capa-

Baldwin model DS-4-4-660 switcher number 663 is working at Glenwood Yard in Raleigh in this view made October 1, 1961. There were three units of this model on the NS, numbered 661-663. By this time, number 663 had been repainted with the "chevy" herald on the cab with unit number in yellow beneath it. In its original paint scheme, the yellow stripe on the body was continued on the cab with unit number in black within the cab stripe. The herald did not appear on the unit at that time. (William P. Nixon collection)

ble of handling both road and yard assignments had been obtained, permitting them to be retired.

As these switchers were being placed in service, NS management was already evaluating diesels for road freight service. Baldwin Locomotive Works demonstrator number 1500 was delivered to the Norfolk Southern at Raleigh on Thursday night, December 26, 1946, by the Seaboard Air Line. Number 1500 was a Baldwin model DRS-6-4-1500, a 1500-horsepower roadswitcher with A1A-A1A wheel arrangement. On Friday morning, the 27th, immediate arrangements were made to put it in test service, with the first run being made from Raleigh to Charlotte that day. On the 28th it returned from Charlotte to Raleigh. On December 29, it ran from Raleigh to Carolina, returning to Raleigh on the 30th. The locomotive was delivered back to the Seaboard on December 31 at 1:25 P.M.

The demonstrator had covered a total of 762 miles during its testing, consuming 2185 gallons of fuel at a total cost of $198.88. Its performance was compared to Norfolk Southern's 500 series 2-8-0 steam locomotives. On the grades of the west end of the line, the diesel proved itself by handling tonnage that at one point exceeded the steamers' timetable listed rating by 47 percent. And on the north end it protected train number 99's schedule, which was the fastest on the railway, from Norfolk to Raleigh. It arrived at Glenwood Yard 49 minutes ahead of schedule, proving the diesel's capability of sustained running with tonnage.

Number 1501, Norfolk Southern's first road diesel, is shown in its original paint scheme on July 11, 1948. It was a 1500 horsepower Baldwin model DRS-6-4-1500. (Bob's Photos)

On January 6, 1947, after having studied the test results, the Mechanical Department recommended the purchase of diesels. In February 1947, an order was placed with Baldwin for ten model DRS-6-4-1500 units similar to the demonstrator.

Although one might guess at this point that NS had by now decided not to consider other locomotive manufacturers, this was not the case. NS did discuss its needs with Electromotive Division of General Motors Corporation (EMD), and scheduled a demonstration of EMD power on its lines, but this was never carried out. The low axle loading of the A1A trucks on the DRS-6-4-1500 model appealed to NS, still hampered by light construction, and EMD did not offer freight locomotives with this wheel arrangement. Alco did offer this with their model RSC-2, but NS saw no reason to prefer this model to the Baldwin offering.

The ten new diesels were given road numbers 1501-1510, again showing their horsepower rating. Number 1501 was delivered in October 1947, but was found to have a crankshaft problem and was returned to Baldwin for correction. This problem may have resulted in a delivery delay for the other nine units. They were not delivered until February and March of 1948, after Baldwin delivered several units with higher serial numbers to the Soo Line. The new NS 1500s were painted in the same scheme as the diesel switchers, except that they had three black stripes on the rear end as well as the front end. They took over through freight operation on the hilly Western District.

Next, NS management turned attention to dieselization of passenger service. They would rather have ignored this, as they had given up hope of making any money with this service. But trains numbers 1 and 2 were still running between Norfolk and Raleigh, and their regular locomotives, Ten-Wheelers numbers 110, 113, and 114, were now forty years old. NS selected unusual but cheap diesel power to replace them in the form of three General Electric 70-ton units. This model was fairly common in light freight service and yard work, but rare as passenger power. This was the first NS purchase of power from a manufacturer other then Baldwin since 0-6-0 number 14 way back in 1900.

These units were delivered in June 1948, and were given road numbers 701 through 703. Since they developed 600 horsepower, they should have been numbered 601-603 to indicate their horsepower, but these numbers were still in use by the Class F 2-8-4s. They were painted the same as the Baldwin switchers except that the black stripes were wider and the road name and numbers were larger.

By the time these units were delivered, train numbers 1 and 2 were mail and express trains only, but they continued in that status, powered by the 70-tonners, until 1951. After that, these locomotives were used in local and branch line service and as switchers at the smaller yards. Their light weight and low power tended to limit their usefulness, however, and number 702 was sold early in 1964, becom-

GE 70-tonner number 702 is shown here at Carolina Yard on April 6, 1952, still in its original paint. Note that the lettering and numbers on these units at this time were larger than those applied to the other NS diesel models, and were also larger than the letters and numbers applied to the 70-ton units when they were repainted. See the photo of number 702 after repainting, taken barely more than a year after this one, later in this chapter. Also, the three black stripes on the nose were wider in this original paint job than in the repaint scheme, although the black stripes above and below the yellow stripe cannot be distinguished from the red in this black-and-white photo. Also note that there were a few steam locomotives remaining on the property in 1952, showing up behind number 702. By the time of this photo, the NS mail and express trains numbers 1 and 2 had been discontinued, and number 702 had limited usefulness. It would be sold in 1964, but its sisters numbers 701 and 703 would survive mainly to work the Bayboro Branch until well into the Southern Railway era. (Thomas T. Taber III photo, Railroad Museum of Pennsylvania, Pennsylvania Historical and Museum Commission)

ing Montpelier and Barre Railroad number 30. The other two spent most of the remaining years of independent NS operations around New Bern, as they were the only locomotives light enough to be permitted on the Bayboro Branch. This continued to be the case under Southern Railway management, so numbers 701 and 703 were repainted with the Southern livery and remained on the roster primarily for this service until 1978.

NS management continued to explore the possibilities for obtaining diesel units more suitable for the lightly constructed branches. In 1948, they held discussions with representatives of the Whitcomb Locomotive Company. That company quoted the NS prices for 80-ton and 70-ton units with 675 horsepower, and 65-ton units with 480 horsepower. The quotation was considered seriously, part-

Baldwin model DS-4-4-1000 switcher number 1001 here is working at Carolina Yard on April 17, 1963. Number 1001 and its sister number 1002 spent most of their time in the Norfolk-Virginia Beach area as they were not permitted to cross the Albemarle Sound bridge. (John Hahn, Jr. photo)

Left: AS416 number 1614 leaves Carolina Yard southbound on its first revenue trip in March or early April 1955. This view shows the shade of red of the first NS diesel paint scheme as delivered, before it began to fade. (Philip P. Coulter, Jr. photo)

Middle Below: AS416 number 1617, the last of NS's Baldwins and one of the last locomotives built by Baldwin, rests near the shop at Glenwood Yard in Raleigh in April 1971. Number 1617 was the last NS locomotive to lose the red, yellow, and black color scheme, and the new colors are still fresh and clean here. Note that the hoods on number 1617 reach almost to the same height as the cab roof. Only this unit and number 1616 had this configuration.(Ed Fielding photo)

Bottom: 70-tonner number 702 is shown here at New Bern on May 28, 1953. It has been repainted recently. Compare the size of the lettering and black nose stripes here with those of the original paint job, shown earlier in this chapter. Note, however, that heralds were not yet applied to the cab sides at this time. (J. David Spanagel collection)

ly because Whitcomb at that time was part of the Baldwin group of companies, and many parts of the Whitcomb units were interchangeable with Baldwin units already on the roster. This included the Westinghouse model 362-D traction motors. No purchases were made, however.

NS even briefly considered replacing the four-wheel trucks on its Baldwin switcher units, both the 660 class and the 1000 class, with six-wheel trucks to make them useable on lighter tracks. This was soon found to be impractical, however, as the frames on these units would not accommodate the longer six-wheel trucks.

Dieselization of freight service produced the expected economies, so the NS decided to proceed with complete dieselization as rapidly as finances permitted. As usual, this was not as rapidly as management would have liked. The next order for road freight power was not placed until 1950. This order was for five Baldwin AS-416 locomotives, that model being the 1600 horsepower successor to model DRS-6-4-1500. They were numbered 1601-1605, again relating road numbers to horsepower. Between 1952 and 1955, NS placed four more orders for AS-416s, raising the total num-

ber on the road to seventeen.

The last NS order for AS-416s, road numbers 1616 and 1617, was notable in several respects. It was the last order Baldwin received for heavy roadswitchers. The appearance of these locomotives was slightly different from numbers 1601 through 1615, as they had higher hoods. Baldwin had changed the design to allow room to install both a steam generator and dynamic brakes in the same unit. This was of little significance to NS as it did not order either option, but the road had no reason to regret having the extra room under the hood.

It did have reason to regret another change, which was not apparent externally. Numbers 1616 and 1617 had General Electric electrical transmission systems instead of the Westinghouse system used in all other NS Baldwin locomotives. Westinghouse had announced in 1954 that it would no longer manufacture components for locomotive electrical transmissions. Baldwin had enough on hand to supply Westinghouse equipment for NS units through 1615, but none were left for 1616 and 1617. The two GE-equipped units did not work well with the Westinghouse-equipped units in multiple unit operation. When NS realized this, they used numbers 1616 and 1617 singly or mu'ed only with each other whenever possible.

These seventeen AS-416s provided NS with enough power to dieselize all operations, so on February 5, 1954, brand new AS-416 number 1611 hauled a funeral train of the last six NS steam locomotives out of Carolina Yard on their way to the scrapyard. It was a proud moment for NS management, which took care to document the event with a photo in their 1954 annual report, but it was not a happy day for railfans.

Actually, NS had determined that the first fifteen AS-416s should be enough to handle all assignments, but they had hardly finished deciding this when locomotive number 1510 was destroyed in a wreck at the Rocky River bridge, near Midland, NC, caused by a trestle fire. This led to the order for the last two units. It is not definitely established why two replacements were ordered instead of one, but it seems likely that the decision was affected strongly by the common knowledge at the time that Baldwin would soon cease accepting new locomotive orders. This would mean that a replacement for any other wrecked unit could not be ordered from Baldwin. As things turned out, no additional replacements for wrecked units were needed until after a new model from another manufacturer had already been ordered.

All the Baldwin and General Electric locomotives were delivered in the red, yellow, and black paint scheme we have described. Eventually, they needed to be repainted, and about 1960 repaint jobs with variations of this paint scheme appeared. The first variation had no yellow stripe on the cab, but a new herald was placed on the cab sides. This was sometimes called the "Chevy" herald because of its similarity to the Chevrolet automobile emblem. The engine number was then placed in yellow below the herald on the cab sides. Otherwise, the scheme was the same as before.

A second variation was to eliminate the yellow and black stripes completely, leaving an all-red body with the "Chevy" herald and yellow number on the cab. The road name was no longer spelled out on the long hood. This variation was used to reduce both cost and shop time for repainting, as one day in the shop was saved by leaving off the stripes. It is not known how many locomotives got this variation, but photos exist of numbers 1504, 1505, 1601, and 1602 with it. It is probably not a coincidence that all these units left the roster

DRS-6-4-1500 number 1504, wearing the simplified solid red paint scheme without stripes, rides the turntable at Glenwood Yard on October 12, 1963. DRS-6-4-1500 number 1505 also carried this paint scheme in its later years on the NS, as did AS416s numbers 1601 and 1602. It is unknown if any other units had this scheme. It is likely that when they were painted this way, NS management had already decided that these units would be among the first to be retired when new power arrived. (Robert C. Reisweber collection)

not long after they received this paint scheme.

The Baldwin and General Electric diesels served the NS faithfully up until 1963, but by then, it was time for new power. Ordering from Baldwin was no longer an option, so NS examined the offerings from EMD. EMD still did not offer an A1A-trucked freight unit, but by this time the main line and several branches had been upgraded to the point that they would tolerate the axle loading of the B-B trucked EMD model GP18. As a result, NS ordered seventeen units of this model. This was the largest single locomotive order in the company's history. Even with the upgrading of the track, keeping axle loading to a minimum was still necessary so these units were ordered with conspicuously small fuel tanks.

NS was still concerned about the axle loading of the GP18s when they were delivered, and placed speed restrictions on them during their initial period of operation. On the Beach District and the Aberdeen Branch, they had to operate at 5 mph less than the timetable authorized speed. On the main line between Carolina and milepost 198 (near Bailey) they operated at 5 mph less than timetable speed except that only 7 mph was permitted over the Albemarle Sound bridge. Between milepost 198 and Charlotte, a speed 10 mph less than authorized timetable speed would be observed, except that only 25 mph was permitted over the trestle at milepost 198.9.

These units represented major changes for the railroad in sev-

eral ways. First, of course, they were from a supplier completely new to NS. Also, their numbering broke with the practice of having numbers indicate the horsepower rating. That practice would have required them to be numbered 1801 through 1817, but the GP18s were numbered 1 through 17 instead. They also received a completely new livery, basically light gray, with black undercarriage, cab roofs, and hood tops, and a series of V-shaped red stripes on the ends. A new logo with a red N and black S, with the latter below and to the right of the former, was applied to the cab side.

The new paint jobs did not meet with universal approval. Some employees at all levels preferred the red, yellow, and black scheme and wanted it continued. Proponents of the new scheme predicted that it would be less affected by fading and dirt accumulation. They

GP18 number 1, the first of this model on the NS, is shown at Glenwood Yard in Raleigh on September 3, 1973. (M. B. Connery photo)

carried the day temporarily, and not only did the new locomotives get the scheme, but also some cabooses and freight cars received it. (Cabooses got the red end stripes but freight cars did not.)

The idea about the wearing qualities of the new paint scheme was not borne out in practice, however. After a few years, the appearance left much to be desired. As a result, the last few boxcar orders were received in a tuscan red paint with yellow doors. All locomotives which survived into the 1970s got the gray paint and kept it until the merger of 1974, however.

It became apparent that the NS had not ordered the new power a moment too soon, as even before deliveries of the new units began in September 1963, unit numbers 1505, 1506, and 1509 were badly damaged in a wreck July 2, 1963 at Marks Creek north of Knightdale. This wreck was caused by a trestle set on fire by a lightning strike, similar to the wreck that had destroyed number 1510. Since the new GP18s were planned to replace the 1500s anyway, the three damaged units were immediately scrapped.

The GP18s took over the major assignments immediately and did so quite successfully, but with business picking up, particularly as the new Lee Creek Branch was about to enter service, additional power was needed. EMD had stopped producing GP18s short-

EMD GP18 number 2, the second of this model on the NS, is shown at Plymouth, NC station almost brand new in December 1963. The order for seventeen of these units initiated the new NS paint scheme shown in the photo. (L. D. Jones, Jr. photo)

ly after delivering NS's seventeen. By the time the additional power was ordered, the GP38 was EMD's light roadswitcher model, so NS ordered seven of these in 1966 and 1967. These units were numbered 2001-2007, resuming the practice of relating road number to horsepower, which was 2000 for these units. The same gray, black, and red paint that had been inaugurated with the GP18s was continued, however.

Baldwin switcher number 661 was scrapped in 1965. The remaining Baldwin switchers and some of the DRS-6-4-1500s were traded in to EMD on the GP38 orders. Three of the 1500s, numbers 1504, 1507, and 1508, were sold to the Durham and Southern Railroad, becoming their numbers 363, 364, and 365, respectively. D&S had recently bought a secondhand Baldwin DRS-4-4-1500 from the Soo Line and liked it. It had kept its Soo Line number, 362. Since the D&S did not need the low axle loading of the A1A trucks, it immediately replaced them with B trucks on the ex-NS units, making them essentially DRS-4-4-1500s also. Their numbering on D&S obviously formed a sequence with the ex-Soo number 362. D&S numbers 363 and 364 later were sold to Rail-to-Water Transfer in Illinois, then apparently went to Central or South America. Number 365 later became a cabless remote controlled coal mine unit in West Virginia.

The right side of the GP18s is illustrated by number 8 at Wilson, NC in January 1964. Note the small fuel tank. (Harold K. Vollrath collection)

At roughly the same time, the lease of the first five NS AS-416s, numbers 1601-1605, expired and NS elected to dispose of these units. They had already been removed from service about the time the GP18s were delivered. They went to Striegel Supply and Equipment Company in Baltimore for possible resale, but there were no takers. This was not surprising, as these units represented one of the least popular models produced by a builder which had now been out of business for ten years.

On January 31, 1966, AS-416 number 1614 was wrecked at Thalia on the Virginia Beach South Route as a result of a derailment caused by a snowstorm, an unusual cause of an accident on the NS. Although the damage could have been repaired, new GP38s would soon be delivered, making the unit unnecessary. As a result, number 1614 was set aside in Carolina Yard, eventually being scrapped in February 1967. The remaining eleven 1600s survived until the 1974 merger, but Southern did not want them. All were soon scrapped except for number 1616, which was purchased by Peabody Coal Company. That unit is now on display in the North Carolina Transportation Museum in Spencer, NC, having been repainted in its final NS paint scheme of gray, black, and red.

All the NS EMD units fit in well with the Southern Railway roster, which contained mostly EMD units, except that they had no dynamic brakes and were therefore excluded from use on some SR lines. Southern still insisted on high short hoods on all its units, however, and all the NS GP18s and GP38s were rebuilt to adhere to this standard, also getting the

The class unit of the Norfolk Southern EMD GP38s, number 2001, is at Wilson, NC in January 1968. NS bought seven of these units in three separate orders, but all were similar. All lacked dynamic brakes and had small fuel tanks, as shown here. (Harold K. Vollrath collection)

Southern Railway black, gray, and gold paint scheme. The control stands were moved to the opposite side of the cabs and turned around, so that the long hood end became the front of the locomotive. This also conformed to Southern Railway practice at that time. The GP18s numbers 1-17 became SR numbers 180-196, respectively, and the GP38s numbers 2001-2007 became SR numbers 2880-2886, respectively. All these units received the small NS initials on the cab, indicating that they were still officially owned by Southern Railway subsidiary Norfolk Southern Railway Company.

The former NS GP18s spent most of their time in their old territory on the original NS. The former NS GP38s, however, could be found almost anywhere on the Southern System. Various older and smaller Southern units took their place on the old NS, including some elderly GP-7s.

All the EMD units from the NS survived to enter the roster of the new Norfolk Southern Corporation in 1982, retaining their Southern Railway numbers but receiving initials CRN on the cab in place of NS, indicating the change of name of the owning company to Carolina and Northwestern. They spent their later years primarily in yard and transfer type service due to their lack of dynamic brakes. All the GP18s were traded in to EMD on newer units in 1985 except 181, 189, 192, and 194 (former NS 2, 10, 13, and 15, respectively), which were sold to Gibbs Railway Equipment Company in 1986, later going to the Otter Tail Valley Railroad in Minnesota. GP38 number 2884, the former NS number 2005, was retired in August 1993 and later was sold to Helm Leasing. The rest of the GP38s continued to serve Norfolk Southern Corporation until the summer of 1995. In later years, one or another of these units was often seen on original NS Virginia Beach lines. The former NS numbers 2002, 2003, 2004, and 2007 now work on the Georgia and Florida Railroad in Georgia, while former numbers 2001 and 2006 are now on the Luxapalila Valley Railroad, a subsidiary of the Columbus and Greenville Railway which operates a former Southern Railway branch from Columbus, Mississippi to Belk, Alabama. These six units all retain their last numbers from today's Norfolk Southern, in the 2880 series.

Three of Norfolk Southern's Baldwin DRS-6-4-1500s found a new home after the NS disposed of them. NS units numbers 1504, 1507, and 1508 wound up on the Durham and Southern, where they were given numbers 363, 364, and 365, respectively. This photo shows number 365 and 363 hauling D&S freight number 11 at Carpenter, NC in August 1972. D&S did not need to distribute the weight of these units over six axles, so immediately replaced the A1A-A1A trucks with B-B trucks, which makes it easy to forget their NS heritage. (Curt Tillotson, Jr. photo)

All-time Diesel Locomotive Roster

Road number	Builder	Const. date	Constr number	Model	horsepower	Weight, pounds	Tractive effort (lbs)	Disposition date	Notes
				Class DE1800					
1	GM-EMD	1963	27772	GP18	1800	241,200	58,930	1974	3
2	GM-EMD	1963	27773	GP18	1800	241,200	58,930	1974	3
3	GM-EMD	1963	27774	GP18	1800	241,200	58,930	1974	3
4	GM-EMD	1963	27775	GP18	1800	241,200	58,930	1974	3
5	GM-EMD	1963	27776	GP18	1800	241,200	58,930	1974	3
6	GM-EMD	1963	27777	GP18	1800	241,200	58,930	1974	3
7	GM-EMD	1963	27778	GP18	1800	241,200	58,930	1974	3
8	GM-EMD	1963	27779	GP18	1800	241,200	58,930	1974	3
9	GM-EMD	1963	27780	GP18	1800	241,200	58,930	1974	3
10	GM-EMD	1963	27781	GP18	1800	241,200	58,930	1974	3
11	GM-EMD	1963	27782	GP18	1800	241,200	58,930	1974	3
12	GM-EMD	1963	27783	GP18	1800	241,200	58,930	1974	3
13	GM-EMD	1963	27784	GP18	1800	241,200	58,930	1974	3
14	GM-EMD	1963	27785	GP18	1800	241,200	58,930	1974	3
15	GM-EMD	1963	27786	GP18	1800	241,200	58,930	1974	3
16	GM-EMD	1963	27787	GP18	1800	241,200	58,930	1974	3
17	GM-EMD	1963	28353	GP18	1800	241,200	58,930	1974	3

Class DE660

661	Baldwin	1946	73361	DS-4-4-660	660	199,980	59,994	1965	1
662	Baldwin	1947	73362	DS-4-4-660	660	199,980	59,994	1967	2
663	Baldwin	1947	73365	DS-4-4-660	660	199,980	59,994	1967	2

Class DE700SC

701	GE	1948	30013	70-ton	600	137,600	41,300	1974	4
702	GE	1948	30014	70-ton	600	137,600	41,300	1964	5
703	GE	1948	30015	70-ton	600	137,600	41,300	1974	4

Class DE1000

| 1001 | Baldwin | 1947 | 72832 | DS-4-4-1000 | 1000 | 242,770 | 72,831 | 1966 | 2 |
| 1002 | Baldwin | 1947 | 72833 | DS-4-4-1000 | 1000 | 242,770 | 72,831 | 1966 | 2 |

Class DE1500SC

1501	Baldwin	1947	73487	DRS-6-4-1500	1500	280,000	56,100	1966	2
1502	Baldwin	1948	73488	DRS-6-4-1500	1500	265,500	53,100	1967	2
1503	Baldwin	1948	73489	DRS-6-4-1500	1500	265,500	53,100	1966	2
1504	Baldwin	1948	73490	DRS-6-4-1500	1500	265,500	53,100	1965	6
1505	Baldwin	1948	73491	DRS-6-4-1500	1500	265,500	53,100	1963	7
1506	Baldwin	1948	73492	DRS-6-4-1500	1500	265,500	53,100	1963	7
1507	Baldwin	1948	73493	DRS-6-4-1500	1500	265,500	53,100	1966	6
1508	Baldwin	1948	73494	DRS-6-4-1500	1500	265,500	53,100	1966	6
1509	Baldwin	1948	73495	DRS-6-4-1500	1500	265,500	53,100	1963	7
1510	Baldwin	1948	73496	DRS-6-4-1500	1500	265,500	53,100	1955	8

Class DE1600SC

1601	Baldwin	1951	75237	AS416	1600	291,460	58,290	1966	9
1602	Baldwin	1951	75238	AS416	1600	291,460	58,290	1966	9
1603	Baldwin	1951	75239	AS416	1600	291,460	58,290	1966	9
1604	Baldwin	1951	75240	AS416	1600	291,460	58,290	1966	9
1605	Baldwin	1951	75241	AS416	1600	291,460	58,290	1966	9
1606	Baldwin	1952	75699	AS416	1600	289,900	57,980	1974	1
1607	Baldwin	1952	75721	AS416	1600	289,900	57,980	1974	1
1608	Baldwin	1952	75722	AS416	1600	289,900	57,980	1974	1
1609	Baldwin	1952	75723	AS416	1600	289,900	57,980	1974	1
1610	Baldwin	1952	75724	AS416	1600	289,900	57,980	1974	1
1611	Baldwin	1954	75938	AS416	1600	288,000	57,600	1974	1
1612	Baldwin	1954	75939	AS416	1600	288,000	57,600	1974	1
1613	Baldwin	1954	75940	AS416	1600	288,000	57,600	1974	1
1614	Baldwin	1955	76037	AS416	1600	289,000	57,801	1967	10
1615	Baldwin	1955	76038	AS416	1600	289,000	57,801	1974	1
1616	Baldwin	1955	76112	AS416	1600	288,000	57,600	1974	11
1617	Baldwin	1955	76114	AS416	1600	288,000	57,600	1974	1

Class DE2000

2001	GM-EMD	1966	31782	GP38	2000	248,200	62,048	1974	12
2002	GM-EMD	1966	31783	GP38	2000	248,200	62,048	1974	12
2003	GM-EMD	1966	32308	GP38	2000	249,500	62,364	1974	12
2004	GM-EMD	1966	32309	GP38	2000	249,500	62,364	1974	12
2005	GM-EMD	1967	32491	GP38	2000	250,800	60,417	1974	12
2006	GM-EMD	1967	32492	GP38	2000	250,800	60,417	1974	12
2007	GM-EMD	1967	32493	GP38	2000	250,800	60,417	1974	12

Notes

In the Builder column above, GM-EMD indicates General Motors Corporation, Electromotive Division. GE indicates General Electric Company. Class numbers ending in SC indicate engines are supercharged (turbocharged).

1 -- scrapped

2 -- traded in to GM-EMD for new power.

3 -- Nos. 1-17 became Southern Railway nos. 180-196, respectively.

4 -- Nos. 701, 703 became Southern Railway nos. 701, 703, respectively.

5 -- Sold to Birmingham Rail and Locomotive Co., then became Montpelier and Barre RR no. 30.

6 -- Nos. 1504, 1507, 1508 sold to Durham and Southern RR as nos. 363-365, respectively. Were rebuilt with B-B trucks instead of A1A-A1A.

7 -- Nos. 1505, 1506, 1509 wrecked at Marks Creek, July 2, 1963, and scrapped.

8 -- Wrecked at Rocky River March 26, 1955 and scrapped.

9 -- Sold to Striegel Supply and Equipment Company.

10 -- Wrecked at Thalia, VA, January 31, 1966. Scrapped February 28, 1967.

11 -- Became Peabody Coal Company no. 1616. Now on public display at North Carolina Museum of Transportation, Spencer, NC.

12 -- Nos. 2001-2007 became Southern Railway nos. 2880-2886, respectively.

Above: An early view of NS electric motor car number 36 at the City Hall Avenue terminal in Norfolk, with the Monticello Hotel behind it. The car was the first of the NS's five largest motor cars, which were built in 1912 and numbered 36-40. It still has its original green paint in this view. (Mrs. John H. Kelly, Jr. collection)

Below: Two of the medium size Norfolk Southern electric cars, numbers 55 and 57. Location is unknown, but is probably somewhere in Virginia Beach. Both cars have the original all-green color scheme. Car number 57 later became an unpowered trailer car. (George Krambles collection)

Chapter 9

Other Equipment

Electric Equipment

In 1904, the Norfolk and Southern Railroad got into the electric railroading business when it electrified its Virginia Beach line to meet the competition of the Chesapeake Transit Company, an electric railroad which N&S bought later that year. From then until 1935, the Virginia Beach lines of the combined companies were operated as a typical interurban electric railroad of the period, with frequent passenger trains between Norfolk and Virginia Beach. The lines formed an Electric Division separate from the remainder of the railroad.

A large amount of electrically powered equipment was operated during these years. A fire in 1922 destroyed the company's records of this equipment. Several attempts were made to reconstruct these records in later years, with some but not complete success. The accompanying table summarizes the best available information from these sources. The information is as accurate as we can make it, given the omissions and contradictions of the data available to us.

Above: Norfolk Southern electric motor cars numbers 36 and 54 at Norfolk Terminal Station, probably in the early thirties. By the time of the photo, both cars had received the newer paint scheme of green and cream, with gray roof. All the largest cars received this paint scheme, as did at least some of the smaller cars. (Tal Carey collection)
Right: Electric car number 45, one of the smaller motor cars, is shown here with an unidentified trailer car at an unknown location and date. The sign on the front of the car says "Virginia Beach direct", which would indicate that it would take the South Route to the beach, rather than the North Route via Cape Henry. (Mrs. John H. Kelly, Jr. collection)

A NS electric train including motor car number 54, trailer car number 50 (formerly a motor car), and two other unidentified cars. Location and date are unknown. (Mrs. John H. Kelly, Jr. collection)

The most important equipment of the Electric Division, of course, was a group of electrically powered passenger cars. These cars all picked up power from overhead lines using roof-mounted trolley poles. All were painted in an olive green color. Later on, the largest cars, numbers 35-40, which remained in service the longest, were painted a cream color from the window sills to the roof, while the smaller cars remained solid green. In addition to the powered cars, several unpowered trailer cars were used. These were divided into open, semi-closed, and closed cars. The open cars had no sides, and wooden seats extending the full width of the car accommodated the passengers. Running boards the full length of the cars on both sides aided the passengers in boarding. Curtains which could be lowered protected the passengers somewhat from bad weather. The closed trailer cars had passenger accommodations similar to the powered cars, with double seats on each side of the central aisle, and end platforms. The semi-closed trailers were similar to the closed trailers but had window openings with removable sashes.

Although the electric lines are best known for their passenger operations, freight operations were always important on these lines as well. During the 1920s, the company owned five freight motors. Two of these, numbers 1 and 2, were conventional steeple-cab units. Numbers 3 and 5 were boxcabs (in the truest sense of the word) which had been rebuilt in the company shops, with old boxcar bodies being applied. The remaining freight motor was a work motor or line car, numbered 8. The freight motors also powered passenger trains hauling Pullman cars to Virginia Beach.

The electric lines also had some miscellaneous equipment, including a baggage trailer numbered 7, and a sprinkler car numbered 6 which was used to wet down the roadbed in the hot and dry summer months to reduce the dust inconvenience to riders.

NS electric freight motors numbers 3 (at left) and 2 (at right). Location is probably Euclid, where the J. C. Jones Sand Company used these motors for a short time after NS discontinued electric operation. Date is probably some time in the late thirties. These motors and much of the other electric equipment remained on the property for several years after operations were ended. Motor number 3 is literally a boxcab motor. It had been rebuilt after an accident some years earlier by installing an obsolete wooden boxcar body on the frame. The number of the boxcar had been 20528, the first three digits of which are showing through the faded paint at the right end of the motor. No photos of number 3 before rebuilding are available, but it was probably originally a steeple-cab type similar to number 2. Motor number 5 had been wrecked at the same time as number 3, and was similarly rebuilt, using boxcar body number 20802 (W. R. Newton collection)

Below: Line car number 8 is shown beside the former electric shop at South Junction, Norfolk, on June 12, 1939. By the time of the photo, NS electrification had been gone for four years, but car 8 was still on the property. The former electric shop was by that time the shop of the Norfolk Southern Bus Corporation. Car number 8 had been built by the Southern Car Company in 1912, along with the last five motor cars numbers 36 through 40. (Allan H. Berner collection)

All the electric equipment was taken out of service by 1935 when electric operations were discontinued, with the exception of two of the freight motors, which were used briefly by the J. C. Jones Company at their sand operations at Euclid. The equipment

Another view of line car number 8 in January 1939, no doubt also at South Junction. (Krambles-Peterson Archive)

remained in storage at the old electric shop at South Junction for several years before finally being scrapped.

Gasoline Powered Equipment

The Norfolk and Southern first experimented with gasoline-powered equipment in 1909 when it purchased McKeen car number 90. This car spent most of its early years in North Carolina, but in 1914 it was shifted to the Currituck Branch to Munden. As we have previously noted, this branch left the Electric Division at Euclid station, but was not electrified. The railroad was not pleased with the performance of the car, as is evidenced by the fact that it was converted to electric operation in 1923. It was then used on the Electric Division lines to Virginia Beach. Apparently its use was discontinued in the late twenties, although some sources indicate that it may not have been disposed of until several years later.

The unsatisfactory performance of number 90 resulted in NS's avoiding the purchase of any additional gasoline powered equipment for several years, although by the mid twenties, it was becoming apparent that the decline in passenger traffic was making railcars a more attractive option. Finally, in December 1934, the railroad took delivery of two gasoline-driven motor cars. These cars were a new product of a partnership of the J. G. Brill Company and American Car and Foundry (ACF). Brill was a longtime manufacturer of electric cars, including some of the NS electric cars.

The two new NS "railbuses" were powered with 168 horsepower Hall-Scott engines, and had seating capacity for 53 passengers. They were given road numbers 101 and 102. Number 101 was named *The Carolinian*, and was put into service between Goldsboro and Beaufort. Number 102 was named *Sir Walter Raleigh*, and was operated between Washington, NC., and Raleigh. They were painted in a green and cream color scheme with aluminum painted roofs, similar to the larger electric cars numbers 35-40. Some

Electric Division Equipment Roster

Road number	Type of equipment	Date obtained	Disposal date	Notes
1	freight motor	1910	1934	1
2	freight motor	1911	?	1
3	freight motor	?	1934	2
4	freight motor	1920	1932	1
5	freight motor	?	1934	3
6	sprinkler car	?	1934	4
7	baggage express trailer	?	1934	5
8	line car	1912	1934	10
10	freight motor	?	?	6
13-15	open trailer cars	1920	1932	7
16-19	semi-closed trailer cars	?	1934	8
20	semi-closed trailer car	?	?	9
36-40	closed motor cars	1912	1936	10
41	closed motor cars	?	1932	11
42	closed motor car	?	1932	12
43	line car	?	1924	13
44-48	closed motor cars	?	1934	14
49-57	closed motor cars	?	1934	15
61-66, 69-74	semi-closed trailer cars	?	?	16

notes

1 Built in company shops
2 Wrecked with #5 in 1922. Rebuilt at company shops using boxcar body #20528.
3 Wrecked with #3 in 1922. Rebuilt at company shops using boxcar body #20802.
4 Purchased from Portsmouth Cotton Oil Co.
5 Formerly open trailer car #68
6 Formerly first #3 freight motor (not the #3 tabulated above)
7 Had transverse seats and running boards.
8 Built as motor cars for Chesapeake Transit Company with same numbers. Rebuilt as semi- closed trailers with double seats, end platforms, removable sash, and fixed sides.
9 Formerly open trailer #67.
10 Built by Southern Car Company, High Point, NC.
11 Rebuilt 1916 in company shops from steam division coaches #204 and 30.
12 Rebuilt 1907 in company shops from steam division coach #31.
13 Rebuilt from Chesapeake Transit Company closed motor car #60.
14 Ex-Chesapeake Transit Company closed motor cars.
15 Built by J. G. Brill Company. Cars nos. 50-53, 56,57 rebuilt as closed trailer cars.
16 Rebuilt from open trailer cars.

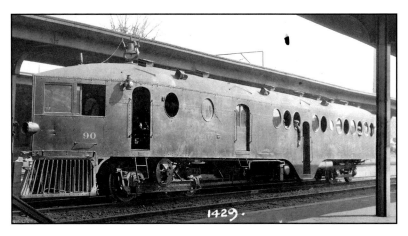

Right: McKeen car number 90 at Norfolk Terminal Station about the time of World War I. At that time, the car was the regular equipment on the Norfolk-to-Munden run, traversing the Electric Division to Clapham Junction by Euclid station, then the non-electrified Currituck Branch. Many different opinions have been expressed as to the disposition date of the car, ranging from 1925 to 1942, with 1934 the most likely date. (Thomas T. Taber photo, Railroad Museum of Pennsylvania, Pennsylvania Historical and Museum Commission)

Above: Norfolk Southern's first railbus, number 101, the Carolinian. *It was delivered in December 1934 by the ACF-Brill combine for use between Beaufort and Goldsboro, but with the termination of NS's lease of that line in 1935, it was withdrawn from that service and placed on the Virginia Beach lines. It is shown here in the latter service, at Park Avenue station in Norfolk, on an unknown date. Note the "cowcatcher" pilot. Apparently this was the only one of the NS railbuses which had it. This is the first paint scheme for the NS railbuses, green below, cream at the window level, and aluminum roof, similar to the large electric cars. (D. P. McDonald collection)*

time later they were given a variation of this scheme in which the cream color curved downward to a point at the bottom front of the vehicle. In later years, a simplified scheme eliminating all the cream color was adopted.

At the time of delivery of numbers 101 and 102, the NS had already ordered two more of the railbuses for use on the Virginia Beach lines. These were numbered 103 and 104, and were named *The Cavalier* and *The Princess Anne*, respectively. They were similar to numbers 101 and 102, but their engines were rated at 180 horsepower.

Railbus number 101 had not been in service for long when NS turned operation of the Goldsboro-Beaufort line back to the Atlantic and North Carolina Railroad. It kept the railbus and moved it to the Virginia Beach lines. Railbus number 102 continued to operate in North Carolina until the big reduction in passenger service in 1938, then it too went into Virginia Beach service.

In 1942, an opportunity arose for NS to add to its railbus fleet when the Seaboard Air Line decided to get rid of three it had bought in 1935, shortly after NS numbers 103 and 104 were built. NS bought two of the

three, formerly SAL numbers 2024 and 2025, and numbered them 105 and 106, but they were never named. These railbuses were 7-1/2 feet longer then NS numbers 101-104 and carried four more passengers, but were mechanically similar so that parts were interchangeable.

Railbus number 104 was badly damaged in an accident in 1943 and was then retired. The other five railbuses continued in service until the end of passenger service to the beach in November 1947. The question then arose as to what to do with them. One idea was to convert one of them (number 106 was the one selected) into a self-propelled business and inspection car, but in the end this was not done. Instead, all five were sold through dealer W. E. Corr to various Cuban railroads. Numbers 105 and 106 were the first to leave the property, being loaded on flatcars and moved from Norfolk on train number 99 on February 24, 1948. They were delivered to the Seaboard Air Line in Raleigh the following afternoon. Numbers 102 and 103 left Norfolk on train number 63 on March 15, 1948, with number 101 the last to go, on June 19, 1948. All were taken to West Palm Beach, Florida, by the SAL, then floated to Havana via the West Indies Lines.

Passenger Cars

In its early days, the Norfolk Southern encouraged passenger business and built up a sizable fleet of passenger cars. By 1921, the steam lines operated 75 first class cars, 25 baggage, express, and mail cars, 12 combination cars, and one parlor car, the *Vance*, which it inherited from the Atlantic and North Carolina. These were all green-painted wood-sheathed cars, although some had steel underframes and structural members, and most were already fairly old. By this time, management was beginning to realize that the passenger business would not be growing, so they had no desire to buy new equipment. As we have noted, by 1932 most passenger service had been discontinued, so the roster of passenger equipment decreased rapidly. By 1938, the roster was down to 12 coaches, 2 combines, and 21 baggage, express, and mail cars, none of which had been built since 1921.

The passenger car fleet continued to shrink slowly until January 31, 1948, when the last true passenger trains operated. This ended the need for coaches and combines, but three of the remaining cars, numbers

A builders' photo of NS coach number 265, built by ACF in 1913. Coaches similar to this were the last word in NS passenger accommodation right up to the end of passenger service January 31, 1948. Three cars of similar vintage, numbers 267, 268, and 269, were then converted into express and crew rider cars and were used on the mail and express trains until December 1951. (ACF Industries, St. Charles, Missouri, Frank M. Ellington collection)

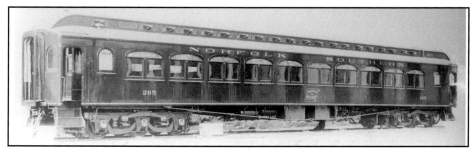

267, 268, and 269, were then converted into combination express and crew cars numbered 290, 292, and 291, respectively, to serve the express and mail trains numbers 1 and 2. Also, three Pullman troop sleepers were purchased from Pullman Standard Company at this time and converted into express cars which were numbered 293, 294, and 295. All this equipment was retired or converted to maintenance-of-way use soon after the discontinuance of the express trains in late 1951.

During the early years of this century, the railroad also owned two officers' cars, the *Virginia* and the *Carolina*. Little is known about the latter car, which left the roster in 1932, but the *Virginia* has had a long and interesting history. The N&S bought it in 1907, after it

Above: Car number 290 is shown here at Elizabeth City after rebuilding as an express and crew rider car. It had originally been a "Jim Crow" combine, number 267, with separate black and white passenger compartments separated by a baggage compartment. (H. T. Crittenden photo, Harry Bundy collection)

Below Left: Car number 291 is shown here at Carolina Yard on July 17, 1948. The car is similar to number 290, shown in the previous photo, but this shows the other side. Before conversion to an express and rider car, this was car number 269. (D. Wallace Johnson photo)

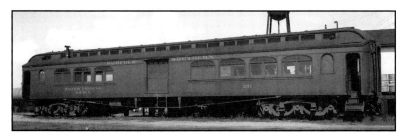

employees. A few years ago, it was moved from there to the North Carolina Transportation Museum in Spencer, NC. Recently, its ownership has been transferred to the Ringling Museum in Sarasota, Florida, which plans to restore

had been part of the Ringling Brothers circus train, where it had been named the *Wisconsin*. It was damaged by fire sometime around 1950, but was rebuilt. It was then sold to the Atlantic and East Carolina Company in 1951, which renamed it the *Carolina*. At some unknown time, it was placed on a disconnected section of track near the site of the Atlantic Hotel, the resort hotel in Morehead City once owned by the NS. There it served as a sort of mini-resort for

Above: The steel office car Mary Lee *appears here at Carolina Yard at an unknown date. The car had formerly been the Pullman car* Mt. Moran, *which was bought by the NS in 1948, rebuilt, and named after President "Major" Kingsley's daughter. After Kingsley left the railroad, it was renamed the* Carolina, *then sold to the Pacific Great Eastern Railway in 1956.(H. A. Stewart, Jr. photo, Tal Carey collection)*

Left: The wood car Virginia *served as the Norfolk Southern's office car for many years. It is shown here at Carolina Yard at an unknown date. It burned in 1950 but was rebuilt. Later it was moved to a permanent location near the station at Morehead City. (H. Reid photo, Tal Carey collection)*

and display it as the *Wisconsin*.

When "Major" Kingsley became president of the railroad, he wanted to establish a more affluent image for himself and the railroad than the ancient wooden *Virginia* would present. He therefore purchased a secondhand all-steel Pullman car named *Mt. Moran*, which he had rebuilt into an office car and renamed the *Mary Lee* after his daughter. Later, he purchased a second all-steel passenger car, the *Canonsburg*, which was also refurbished and named the *Virginia*, replacing the wooden car which had been shipped to Morehead City. The *Mt. Moran* had been a 10 section, lounge, observation car built in October 1924. The *Canonsburg* had been a 12 section, drawing room car, built in October 1910, which saw service on the Pennsylvania Railroad.

After Major Kingsley departed from the railroad under less than cordial circumstances, the railroad was not anxious to perpetuate the name *Mary Lee*, so the car was renamed the *Carolina*. After a few years, the company decided that owning official cars was a luxury it could no longer afford, so the *Carolina* was sold to the Pacific Great Eastern Railway, while the *Virginia* was converted into a maintenance-of-way car and given the number 912 in place of its name.

Cabooses

Essentially no information is available concerning the cabooses used on the Norfolk Southern and predecessor roads in the earliest years. Not long after the comprehensive locomotive classification and renumbering was initiated, the 300 number series was established for cabooses. About the same time, a program of rebuilding wood boxcars into cabooses in the

Wooden caboose number 316 was ordered from American Car and Foundry by the Virginia and Carolina Coast Railroad, but was delivered to the Norfolk and Southern, which had taken over the V&CC by the time it was ready for delivery. (ACF Industries, St. Charles, Missouri, Frank M. Ellington collection)

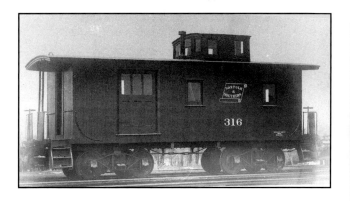

Above: Caboose number 335, shown here at Carolina Yard in January 1957, was one of the last wood cabooses on the road. It is presently owned by the North Carolina Railroad Museum in Bonsal, NC. (H. Reid photo)

Below: Wood cabooses remained in service up until the end of the NS. Here caboose number 306 brings up the rear of the Virginia Beach local freight in April 1972. (Felix Freeman photo)

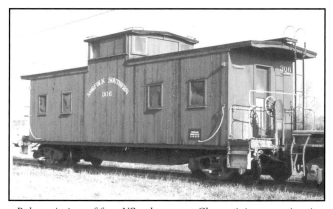

Below: A view of four NS cabooses at Chocowinity some time in the 1940s. Twelve steel cabooses were purchased from Magor Car Company in 1940, and numbered 365 through 376. The first, second, and fourth cabs in this row were part of that group. The third cab is an unidentified earlier wood caboose. Some sources say cabs 365 through 376 were originally painted an aluminum color, but today they are remembered only as having first been light gray. This may have been due to weathering of aluminum paint. They were later painted in at least two different shades of red, one dark and one bright. In this photo, cab 372 has its original paint. The other two steel cabs may be red, but more likely are light gray with a coating of dirt. (Tal Carey collection)

Above: A photo of steel caboose number 365 at Charlotte at an unknown date after repainting in the gray color scheme with red stripes. A few of these cabooses got this scheme, but several remained in red up to the merger. (D. P. McDonald photo)

Upper Below: Cabooses numbers 373 and 375, shown at Carolina Yard on May 9, 1964, show the bright red paint applied to some of the steel cabs in later years. The photo also shows that different lettering schemes were used, and the shade of red may also be different, although the one on the right may just be faded. (H. Reid photo)

Lower Below: The first caboose numbered 391 on the Norfolk Southern was this wood cab shown at Star at an unidentified date. This was one of five that had been bought secondhand from Seaboard Air Line, where it had been cab number 49517, in December 1952. It had apparently left the roster by 1969, at which time the last of the NS steel bay window cabs was given number 391. (Marvin Black collection)

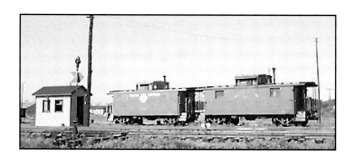

company shops was started. Records are available on part of this program, and the information is included in the following caboose roster.

In 1923, the NS began to build new wood cabooses in the New Bern shops (formerly and later the Atlantic and North Carolina Railroad shops). Later, four cabooses were purchased secondhand from the Richmond, Fredericksburg, and Potomac Railroad.

In 1940, the NS modernized its caboose fleet by buying twelve new steel cabooses. These were numbered 365-376. They were originally painted aluminum or light gray color, but were later repainted red.

By the early 1950s, the NS was short of cabooses and was leasing five from the Seaboard Air Line. The railroad soon realized this was an expensive solution, and improved on it by buying these five secondhand wood cabooses from the Seaboard in December 1952. The purchase price was little more than the one-year lease fee the NS had to pay, and the

Above: Norfolk Southern obtained six steel bay window cabooses in 1967, numbered 380 through 385. Number 385 is shown here at Raleigh shortly after delivery. They were originally painted in this bright red color with yellow and white lettering, but eventually several were painted gray to match the diesel color scheme. Cabs numbers 380 through 385 were rebuilt from boxcars. In 1969, six more similar cabooses also rebuilt from boxcars were obtained and numbered 386 through 391, but these were originally painted gray rather than red. Cab number 387 is now in the North Carolina Museum of Transportation at Spencer, NC. (Wharton G. Separk III)

Below: This view of caboose number 382 shows how the bay window cabooses looked in the gray paint scheme. (Ed Fielding photo)

railroad got much more than one year's use out of them. These cabooses were originally planned to carry the numbers 377-381, the next numbers available. Before they were actually put into service, it was decided to number them 391-395, leaving the lower numbers for newer steel cabooses which would probably be obtained later.

NS management proved to be correct in this assumption, as beginning in 1967, they had a series of steel boxcars rebuilt into bay window cabooses by Southern Iron and Equipment Company. Apparently management felt that these were sufficiently different from cabs numbers 365-376 that they were numbered starting at 380 rather than 377, the next number available. The first six, numbers 380-385, were built in 1967, with six more, numbers 386-391, following in 1969. The last number replaced the one-time SAL cab which had first carried number 391. All these bay window cabooses were retired after the merger with Southern Railway because they were too wide for SR clearance standards.

Two different paint schemes were used on the bay window cabooses. The first group of six were delivered in a bright red scheme with yellow and white lettering. However, the railroad soon began to repaint these into a light gray scheme with red end stripes and black lettering, similar to the scheme used on the EMD locomotives. A photo of caboose number 382 in this scheme and dated only one year after delivery has been found. However, at least one of this group was still in red at the time of the merger into Southern Railway. The second group of six was delivered in the light gray scheme and retained this scheme until the merger.

The following roster includes all the information we have been able to assemble on the NS cabooses after the numbering into the 300 series began. It is not claimed to be complete, but is believed to be accurate as far as it goes. In particular, numbers missing from the roster do not necessarily mean that no NS cabooses carried these numbers, only that we have no information about them. Also, more than one caboose may have carried some of the numbers in the roster, although we do not know of any instance of this except number 391.

In regard to the NS cabooses, it is also of interest to note that NS assigned specific cabooses to individual conductors up until the merger with Southern Railway. If a conductor left one job for another, his cab would be moved with him. Most of the conductors took pride in their cabs and kept them exceptionally clean

In the early years, Norfolk Southern rostered many of these ventilated boxcars. These are sometimes called "watermelon cars", but they were used for a wide variety of perishable agricultural products. This photo is identified as the first carload of eggs shipped from Craven County, NC (The New Bern area). (New Bern Area Chamber of Commerce collection, NewBern-Craven County Photographic Archive, New Bern-Craven County Public Library)

and neat. Some added special equipment to their cabs. For example, conductor Joe Jeffries wanted an electric light in his cab instead of the kerosene lamps installed in most of the steel cabs. He installed a 12-volt marine type battery in the storage area under one of the bunks in his cab. He attached a battery charger to it and ran an extension cord thought a small hole in the floor. He then mounted a 12-volt light fixture on the wall above his seat. When the cab would be placed in a cab track, the extension cord would be pulled out the bottom and plugged into an outlet to charge the battery. Mr. Jeffries also installed an electric flashing marker on his cab by having special brackets made and placed on the ends. He bought a rechargeable highway barricade light and would place it in the brackets as his marker.

Norfolk and Southern boxcar number 2300 was built by American Car and Foundry at their Milton, PA plant. The date is unknown, but presumably was before May 1910, when the company again became Norfolk Southern, and the ampersand was no longer used in the herald. (ACF Industries, St. Charles, Missouri, Frank M. Ellington collection)

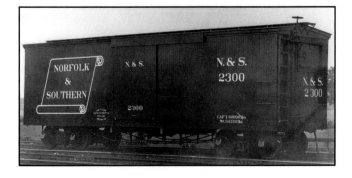

Above: NS boxcar number 4557, shown at an unidentified location in 1934. (North Carolina Division of Archives and History)

Below: Biggest boxcars owned by the NS were the twenty 60-foot double plug door car numbers 550-569. They had D. F. (Damage Free) equipment and 20-inch cushion underframes, and all were assigned to Plymouth for paper loading. Number 554 was photographed at Raleigh, NC on July 5, 1975.(Robert Graham photo)

Above: Boxcar number 1434 was built by the American Car and Foundry St. Louis plant in June 1959. It was one of 250 similar cars, numbers 1201-1450, with one sliding door and one plug door on each side. These cars were bought for paper service. Several of the cars in this group had special equipment, such as cushion underframes, added. In some cases, this equipment was removed later in response to shipper requests. (ACF Industries, St. Charles, Missouri, Frank M. Ellington collection)

Below: Boxcar number 1411 is shown at Charlotte, NC on April 21, 1973 after repainting into the new gray paint scheme first applied to the GP18 locomotives. (Larry Goolsby photo)

Above:Boxcar number 1428 is shown at Raleigh, NC on January 5, 1975, in the final NS boxcar paint scheme of tuscan red with yellow doors and lettering. Note this car had D. F. equipment added. (Robert Graham photo)

Below: 40-foot boxcar number 1599 was one of a group of 225 cars built in 1947, all of which had D. F. equipment, as shown by the letters to the left of the door. It is seen here in Wilson, NC in 1966. (Tom King photo, Robert Graham collection)

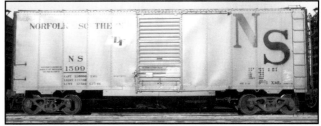

Freight Cars and Work Equipment

Throughout its history, the Norfolk Southern owned and operated freight cars of most of the usual types, such as box, flat, hopper, and gondola cars. In later years when special purpose cars designed for a specific service became popular, the NS added these when desirable for the traffic it handled. This included cushion underframe box cars, plug-door boxcars, covered hopper cars, and high volume hopper cars for woodchip service. The accompanying photographs illustrate some of the freight cars used over the years.

Before 1935, NS boxcars were painted green, as that color was a "trademark" of the railroad. Structures such as depots were also painted in green, with a darker green trim. It is not definitely known that all freight cars were green, but it seems likely that many were. In 1935, the railroad switched to the more common "boxcar red" as a cost-cutting measure. After 1963, the railroad began to paint boxcars and most other freight cars in the light gray paint initiated on the GP18 locomotives, but switched back to red for boxcars later. The newest paint jobs on the boxcars had bright yellow doors.

Above: Fifty-foot boxcars numbers 1800 through 1859 had one plug door and one sliding door on each side, and also had four roof hatches. The roof hatches were supposed to be for use for phosphate loading at Lee Creek, but they were seldom used for that. It is said that the real reason for ordering them with the roof hatches was to make them special cars to be returned immediately to the NS, so that they would not spend long periods of time on other railroads. (Ed Fielding photo)

Below: In the 1920s, NS began to number newly acquired boxcars from 20000 up. The numbers eventually reached 28236, but not all intermediate numbers were used. Numbers for new boxcars went back down to 1201 in 1959. Car number 25212, shown in this photo, was one of a group of 500 boxcars numbered 25000-25499, built by Pullman Standard Car Manufacturing company in its Richmond, VA plant in 1935 and January 1936. It was one of four of this group of cars given this special lettering for the new "tarwheel" LCL service in 1959. The other cars with this lettering were 25045, 25242, and 25394. (Robert Graham collection)

Top left: 40-foot boxcar number 1906 shows the final boxcar color scheme of tuscan red with yellow lettering and doors, at Raleigh on March 17, 1974. This car is one of a series of 100 cars numbered 1900-1999. These cars may be unique to the NS as they were modern outside braced boxcars of 40-foot length built in 1971 when the industry standard boxcar length had become 50-foot. NS had these cars built using the frames and running gear from a like number of obsolete 40-foot gondolas, hence the 40-foot length. (Robert Graham photo)

Above left: 50-foot boxcar number 2170 in red and yellow, shown at Star, NC on June 2, 1983. Note that the NS letters of the herald are smaller on this car than on most others. This group of cars included numbers 2100-2249, and were built by ACF Industries. They entered service on the NS in the latter part of 1971. (Robert Graham photo)

Below left: 50-foot boxcar number 2339 at Greensboro, NC on October 21, 1977. This group included car numbers 2300-2449, and were built by Southern Iron and Equipment Company of Atlanta, GA in 1972. They were similar to car numbers 2100-2249 except for small differences in dimensions. The last group of NS boxcars, numbers 2500-2559, was also similar, again excepting small dimensional differences. (Robert Graham photo)

Bottom left: This boxcar, number 1257, is one which had a cushion underframe added. It was given this special paint scheme with the figure of a swan, and the lettering "3C" and "Cushion Cargo Car". (John Sullivan photo)

Below: Number 26007 was a 40-foot, 40-ton capacity car with two sliding doors on each side. This was one of a 25-car group with numbers 26000-26024, and was photographed in Raleigh on July 23, 1973. (Robert Graham photo)

Below: 40-foot boxcar number 28134 with the "chevy" herald. Note that this car had 44-ton capacity, but some of the other cars in this series (numbers 28000-28236) had capacities of 50 and 55 tons. Photo was made in Raleigh on September 16, 1973. (Robert Graham photo)

2nd below: This is one of four Fruit Growers Express reefers which had NS reporting marks. The four cars were numbered NS 92161, 92162, 92329, and 92330.(D. P. McDonald photo)

2nd above: 55-ton open hopper car number 9120, seen at Chocowinity in January 1970, from a series of 75 cars numbered 9100-9174. (Robert Graham photo)
Above: Number 9394, one of two hundred 55-ton hopper cars numbered 9200 through 9399, was photographed in Charlotte on November 26, 1972. (Larry Goolsby photo)

Above: Open hopper cars with 70 to 77-ton capacity were numbered in the 8000 series, which also included some older covered hopper cars of similar capacity. Number 8460, a 77-ton car seen at Lillington, NC on January 12, 1975, was one of a group of 70 cars numbered 8400-8469. (Robert Graham photo)

Below: Number 8678 was one of 125 70-ton hoppers obtained secondhand from the Bessemer and Lake Erie Railroad, numbered 8600 through 8724. The distinctive trucks on these cars indicate their B&LE heritage. Photo was taken at Raleigh on July 22, 1973. (Robert Graham photo)

Above: Number 8292 was one of fifty high-capacity 77-ton hopper cars for wood chip service, numbered 8250 through 8299. It was photographed in Charlotte on December 2, 1973. (Larry Goolsby photo)

Below: NS rebuilt several 70-ton hopper cars such as number 8219 with extended sides to accommodate the high volume of wood chips. (Tom King photo, Robert Graham collection)

Above: An example of an early application of wooden side extensions for wood chip loading to a 70-ton hopper car. The 30 cars in this series were numbered NS 101-130 and were retired and returned to their owner, Chicago Freight Car Leasing, when their lease expired in 1966. (Tom King photo, Robert Graham collection)

Below: Some of the 55-ton hopper cars also had extended sides added for woodchip service. Number 9106, shown here at Mackeys, NC, on April 9, 1966, is an example of these. (No, these cars were not equipped with brick chimneys. They are part of the depot behind the car.)(Tom King photo, Robert Graham collection)

Above: Builders' photo of NS covered hopper car number 8001, built at the ACF Berwick, PA plant in January 1952. This was the first of five such cars, built for cement service. (ACF Industries, St. Charles, Missouri, Frank M. Ellington collection)

Right: Norfolk Southern's car shops were adept at making useful new equipment out of worn out cars. This is one of a series of pulpwood cars built up on the frames of obsolete gondolas. The floor of the car is supported on lengths of old light rail replaced by heavier rail on the company's lines. This photo was taken at Carolina Yard in 1955. (Robert Reisweber collection)

Top above: Number 8301, shown at Charlotte on April 7, 1974, was the first of a series of five covered hoppers built in April 1961. These were painted light gray with black lettering and herald. (Larry Goolsby photo)

Above: Number 5120, photographed at Wilson, NC on February 20, 1966, was one of a group of 300 2929 cubic foot 100-ton covered hopper cars numbered 5000-5299 on the NS roster. All were assigned to Lee Creek for phosphate loading with the exception of numbers 5094 and 5097, which were assigned to Ohio Blenders of Toledo, Ohio, on the Norfolk and Western, for feed loading. The paint scheme was similar to that of the EMD locomotives, but the gray was a lighter color, almost a cream color. (Tom King photo, Robert Graham collection)

Below: Number 5327 was a 100-ton covered hopper car, one of a group of 150 cars numbered 5300-5449. These were built in 1973, the last new cars to be bought by the independent NS. They were also bought for phosphate service on the Lee Creek Branch. Like most NS cars, they did not stay this clean for long. Photo was taken at Fayetteville, NC, in October 1973. (Robert Graham photo)

Top: NS 10534, photographed at Charlotte on October 28, 1973, is a pulpwood car. NS had several different series of these cars. This car is one of forty, numbered 10500 through 10539. These cars were 47 feet two inches long between bulkheads, which were 8 feet 3 inches high. Pulpwood cars, which had AAR car type code LP, differed from bulkhead flat cars in that the floor was sloped downward toward the center from both sides. Bulkhead flat cars, AAR car type code FB, had a flat floor.(Larry Goolsby photo)

Above: Number 10915 was another pulpwood car, one of a series of 80 cars numbered 10901-10980. They had inside dimensions of 35 feet length and 9 feet height. Number 10915 still had NS reporting marks when photographed in June 1984 in Charlotte. (Paul Faulk photo)

Below: Number 652, at Raleigh on December 29, 1973, is a bulk-head flat car, with the flat floor. These cars were used mainly for lumber. This is one of 15 similar cars numbered 650-664 which were converted to flat cars from 10500 series woodracks by NS shop personnel. (Robert Graham collection)

Although the NS was always one of the smaller railroads and certainly not one of the wealthiest ones, it spent time and money in keeping up with freight car development, and in some cases taking the lead in this

Above: Tank car number 3008, shown at Plymouth. NS did not have any tank cars in revenue service, but had a few for company service for water, fuel, etc. (L. D. Jones, Jr. photo)

Below: Gondola number 7802 was one of 150 40-foot gondolas numbered 7700-7849. It is seen at Charlotte on March 4, 1973. (Larry Goolsby photo)

Bottom: Gondola number 7604 was one of 150 40-foot gondolas numbered 7500-7649. (Marvin Black collection)

development. As John H. White points out in the book, *The American Railroad Freight Car*, when Mr. G. R. Joughins was superintendent of motive power for the N&S in the 1890s, he devised a new type of truck, primarily for all-steel cars. This was somewhat similar to the better known Fox truck but was easier to assemble and disassemble.

Of course, the NS required a roster of equipment for maintenance of way and other work duties. Like most railroads, the NS created some of this equipment in its own shops from obsolete passenger and freight cars. We include illustrations of some of the more interesting items of work equipment.

Above: Car number 762 was photographed at Raleigh on March 23, 1974.. (Larry Goolsby photo)

Below: Wheel car number 767 at Duncan, NC on October 21, 1973.(Robert Graham photo)

Top: Rogers ballast plow number 500 was built for NS by ACF in September 1915. (ACF Industries, St. Charles, Missouri, Frank M. Ellington collection)

Above: The NS scale test car number 479 is shown at Wilson, NC, August 4, 1973. (Robert Graham photo)

Below: Maintenance-of-way car number 711 is shown at Raleigh on March 17, 1974. This car is now in the North Carolina Railroad Museum at Bonsal, NC. (Robert Graham photo)

Bottom: A view of the opposite side of car number 711, photographed at Raleigh on March 23, 1974.. (Larry Goolsby photo)

Above: The other side of wheel car number 767 is seen at Raleigh on September 16, 1973. (Robert Graham photo)

Below: Foreman car number 786 at Marsden, NC October 31, 1965. (Tom King photo, Robert Graham collection)

Right: Kitchen and dining car number 851 at Camden, NC, date unknown. (Tom King photo, Robert Graham collection)

Below:Dump car number 839, seen at Raleigh on March 23, 1974. (Larry Goolsby photo)

Above: Derrick number 900 is hard at work changing out a diesel engine in one of the Baldwin roadswitchers. Derrick operator Fred Curling gave his camera to one of his coworkers to take this photo. Fred is shown standing on the front corner of the derrick. This derrick was originally steam-powered and was owned by the U. S. Army at Fort Eustis, Newport News, VA. NS bought it and converted it to diesel power in 1957. (Fred Curling collection)

Below: Maintenance of way car number 901 was photographed at Raleigh on January 24, 1976. (Paul Faulk photo)

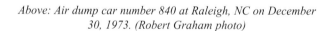

Above: Air dump car number 840 at Raleigh, NC on December 30, 1973. (Robert Graham photo)

Below: Foreman car number 850 at Raleigh, NC on June 24, 1973. (Robert Graham photo)

Bottom right:Car number 902 at Raleigh, NC on December 25, 1975. (Robert Graham photo)

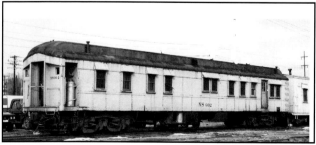

Above: Pile driver number 905 at work rebuilding the Charles Boulevard underpass in Greenville, NC. (Scott Burns photo, Bruce H. Baker, Jr. collection)

Below: Sleeping and dining car number 910 at Raleigh, NC. December 15, 1973. (Robert Graham photo)

Above: No. 1 extra force car number 911 at Charlotte on August 20, 1972. (Larry Goolsby photo)

Above: Derrick number 915 photographed at Carolina Junction in July 1971. (Ed Fielding photo)

Below: Wheel car number 11010 at Raleigh, NC on July 22, 1973. (Robert Graham photo)

Above: Inspection car number 1, purchased from Willys in December 1950 and converted in NS Carolina shops for use on rails. (W. R. Newton collection)

Below: NS electric truck number 4 at Carolina Yard in 1948. (H. Reid photo, Harry Bundy collection)

Chapter 10

Operations

Norfolk Southern was similar to other Class I railroads in that it was split into divisions or districts for operating purposes. Also, like most other railroads, many changes took place in the division alignments over the years as the railroad grew and traffic patterns changed.

When the railroad ran only from Norfolk to Edenton, it was short enough that no division of operations was needed. In 1891, however, when the NS was combined with the Albemarle and Pantego to form the new Norfolk and Southern Railroad, the need for two separate divisions became obvious, since the two formerly independent railroads were still separated by Albemarle Sound. They became the Norfolk and Pamlico Divisions, respectively, the former headquartered at Berkley (later Norfolk) and the latter first at Roper, NC, five miles south of Mackey's Ferry, and later at Belhaven. When the Washington and Plymouth Railroad was added to the N&S, it became part of the Pamlico Division. Headquarters of the division then moved to Washington.

A third division, the Electric Division, was created to cover the Virginia Beach lines when they were added to the railroad. However, the Currituck Branch from Euclid to Munden and the branch from Euclid to Providence, which were operated by steam rather than electric power, were added to the Norfolk Division. The Electric Division was also headquartered at Norfolk.

The big expansion of the railroad in 1906, which added the Virginia and Carolina Coast, the Atlantic and North Carolina, and the Raleigh and Pamlico Sound to the system, added three new divisions. These were the Suffolk, the Beaufort, and the Raleigh Divisions, which corresponded roughly to the three predecessor railroads mentioned above. The Chocowinity-to-Bridgeton line of the R&PS was added

to the Pamlico Division along with the Columbia Branch of the V&CC and the Pamlico, Oriental, and Western Railroad.

The extension to Charlotte added three new divisions to the railroad, called the Raleigh and Southport, the Durham and Charlotte, and the Aberdeen and Asheboro Divisions. Obviously, these corresponded to the predecessor railroads of the same name.

At this point, management decided to streamline the organization, and created four new divisions. The Northern Division covered everything north of Chocowinity, the Western Division included everything south of Raleigh, and the Central Division included everything in between. The Electric Division remained as it had always been. Headquarters of the three new steam divisions were at Norfolk, Raleigh, and New Bern, respectively.

In 1922, the Central Division was eliminated. The part of the main line between Marsden (as Chocowinity was then known) and Raleigh was added to the Western Division, and the rest of the former Central Division became part of the Northern Division. In January 1934, this division system was eliminated. The Northern and Western Divisions were then called the Northern and Western Districts with a single superintendent over both of them.

The next change occurred in September 1936 when all the steam lines became the Steam Division. The main line from Norfolk to Marsden became the Norfolk District, from Marsden to Raleigh the Raleigh District, and from Raleigh to Charlotte the Charlotte District. At this point the NS was being operated with an Electric and a Steam Division. This lasted until late 1947 when both these divisions were dropped. From this time on the railroad was operated in its entirety without divisions. The North and South Routes that had comprised the Electric Division were now the Virginia Beach District. In March of 1954 this name was shortened to Beach District.

The last major change occurred in February 1948, when the District names were changed. The Norfolk became the Northern, the Raleigh became the Central, and the Charlotte became the Western. With this change the railway had come full circle as these districts were identical to the three divisions of the same names that had existed prior to 1922, minus the trackage no longer operated. This district arrangement continued until the end of the NS as an independent railroad.

One further point should be mentioned with respect to the districts. While Marsden (later once again to be known as Chocowinity) was the point at which through trains exchanged Northern District and Central District crews, Jacks Creek in Washington, just north of the Washington station, was the official line of demarcation for the crews. So twice a year the railroad added up the train miles northern District crews had accumulated between Jacks Creek and Marsden, and assigned Central District trainmen to the Northern District to equalize mileage. Another consequence was that Lee Creek trains were normally operated with a Northern District engineer and remaining crewmen from the Central District.

We will not attempt to provide a comprehensive description of all the individual train operations throughout the history of the railroad. However, we will now proceed to include a description of "normal" train operations, recognizing that exceptions to these "normal" operations were frequent. We will concentrate mainly on the last few years of independence for the Norfolk Southern. As we have already mentioned, passenger operations on the NS ceased long before the end of the railroad except for a few very abnormal special trains. Consequently, the following description includes only freight and yard operations. Previous chapters contain information about the most significant passenger operations when they existed.

Through Freights

With the westward extension of the railroad completed in late 1913, the NS had a main line running from Berkley, VA to Charlotte, NC, but it would be over a year later before a permanent train would be established to operate between those points. Norfolk Southern's first through freights to run between Berkley and Charlotte were trains numbers 62 and 63, which began on April 11, 1915. Train number 63 was scheduled to depart Berkley at 6:45 P.M. and arrive at Charlotte at 10:10 P.M. the next day, 27 hours and 25 minutes later. Its northbound counterpart, number 62, departed Charlotte at 8:00 A.M., with arrival at Berkley scheduled for 6:30 P.M. the following day, 34 hours and 30 minutes later.

By 1926, Norfolk Southern's business had grown to the point that a second pair of through freights were needed. So, on May 2 of that year, train numbers 61 and 64 were added to the timetable. Trains no longer operated out of Berkley and downtown Charlotte by this time, but instead originated and terminated at the railroad's classification yards at Norfolk and Charlotte.

In the later years of the Norfolk Southern as an independent railroad, train number 63 was the only scheduled southbound through freight. Here number 63 led by four AS416s traverses the rural territory just south of Wilson in March 1965. The locomotives cannot be identified, but the third unit appears to be either number 1616 or number 1617, since it seems to have the higher hood which only these two units on the NS had. (Harry Bundy photo)

Number 61 was scheduled to leave Carolina Yard in Norfolk at 9:00 P.M. and arrive in Charlotte at 8:10 A.M. on the second morning, or 35 hours and 10 minutes later. Number 64 departed Charlotte Yard at 8:00 P.M. and arrived at Carolina Yard at 5:00 A.M. on the second morning for an elapsed time of 33 hours.

Train numbers 61, 62, 63, and 64 would handle the Norfolk Southern's through freight business between Norfolk and Charlotte for the next twenty years. The only change came in the mid-thirties when local freights replaced number 61 on the Central District between Marsden and Raleigh. In addition to the aforementioned trains, trains numbers 65 and 66 operated on the Western District between 1935 and 1948, as the hilly terrain on that district often necessitated additional trains to help move tonnage.

The next change in the through freight trains occurred after World War II, when trains numbers 98 and 99 were added to the schedule, as mentioned in Chapter 6. Number 99 was a first class train and the hottest one on the railroad. It ran on a 19-hour schedule, leaving Norfolk at 2:00 P.M. and arriving at Charlotte at 9:00 A.M. The second class number 98 departed Charlotte at 3:00 P.M. and arrived at Norfolk at 1:30 P.M. the next afternoon. Trains numbers 61 and 62 were removed from the schedule when numbers 98 and 99 were added.

Almost from the moment of the inception of trains number 98 and 99, the NS was trying hard to improve upon their schedules. With nearly every successive timetable would come an incremental improvement in the trains' running times. Fast freight service on the NS reached its zenith when timetable number 2 of May 15, 1955 was issued. Train number 99 was then scheduled to depart Norfolk at 1:00 P.M. and arrive Charlotte at 5:20 A.M., or 16 hours and 20 minutes later. This would be the fastest scheduled train ever to run on the Norfolk Southern. In 1957, the schedules were changed twice with the final result being 40 minutes added to number 99's running time. While it still departed Norfolk at 1:00 P.M., the Charlotte arrival time was now 6:00 A.M.

The fast freight era on the NS ended in January 1962 when trains 63, 64, 98 and 99 were all removed

from the timetable. They were replaced by a single train in each direction, numbered 3 and 4. Number 3 was then scheduled to run from Norfolk to Charlotte in 19 hours. The numbers of these trains returned to 63 and 64 in July 1964.

In the final years of the independent Norfolk Southern, Northern District number 63 was due to leave Carolina Yard in Norfolk at 12:30 A.M. The normal consist would include two engines and cars blocked for Elizabeth City, Plymouth, Chocowinity, Farmville, Wilson, and Raleigh. The crew would normally stop at Elizabeth City and Plymouth to make setouts and pickups before reaching the crew change point at Chocowinity. This was also the timetable scheduled meeting point with number 64, but in actuality this meet seldom occurred there. Depending on how the trains were running, the meet could take place anywhere from Greenville or Simpson on the Central District to Alligoods or Plymouth on the Northern.

There was no yard engine at Chocowinity so about an hour before the arrival of Northern District Number 63 the Central District crew that was to take over the train would report for duty. This crew would use an engine off one of the locals tied up there to begin building their train. They would get their caboose and all the cars for Raleigh and points south from the yard. This would be the rear of their train leaving

Train number 63 and its northbound counterpart number 64 pass on the main tracks at Glenwood Yard. The view is toward the north. The locomotives of number 63 are at the bottom of the photo, with train number 64 to the left of them.
(D. P. McDonald photo)

Train number 63 with GP18 number 6 in the lead heads south out of Raleigh on October 29, 1967. Note that the consist includes several Baldwin diesels, still in the red paint scheme. On Sundays, Norfolk Southern usually used train number 63 to ferry freshly serviced units to points on the Western District for the weekday locals. (David Burnette photo)

Chocowinity. Upon the arrival of number 63, the Northern District crew would make Chocowinity setoff and then the head end crews would trade places with each other. The Northern District crew would then be on the local engine and Central District crew on Number 63's engines. These crews would work in conjunction with one another to drop the Northern District caboose and add the Central District cab and Raleigh block to the rear of Number 63. The Central District crew was then ready to depart. Scheduled departure time was 6:30 A.M.

There were normally two stops made on the Central District before reaching Raleigh. These were to set off and pick up at Farmville and Wilson. Arrival at Raleigh which was the crew change point with the Western District could be anytime from late morning to mid-afternoon. There the Raleigh yard engine would reswitch the train extensively before it would be ready to depart on the Western District.

Number 63 was scheduled out of Raleigh at 12:30 P.M., but it usually departed sometime between 1:00 P.M. and 3:00 P.M. Its normal consist would include four engines, a mix of GP18s and GP38s, and cars blocked for Varina, Duncan, Star, and Charlotte. After setting off and picking up at Varina and Duncan, Number 63 might be required to stop at Brickhaven to pick up empty coal hoppers for return to the Winston-Salem Southbound at Norwood. Otherwise, the next stop would be Star. It was at Star that Number 63 was scheduled to meet its northbound counterpart Number 64 on the Western District. After this meet took place, Number 63 would have a straight run to Charlotte unless it had cars to set off for the Winston-Salem Southbound at Norwood.

Upon arrival at Charlotte there would be a flurry of hurried activity as the crew began to break up their train and to deliver to the connections. On the Western District Number 63 was a per diem train and it was imperative that they arrive at Charlotte in time for the crew to get their cars off the NS and onto the connecting roads before midnight to save another day's per diem charges. The NS crews called this "making the market."

The first move on arrival at Charlotte was to fill up one of the interchange tracks to Southern with cars. At the same time, the operator-clerk was using the waybills the conductor had brought in to make overhead and interchange reports. Delivery to the Seaboard Air Line followed. SAL forwarded any cars destined to Piedmont and Northern from NS.

Western District Number 64 was scheduled to depart Charlotte at 1:30 P.M. The crew and engines would be the same ones that had arrived on Number 63 the previous night. In addition to the four engines, the consist normally included cars blocked for Star, Duncan, Varina, and Raleigh. After departing Charlotte the first stop would be at Norwood to pick up cars lined up there by the Charlotte local. Often this pickup would include coal coming off the Winston-Salem Southbound destined for Brickhaven. The next stop would be at Star to set off and pick up and meet Number 63. Then it was on to Brickhaven to set off any coal that had been picked up at Norwood.

After stops at Duncan and Varina the train would arrive at the crew change point of Raleigh. This was usually a couple of hours later than its 7:55 P.M. scheduled arrival time. At Raleigh, the train would be reclassified by the Raleigh yard engine and made ready for its 2:01 A.M. scheduled departure on the Central District. When it left Raleigh, it would have cars blocked for points all the way to Norfolk, including blocks for Wilson, Farmville, Chocowinity, Plymouth, and Elizabeth City as well as Norfolk.

On the Central District there would be stops to set off and pick up at Wilson and Farmville before reaching Chocowinity, where a Northern District crew would take over the train. Departure was scheduled for 7:30 A.M. If Number 63 had not been met on the Central district, then the Northern District crew would meet it at Alligoods or Plymouth. Then after stops at Plymouth and Elizabeth City, Number 64 was scheduled into Norfolk at 12:20 P.M., but arrival was usually much later.

Local Service

The NS used two types of trains to provide service to customers at intermediate points along the line. The two types were called switchers and locals. The only differences between them were that the switchers spent a considerable amount of time working at one geographic location, and their crews were paid at a slightly higher rate than crews of the locals.

Local service on the Northern district was provided by four trains, two on the main line, and one each on the Beach District and Belhaven Branch. The Beach local, reporting at 2:00 A.M., served what was left of the old electric lines, now known as the Beach District. This consisted of 9.6 miles of the former North Beach Route from Norfolk to Shelton, and 17.1 miles of the South Beach Route from Tidewater to Virginia Beach station, which in later years was the end of track, about one-half mile west of the oceanfront. Also worked by the Beach local was a two-mile spur track from Tidewater to the former Park Avenue station site, which served a few commercial customers. The North Route did not have a lot of business. Company records show that in 1969 only 282 revenue cars were handled, with the U. S. Navy at Shelton being the largest customer, accounting for over half that total. The South Route had a good mix of traffic with more than two dozen accounts in its seventeen miles. Records from 1969 show that the three largest accounts all received sand and gravel for the construction industry. Others included building supply companies, a beer distributor, steel, coal, and LP gas companies.

The first of the main line trains was the Elizabeth City switcher. This crew, working out of Elizabeth City, NC, went on duty at 7:00 A.M. and ran as far north as Moyock and as far south as Mackeys. They also worked the seven-mile long Weeksville spur

Above: Northbound through freight number 64 passes Boylan Tower with GP18 number 14 in the lead. It is running as an extra at this point, as indicated by the white flags, due to having fallen more than twelve hours behind schedule. It was scheduled to arrive at 7:55 P.M. the evening before. It was usually an hour or two late, which put it by Boylan in darkness, but on this occasion, it has not arrived there until the morning after.
(D. P. McDonald photo)

Below: GP18 number 9 is hauling the Beach local near Rosemont station in this photo made in April 1972. This unit suffered a crankcase explosion earlier but was rebuilt and returned to service. (Felix Freeman photo)

General Electric 70-tonner number 702 works as the Elizabeth City switcher in 1960. With the end of the mail and express trains numbers 1 and 2 in 1951, number 702 and its two sisters were relegated to light switching duties. Three units of this size were more than the railroad could use efficiently, so number 702 was sold in 1964. Note that number 702's consist in this photo includes three open hopper cars which have been rebuilt with extended sides for wood chip service. (Harry Bundy photo)

track which ran out of Elizabeth City. The two largest cities served by this job were Elizabeth City and Edenton, and it was in this area that it spent most of its time. Accounts in Elizabeth City included several beer distributors, scrap yards, a brick company, a plywood manufacturer, and on the Weeksville spur, a cabinet company. At Edenton there were two peanut dealers, a couple of fertilizer companies, a cotton mill, and a pallet manufacturer. Most of the smaller stations served, such as Moyock, Shawboro, and Camden, had customers who shipped grain and/or received fertilizer.

The second train which operated on the main line was the Plymouth switcher. This job went on duty at 3:00 P.M. and spent its tour of duty switching Weyerhaeuser's large Plymouth pulp mill, which was jointly served by the Seaboard Coast Line. This crew used a single engine, either Baldwin or EMD.

The last of the Northern District jobs was the Belhaven local. This crew had operated out of Chocowinity as trains Numbers 26 and 27 until mid-1973, but then had their home terminal moved to Plymouth. There they went on duty at 3:00 A.M. and worked between Plymouth, Chocowinity, and Belhaven using the same engine that had been used on the Plymouth switcher. Among the accounts served by this

crew were companies shipping grain from Plymouth, Washington, Bishop Cross, and Belhaven, and fertilizer dealers at Plymouth and Pantego. At Washington, Moss planing mill received lumber and shipped out wood chips, and on the Belhaven line, both Howell and M&L siding had saw mill type operations shipping chips. All the cars picked up by this crew were taken back to Plymouth and lined up along with those from the Plymouth switcher for pickup by trains Numbers 63 and 64.

On the Central District, local service was provided by five trains, one on the Lee Creek Branch, two on the New Bern Branch, and two on the main line. The Lee Creek Branch was worked by a turn operating out of Chocowinity on duty at 9:00 A.M. This crew served Texas Gulf's phosphate mining operation at Lee Creek, for which this line had been built. Usual power on this train was two or three EMDs.

The first of the two trains serving the New Bern branch was the New Bern-Weyco switcher. This crew, on duty at 8:00 A.M. at New Bern, worked the local industries, A&EC and SCL interchanges, and then ran to Weyco where they served Weyerhaeuser's large pulp mill before returning to New Bern. About twice a week they would make a side trip on the Bayboro branch to

The Elizabeth City switcher crosses the Albemarle Sound bridge to Mackeys in August 1962. (J. Parker Lamb photo)

switch the customers located on that line. This train's normal power was the Norfolk Southern's last two GE 70-tonners which were necessitated by the light rail on the Bayboro line.

The other train operating on the New Bern Branch was the Weyco local. This crew went on duty at 12:01 P.M. at Chocowinity. It was assigned to work between Chocowinity and New Bern, but usually turned around at Weyco. There was little business on the branch between Chocowinity and the New Bern area, except the pulp mill at Weyco. This crew's main purpose was to act as a connection between the main line and the New Bern-Weyco switcher, bringing down cars for the switcher and taking back to Chocowinity those cars left by the switcher. This interchange of cars took place at Weyco or Askin. Only occasionally when there was a special move or the hours of service law got the switcher did this job go all the way into New Bern.

The section of the Central District main line between Chocowinity and Wilson was served by the Farmville switcher. This crew reported for duty at 9:00 A.M. at Farmville. Most of the local business was concentrated in the cities of Farmville and Greenville. This area of North Carolina is known as the tobacco belt and much of the Norfolk Southern's traffic here was related to that crop. Accounts at Farmville included a Formica plant, FCX feed mill, LP gas and fertilizer dealers, two grain shippers, and a pair of tobacco warehouses. In Greenville there were tobacco warehouses owned by American, Liggett, Reynolds, and Export tobacco companies. In addition to the tobacco companies there were a toy and game maker, food wholesaler, building supply company, and Unichem(a soap company). This

Above: AS416 number 1611 handles the Belhaven local in August 1971. Note the woodchip cars. (Ed Fielding photo)

Below: A Lee Creek turn, the "Phosphate Flyer", is seen headed for Chocowinity in October 1967. The nickname came from J. R. Pate, one of the Central District trainmen. When the Lee Creek Branch was under construction, the crew had to use a "hobo caboose" instead of a caboose regularly assigned to a specific conductor. The "hobo caboose" was not nearly as well kept up as the other cabs. On the first revenue run to Lee Creek, Mr. Pate wrote "Phosphate Flyer" in the accumulation of grit on the cab. So afterward, the Lee Creek trains were called "Phosphate Flyers". This one has number 1616 and another unidentified AS416 on the head end. Number 1616 still has its initial paint scheme, having not yet gotten a "chevy" herald. (Harry Bundy photo)

crew used a single unit as its power, and lined up the cars to be moved by through freights Numbers 63 and 64 at Farmville.

The Central District local service from Wilson to Raleigh was provided by the Wilson switcher. This crew went on duty at 8:30 A.M. at Wilson and worked south to serve the towns of Bailey, Middlesex, Zebulon, and Wendell before returning to Wilson. Occasionally this job would run all the way to Raleigh, but this would be to carry or pick up tonnage as there were no active accounts to switch between Wendell and Raleigh. The largest concentration of business served by this switcher was in Wilson where customers included Reynolds, American, and Export tobacco warehouses, Nutrena and Cargill feed mills, Royster fertilizer, a building supply company, a coal dealer, a lumber company that shipped loads of chips, and a busy interchange with the SCL. Outside of Wilson, accounts

Left: GE 70-tonner number 703 is at milepost 5 on the Bayboro Branch on December 1, 1973, having been left there when the crew of the New Bern-Weyco switcher outlawed. The 70-tonners were the heaviest locomotives permitted on the Bayboro Branch because of its light construction, and even these light locomotives were limited to fifteen miles per hour on the branch. By this date, Norfolk Southern had already applied for permission to abandon the branch, but the application had been denied. (Robert Graham photo)

Below: The Gulf turn is shown here at Duncan with AS416s numbers 1610 and 1613 in the lead on October 22, 1973. (Louis Saillard photo)

included the large gravel quarry at Neverson, a feed mill at Bailey, Illinois Tool Company at Zebulon, and Bridgers Coal and Kemp Furniture in Wendell. All cars picked up on the road were taken to Wilson and lined up for movement by the through freights.

The Western District, which was the largest, worked three locals on the main line, two on the Fayetteville Branch, and one each on the Durham and Aberdeen Branches. A local operating as a turn out of Glenwood yard at Raleigh, and assigned as far south as Carbonton, worked the industries on the north end of the Western District main line. This train, commonly known as the Gulf Turn, was called to depart between 8:00 and 10:00 A.M. The largest account served by this train was the Carolina Power and Light steam powered electric generating plant at Brickhaven, which was jointly served by the SCL. The Norfolk Southern received coal bound for this plant from the W-SSB at Norwood and the Durham and Southern Railway at Varina, and in 1969 this amounted to 7,781 cars. Other major accounts included several brick plants and pulpwood yards, plus interchanges with the D&S at Varina and Southern Railway at Gulf.

The middle section of the Western District main line was served by the Star Night Local, which reported for duty at 7:00 P.M. at Star. This train worked both north and south of Star, being assigned between Troy and Glendon. It did not switch any single large shipper, but instead served numerous small accounts. These included mobile home manufacturers at Troy and

Robbins, feed mills at Purwat, Robbins, and Parkwood, pulpwood yards at Putnam and Parkwood, pyrophyllite mines at Glendon and Pyrax, and a crosstie dealer in Robbins. All cars picked up by this crew were taken to Star and classified for movement by through trains Numbers 63 and 64. Power on this local was usually a single unit, either EMD or Baldwin, which was the same engine that had been used during the day by the Aberdeen Branch crew.

The Charlotte local, on duty at 2:00AM, worked out of Charlotte yard as a turn to handle the local business on the south end of the main line. This crew used two engines, GP18s or GP38s, from Number 63's train which had arrived at Charlotte earlier in the night. It was assigned to work between Charlotte and Star, but usually ran only as far north as the Mt. Gilead area. The largest account served by this crew was Carolina Solite, located a mile south of Aquadale. This plant, built in the fifties, received inbound loads of coal and shipped out cinders for the construction industry, accounting for more than 6,000 cars in 1969. Other accounts included several pulpwood yards, a brick plant, fertilizer and scrap metal dealers, and the Winston-Salem Southbound interchange at Norwood. All cars picked up for the north were left at Norwood for movement by Number 64, and all south cars were taken back to Charlotte. Occasionally, if tonnage was accumulating at Norwood due to heavy coal interchange coming off the W-SSB, then this crew would run all the way to Star to help move this tonnage. When this occurred, the crew would run the engines light back to Norwood where they would be left for pickup by Number 64.

Operations on the Fayetteville Branch consisted of two locals operating out of Lillington. The morning job went on duty at 7:00 A.M., and worked from Lillington to Fayetteville and back. This crew switched the Kelly Springfield tire plant located about eight miles out of Fayetteville and ran on into the city to serve some smaller accounts and work the Aberdeen and Rockfish and SCL interchanges. One the return trip from Fayetteville they would leave their train at Senter, a few miles south of Lillington, and take their caboose

and engine on to Lillington to tie up. Normal power on this job was a single Baldwin AS416. EMD engines were restricted from operating on the Fayetteville Branch.

The afternoon job reported at 4:00 P.M. and worked between Senter and Varina. This crew switched Becker Sand and Gravel Company's two pits located in the Lillington area. They would first run north of town to pull the loads from the Becker pit and take them back to the Senter pit. Here all the loads from both pits would be weighed and classified. This sand business was quite good and in 1969 amounted to more than 15,000 loads. This crew's normal power was two Baldwins. After the pits had been worked, this crew would pick up the morning job's engine and cars. They were then ready to make their run to Varina, but one

Left: The Fayetteville local with number 1610 in the lead is southbound on Hillsboro Street in Fayetteville. The NS runs down the middle of Hillsboro Street for about one-half mile. Just to the rear of the train is the traffic light at the intersection of Hillsboro and Cumberland Streets. NS crews heeded the signal displayed by this light. Should it be red on their approach, they would stop along with the vehicular traffic and wait for it to turn green before proceeding. (Robert Graham photo)

Below: The Durham Branch local has arrived back in Duncan and, after setting off the caboose, is switching the pulpwood yard located at the rear of the wye. After the pulpwood has been added to the train, it will be placed in the yard for pickup by the through freights and the engine will be put in the team track for the night. (Marvin Black photo, M. B. Connery collection)

153

Norfolk Southern's lucrative passenger business to Pinehurst is long gone, but there was freight business there up until the end of the railroad. Here AS416 number 1607 with train number 39 is working near the depot site. (D. P. McDonald photo)

obstacle stood in their way, Kipling Hill. Its nearly three miles of slightly more than one percent grade quite often required the train to double to its crest. When they arrived at Varina a setout and pickup would be made. Before departing, several hours would be spent lining up the cars picked up for both the morning and evening jobs as there were no tracks at Lillington suitable for classification work. Upon arrival back at Lillington the train would be set off on the three-mile long spur track leading to the Becker sand pit as this was the only track in town long enough to handle it.

Operations on the Durham Branch consisted of a turn originating at Duncan, on duty at 7:30 A.M., and running to Durham and back. EMDs were prohibited from operating on this line, so it was Baldwin territory, with one or two units being the norm. From the early thirties to the mid sixties cigarette business from American Tobacco Company's plant located on this line in Durham had been its mainstay, and one of Norfolk Southern's most valued sources of revenue.

During its peak, two trains a day operated across this line. But, by the final years the American Tobacco business had dropped dramatically. By this time, only a handful of cars was spotted at the plant each day, usually two cars of coal for the boilers, a box for cigarette loading, and an occasional tank car of liquor used to flavor the cigarettes. Other accounts on the branch included a pulpwood yard at Bonsal, a sawmill at Farrington, and a cinder distribution facility located near Keene Yard at Durham. This job also handled interchange business in Durham with the city's four other railroads.

The Aberdeen branch was served by a turn working out of Star as trains Numbers 38 and 39. Number 39 was scheduled to depart Star at 7:00 A.M. daily except Sunday. Normal power for this crew was a single unit, EMD or Baldwin. This line in years past had seen solid trains of both peaches and sand, but by the final years, the peach business was gone and only a single sand pit remained. Despite these losses, the line

GP18 number 15 is serving as the Carolina Yard engine and is working the north end of the yard in this view. The GP18s were really general purpose locomotives on the NS. They replaced the Baldwin DS-4-4-660s and DS4-4-1000s as yard engines as well as working main line trains and branch line trains wherever the line was heavy enough to hold them. They even worked the few special passenger trains the railroad operated. (J. Raymond Pritchard, Jr. photo)

DS-4-4-660 number 661, NS's first diesel, is shown here working as the Glenwood Yard engine. Before the GP18s were purchased, the 660 class engines usually worked Glenwood Yard since the 1000 class engines were not permitted to cross the Albemarle Sound bridge (David Burnette photo)

still had numerous shippers and a varied traffic mix. The major accounts were the Sandhills furniture plant at West End and J. P. Stevens carpet mill at Aberdeen. Others included a couple of pulpwood yards, building supply companies, an LP gas dealer, fertilizer dealer, and a foundry. In Aberdeen there were interchanges with both the SCL and Aberdeen and Rockfish Railroads.

Yard Service

Norfolk Southern operated yard engines at three locations. These were Norfolk, Raleigh, and Charlotte.

Norfolk was the home of Carolina Yard, which was the largest on the system. The yard crews here had to build train number 63 for its 12:30 A.M. departure, and break up number 64 upon its arrival, also doing the same for the Beach local. In addition to this classification work, the company's back shops at Carolina and piers at Berkley had to be switched. There were transfer runs to interchange with the connecting roads. In Norfolk the NS connected either directly or through the

Norfolk and Portsmouth Belt Line Railroad with seven other lines. These were the Chesapeake and Ohio, Norfolk, Franklin, and Danville (formerly Atlantic and Danville), Seaboard Coast Line, Penn Central (formerly Pennsylvania), Norfolk and Western, and Southern, in addition to the Belt Line. Historically the Pennsy and its successor Penn Central were the primary interchange partners of the NS at Norfolk. To handle all their business in Norfolk, the NS operated three yard and transfer crews. These went on duty at 7:30 A.M., 10:30 A.M., and 5:30 P.M. These crews often worked long hours, occasionally up to the 12 hour federally mandated limit.

Raleigh, NC was the location of Glenwood Yard, which was the second largest on the railroad and the main classification point of the line between Norfolk and Charlotte. It was the crew change point between the Central and Western Districts and the location of their extra boards as well. Normal operations at Glenwood consisted of three yard crews per day. The first of these reported for duty at 7:00 A.M. This crew would immediately begin building the Western District

AS416 number 1506 switches the yard at Charlotte. As noted in the text, the Charlotte Yard job used a locomotive which had come in with train number 63 the night before as its power. (Robert C. Reisweber collection)

Gulf Turn local which would be called to depart as soon as it was finished. After its departure, the yard engine would continue to do classification work in the yard and switch some of the industries located nearby while awaiting the arrival of Central District through train 63. Upon its arrival, 63 would be extensively reswitched and made ready for the 12:30 P.M. scheduled departure on the Western District. Then there would be a lull in activity that would last into the evening hours until the arrival of the Gulf Turn and later Western District through train 64. Then at 10:30 and 11:00 P.M., the two night shift yard crews would report for duty. With one crew working on the north end of the yard and the other on the south end, they would go about the task of breaking up the local and reclassifying number 64 which was scheduled to depart on the Central District at 2:01 A.M. In addition to these duties there were the SCL and Southern interchanges to be worked and numerous commercial accounts to be switched. These on-line industries serviced by the Raleigh yard engines accounted for more than 7000 cars in 1969.

Charlotte, NC was the largest city to be served by the NS and was the southern end of the line. Here the NS had a five-track classification yard bordered on one side by Brevard Street and by the Southern Railway's yard on the other. Interchanges were maintained here with the Southern and SCL railroads. In addition to the yard, the NS owned a tract of land adjacent to the main line on the edge of the city which it was developing as

AS416 number 1612 is serving as the AT switcher at the American Tobacco plant in Durham in this view.
(David W. Younts collection)

an industrial park. This area was called "the farm" by the train crews as that was what it had been before the NS purchased it. A single yard engine taken from train number 63's power took care of Norfolk Southern's business in Charlotte. This crew went on duty at 5:00 A.M. Monday through Saturday, with no yard service on Sundays. It must be noted here that by contract, NS yardmen had a five day work week, and in order to provide this six-day service, a local agreement was negotiated between the company and union. This agreement specified that the Charlotte yard crew would work six days a week for five weeks and have every sixth week off. So every six weeks a crew would be called from the Raleigh yard extra board to go to Charlotte. The duties of the yard engine were to work the interchanges, switch the local industries, and build train number 64, which was scheduled to depart at 1:30 P.M. Any trains that arrived or departed Charlotte when the yard engine wasn't on duty had to do all their own switching.

One other yard operation on the NS that ended before the final years, but is still worthy of note was at Durham. Its primary purpose was to do the in-plant switching at the large American Tobacco Company cigarette factory located on the NS. This plant was one of the first large manufacturing concerns to locate on the NS, and for a railroad whose stock in trade had been hauling logs, sand, and gravel, this traffic was valued highly and given preferential treatment. This job, known as the AT switcher, began in 1930 and lasted until the mid sixties, by which time trucks had made enough inroads into Norfolk Southern's business to allow the switcher to be dropped and its duties to be taken on by the local freight out of Duncan. Although the American Tobacco plant was located almost adjacent to both the Seaboard Air Line and Southern lines in Durham, the only rail access to it was by means of a three mile long spur track from NS's Keene Yard on the outskirts of the city. The AT switcher reported for duty at Keene Yard at 7:00 A.M. Monday through Friday and in addition to the plant switching, it also performed the interchange work with the city's four other railroads, the Southern, SCL, Norfolk and Western, and Durham and Southern. The diesel locomotive class most associated with the AT switcher would be the Baldwin DS4-4-660. One of them went to it immediately upon delivery, which made this the one of the first assignments to have a diesel for its power.

Chapter 11

A Tour of the Railroad

The Norfolk Southern Railroad originated from a group of short lines. Most of these were primarily logging railroads. As such, they shared most of the characteristics of short lines, which can be generalized as low cost construction. NS was not unique in this respect, but most Class I railroads which began in this way underwent extensive upgrading as they achieved Class I status. NS was also upgraded as it grew, but the upgrading could hardly be called extensive. The reasons for this have already been mentioned at several points in the history of the line; little capital was available for upgrading, and the traffic volume never required it.

Norfolk Southern was almost completely a single track railroad. The only exceptions were a few short stretches of double track on the Beach lines. The company actually operated more double track through trackage rights than on owned track. This included trackage rights over the Virginian Railway from Carolina Junction to Coleman Place in Norfolk, about 3 fi miles, plus three miles of jointly owned double track between Coleman Place and Camden Heights, utilizing the Pennsylvania Railroad's track along with the one-time Chesapeake Transit Company track.

NS never had any CTC (Centralized Traffic Control) or even an automatic block signal system. Traffic was controlled entirely by timetable and train orders. The only signals were at drawbridges, crossings of other railroads, and train order signals at stations. The traffic was never heavy enough to justify a more sophisticated system, as evidenced by the fact that there were few accidents involving collisions of two trains.

Rails originally laid on the system were light weight, typical of logging railroads and other short lines. The Elizabeth City and Norfolk Railroad was originally laid with 45- and 50-pound rail. Some of the rail on the Albemarle and Pantego Railroad was as light as 25-pound, and several other of the absorbed short lines had 30-pound rail. Over the years, heavier rail was laid, but again at a very gradual pace. By 1942, when the "heavy" 2-8-4 locomotives were already heading the through freight trains, the main line still included 80 miles of 70-pound rail. Some of the branches still had 45-pound rail. The company never installed any rail heavier than 100-pound.

When Southern Railway took over the line in 1974, a program to install 132-pound continuous welded rail on the main line between Norfolk and Raleigh was initiated. This program was not quite complete when Southern merged with Norfolk and Western to create the new Norfolk Southern in 1982. The program then stopped as the original NS main line was no longer to be a main line.

An interesting feature of the construction in early years was the use of oyster shells for ballast on the eastern end. This material was very cheap and readily available in that area at the time. As late as 1914, the railroad installed 58,500 bushels of new oyster shell ballast. Some of the trackage on the Virginia Beach lines still rested on oyster shells at the time of the Southern Railway takeover.

Depots along the line were mostly of wood frame construction, of the usual general form of railroad depots, i.e., a narrow, one story rectangle with a bay window in roughly the center of the track side for the agent. Size varied considerably with the size of the town served, and many of the smaller stations were combination passenger and freight stations. After passenger service ended, the passenger ends of some stations were torn down. In early years, the frame stations were painted green with darker green trim, but some of these were repainted into other colors in later years. A

Northern end of the NS main line, milepost zero, was established at Berkley when the road was first built as the Elizabeth City and Norfolk Railroad. By 1888, passenger trains originated and terminated at the N&W station in downtown Norfolk, but in 1940 they returned to Berkley as a result of the railroad's decision to discontinue use of Norfolk Terminal Station. This view shows train number 2 arriving at the Main Street station in Berkley in August 1947. (William Gwaltney photo, David Burnette collection)

few of the larger stations such as Elizabeth City and New Bern were brick. Even some of the smaller stations on the west end were brick as a thriving brick business existed there. An example is the Colon station, one of the smallest brick stations on any railroad, which served little other than a brick plant. Several of the larger cities such as Norfolk, Raleigh, Durham, and New Bern were served by union stations also serving the other railroads of the city. As we have mentioned, the one at New Bern was built and owned by the NS until the lease of the A&NC ended. A few smaller stations such as Plymouth, Aberdeen, and Asheboro were also union stations. The photographs in this book were selected to include views of several of the stations, but available space did not permit us to provide a full set of views of any of these.

As we have noted several times previously, the Norfolk Southern was divided into operating divisions or districts. This was also true of most class I railroads. For some of these, the end of a division and beginning of a new division meant little more than that a distance which a train crew could reasonably cover in one working day had been reached. On the NS, however, the divisions (and later the districts) had much more to distinguish themselves. First, they represented to a large degree a chronological breakdown according to when the lines became part of the system. The Northern District included the earliest lines of the railroad. The Beach District covered the trackage added in the first years of the twentieth century. The Central District was mainly composed of the trackage added by the merger of 1906. The Western District consisted of the trackage of the western extension to Charlotte and associated branches. The districts also differed in the type of terrain through which they passed. The Northern and Beach Districts, along with much of the Central District, traversed the coastal plains of Virginia and North Carolina, while the remainder of the Central District and all of the Western District were located in the hilly Piedmont Region of North Carolina. In addition, the Beach District, in its early years, was much different from the others in its traffic mix and its means for providing for it. We will now discuss these differences in more detail, illustrating them as much as possible with photographs.

The Northern District

The Northern District included the main line from Berkley to Chocowinity, plus the Belhaven branch and Weeksville spur. As such, it included the original line of the Elizabeth City and Norfolk Railroad from Norfolk to Elizabeth City and Edenton, which became the first track of the Norfolk Southern Railroad in 1883. It also encompassed the remaining portions of the former Albemarle and Pantego, Suffolk and Carolina, and Washington and Plymouth Railroads. It had included the Suffolk, Columbia, Currituck, and Providence branches in earlier years, when it had been the Northern Division. As we noted earlier, technically the southern end of the district was just north of the Washington station, but for all practical purposes, Chocowinity was treated as the south end.

The country traversed by this district is uni-

Ten-Wheeler number 110 is ready to depart from Berkley with train number 1 on the morning of July 27, 1947. As you can see, the platform erected by the NS in 1940 when the Norfolk passenger terminal was moved back to Berkley was quite small. NS managers did not expect many passengers to use it, and their assumption was correct. (D. Wallace Johnson photo)

Switcher number 1002 works the interchange with the Norfolk and Western at Berkley Junction. The roof of the interlocking tower is seen at the bottom of the photo. Norfolk Southern called this spot Berkley Junction but N&W called it NS Junction, and that name is used today (James A. Ramsey photo)

formly low and mostly swampy. The track elevation never gets higher than 55 feet above sea level. As a result, ruling grades are moderate, never exceeding one-half of one percent. Curves are few, and never exceed five degrees of curvature, until the curve at Chocowinity joining the Northern District to the Central District line to Raleigh is encountered. That curve is ten degrees.

Although grades and curves in the district are negligible, one should not conclude that construction of the line presented no problems. Much of the ground is swampy, and crossed by many streams of all sizes. In addition, numerous canals have been dug in the area to drain swampland for agriculture. All these had to be crossed with bridges or culverts. A much greater expense for the railroad was the fact that many of the streams were navigable, and required drawbridges. In

AS416 number 1610 is just south of Carolina Junction in September 1958. Crewmen Tommy Coates and Ben Moore ride the pilot of the locomotive. Carolina Yard is just to the rear of the photographer. (H. Reid photo)

Above: Although little business remains on the old NS line north of Carolina Junction, Norfolk and Portsmouth Belt Line continues to operate over the line to access their Berkley yard. Here a Belt Line train with SW1200 number 102 on the point crosses the N&W at NS Junction in June 1987. (Kurt Reisweber photo)

Below: A March 1980 view of the crossing of the former Norfolk Southern and former Virginian at Carolina Junction. Southern Railway GP38AC number 2826 is heading south on the former Norfolk Southern. The former Virginian track leads to Sewells Point in the distance. (Kurt Reisweber photo)

this district, the Albemarle and Chesapeake Canal, the Northwest River, the Pasquotank River, Knobbs Creek, Perquimans River, Albemarle Sound, Mackey's Creek, and the Pamlico River on the main line all required drawbridges when the railroad was built, as did the Scuppernong River on the Columbia Branch. The

A 1937 view of the engine shop and part of Carolina Yard. (John W. Barriger III photo, Barriger Railroad Collection, St. Louis Mercantile Library)

2-8-4 number 601 is at the Carolina Yard locomotive servicing facilities on May 17, 1947. This photo shows a good view of the Fairfield conveyor used to coal locomotives at that location. It is unusual for a class I road not to have larger coaling facilities at a major terminal. (H. Reid photo, D. Wallace Johnson collection)

2-8-0 number 215 switches Carolina Yard in July 1951. Shops and locomotive servicing area are out of the photo to the right. Diesels are on the property and number 215 will soon be unemployed. Several of her E2 class sisters, plus all of the 0-6-0 steam switchers, have already been scrapped. (H. Reid photo, D. Wallace Johnson collection)

drawbridges at the Pasquotank and Pamlico Rivers and the A&C Canal remain active today.

In 1907, when the Norfolk and Southern had high hopes for its passenger service between Norfolk and Raleigh and New Bern, a sixty mile per hour speed limit was established for passenger trains on the Norfolk-Marsden main line. This was later lowered to forty-five miles per hour. Freight trains were limited to forty miles per hour north of Edenton, and thirty-five miles per hour south of there. Of course, there were

During the last year of independence for Norfolk Southern, a sampler of all the types of diesel locomotive operated by NS at the time lines up by the sand tower at Carolina Yard. From front to back, we see AS416 number 1613, 70-tonner number 701, GP38 number 2003, and two unidentified GP18s. (Tal Carey photo)

many speed restrictions at spots such as the many long wood trestles. Branch line speed limits were also considerably lower.

The main yard and shops for what eventually became the Northern District were located at the Berkley waterfront in early years. As we have noted, however, these were moved to Carolina Junction, three miles south, beginning in 1911. Berkley declined in

A view north from the Carolina Yard engine shop shortly after the merger into Southern Railway. The Baldwin diesels shown in the photo will run no more, and will soon be on their way to the scrapyard. (J. David Spanagel photo)

Right: Baldwin DS-4-4-1000 number 1002 switches Carolina Yard in June 1962. This view looks south, with the locomotive shop at the right. Numbers 1001 and 1002 generally stayed in the Norfolk-Virginia Beach area. They were popular with crews because of their pulling power (Jim Wade Collection)

Below: Switcher number 1001 switches cars in Carolina Yard on September 1, 1960. The aircraft fuselage in the gondola has probably come from Oceana Naval Air Station on the NS Virginia Beach South Route. (James Ramsey collection)

Below: DS-4-4-1000 number 1001 works the south end of Carolina Yard in South Norfolk, VA. (H. Reid)

Above: Two AS416s head north into Carolina Yard in February 1962. Norfolk Southern rarely had to contend with more snow than this. (Harry Bundy photo)

2-8-0 number 542 is followed by a string of reefers with ice hatches open. Exact location is unknown, but the configuration of the crossing sign indicates it is somewhere in Virginia. (John Barnett collection)

importance gradually over the years, then precipitously during World War II, when connecting water traffic essentially disappeared. The former site of the Berkley Yard is now occupied largely by Norshipco (Norfolk Shipbuilding and Drydock Company), a company founded by the descendants of John L. Roper. Today's Norfolk Southern Corporation continues to operate the track to Berkley as needed to serve a few commercial customers, but this is very infrequent.

Carolina Yard soon became the major yard in the District and for the entire railroad. It contained a large rectangular building used in steam days for locomotive service and back shop. When diesels took over, the building was converted to serve the same purpose for the diesels. The area also included several other shop buildings such as a car shop and an office build-

ing housing the Mechanical Department offices. In steam locomotive days, a large water tank and 70-foot turntable were located there. A coaling conveyor was used for coaling locomotives. At the time the shop facilities were built, a major coaling station existed at Northwest, VA, eighteen miles south of Carolina Yard, so there was no need for a coaling tower at the yard. The turntable remained in place after the steam days for use in turning diesel locomotives.

Carolina Yard was the site of the railroad's main servicing facilities until the merger with Southern Railway in 1974, but changes came soon after that. The locomotive shop was torn down and all locomotive repair functions were moved to other Southern shops. The car shop was closed soon afterward but the building remained in place until very recently. Southern set

Above: A Chesapeake and Albemarle Railroad train crosses the Albemarle and Chesapeake Canal drawbridge just north of Fentress, VA on the former NS main line October 28, 1994. Train is headed for Elizabeth City and Hertford. The CA took over operation of the NS main line between Carolina Yard and Edenton on April 2, 1990. (Robert C. Reisweber photo)

Above: Apparently the engineer of 2-8-4 number 602 did not see the signal set against him when he approached the Albemarle and Chesapeake Canal, seven miles south of Carolina Yard, on April 5, 1943, with the disastrous result shown. The engineer paid for his mistake with his life. Number 602 was luckier. It was rebuilt and returned to service. (Fred Curling photo)

Below: Freight train number 64 led by number 1608 and another AS416 passes Fentress station, near milepost 12 on the NS main line, headed for Carolina Yard in September 1961. Fentress was known as Centerville in the early days of the railroad. It is now a part of the city of Chesapeake, Virginia, which absorbed the city of South Norfolk and Norfolk County, Virginia.(This does not include the independent city of Norfolk.) (Harry Bundy photo)

up a piggyback terminal at the yard immediately after taking over, but it was removed after the merger with Norfolk and Western.

Activity at the yard declined after that merger in 1982 as most remaining functions were transferred to N&W's Portlock Yard nearby. A new connection track in the southeast quadrant of the crossing at Carolina Junction was installed to provide easy access from Carolina Yard to Portlock Yard. By 1999, Carolina Yard was used only for interchange between Norfolk Southern and the Chesapeake and Albemarle Railroad, and occasionally for freight car storage. Then, in 2000,

Below: A Norfolk Southern freight passes Hickory Ground depot about 1920. The locomotive cannot be positively identified, but the headlight centered on the smokebox front makes it likely that this is one of the "bohunk" 2-8-0s purchased from the New York Central system. Eventually most if not all of these had their headlights moved to the top of the smokebox front. (Harry C. Mann collection, Library of Virginia)

Above: It is August of 1974 and Norfolk Southern has been a part of the Southern Railway System for eight months. A northbound freight crosses the Northwest River, headed by Southern Railway GP18 number 191, formerly NS number 12. SR GP30 number 2583 and the future SR GP18 number 193, still wearing NS colors as number 14, follow. (Kurt Reisweber photo)

Below: Moyock depot in 1937. Moyock, the first town in North Carolina on the southbound main line out of Carolina Yard, was settled as early as 1753 since it was accessible by water traffic at Shingle Landing Creek. (John W. Barriger III photo, Barriger Railroad Collection, St. Louis Mercantile Library)

Above: A freight train with E3 class 2-8-0 number 530 as power works near the Moyock depot in June 1949. The girder bridge crosses over Shingle Landing Creek. The last spike of the Elizabeth City and Norfolk Railroad was driven near here on May 12, 1881. (H. Reid photo, D. Wallace Johnson collection)

Below: Shawboro station and surroundings in 1937. The water tank to the left of the track was replaced by a new 50,000 gallon tank in 1947, just in time to be rendered obsolete by complete dieselization. (John W. Barriger III photo, Barriger Railroad Collection, St. Louis Mercantile Library)

a new facility for loading trucks from the Ford plant in Norfolk onto auto-rack cars was constructed at this location, which was given the name Crescent. Chesapeake and Albemarle trains continue to run into the yard, but now usually proceed on to Portlock for interchange.

Below: Southbound freight train number 99 led by AS416 number 1604 approaches the Camden depot in May 1961. Linda Morrisette, the agent at Camden for many years, prepares to give the train a rolling inspection and to hoop company mail for Raleigh to the flagman. This internal mail service saved the company postage and gave faster delivery. (Harry Bundy photo)

Above: GP18 number 13 is shown setting out a car by the grain elevators near Camden station. These elevators were always a good source of revenue for the railroad. (Tal Carey photo)

The yard at Chocowinity, the south end of the District, became very important to the railroad soon after the merger that extended the lines to Raleigh and New Bern, and continues to be so today. We have already noted that this was the actual crew change point between the Northern and Central Districts, even though the official dividing point was in Washington. Also, through freight trains numbers 63 and 64 were

Above: A northbound freight headed by three AS416s and a Baldwin switcher has just come across the Pasquotank River drawbridge south of Camden station in November 1961. The switcher is probably going to Carolina shop for service. The semaphore at the right of the photo protects the drawbridge. (Harry Bundy photo)

Below: John W. Barriger III's special train pauses at the Elizabeth City Main Street passenger depot in April 1937. Ten-Wheeler number 113 pulled the two-car train. This brick depot was built shortly before World War I, replacing a frame depot which had been built in this same area shortly after the Elizabeth City and Norfolk Railroad was extended to Edenton in late 1881. The newer depot still exists, but is no longer used by the railroad. (John W. Barriger III photo, Barriger Railroad Collection, St. Louis Mercantile Library)

Above: A northbound freight led by number 1616 and two other units crosses the Pasquotank river near Camden, NC. Notice the high hood on number 1616, reaching almost to the highest point of the cab, in contrast to the unidentified earlier AS416 behind it, which has the slightly lower hood. Number 1616 is now in the North Carolina Transportation Museum at Spencer, but is now painted in the more recent paint scheme of gray with red end stripes. (Harry Bundy photo)

Below: Ten-Wheeler number 110 switches cars by the Elizabeth City station platform. Note that this station is at milepost 46, from Berkley. (H. Reid photo, Tal Carey collection)

scheduled to meet here, and locals to Belhaven, Lee Creek, and Weyco operated from here.

In late steam days, the Northern District had coaling stations at Carolina Yard and Edenton. Earlier, there had been coaling stations at Park Avenue (Norfolk), Euclid, Northwest, Mackeys, Suffolk, and Elizabeth City. Water stations on the main line were located at Carolina, Northwest, Shawboro, Elizabeth

City, Perquimans River, Edenton, Mackeys, Hinson (near Pinetown), and Marsden(Chocowinity). Branch line water stations were located at Euclid, Munden, and Providence on the Currituck and Providence Branches, and at Columbia and Belhaven on their branches. The Suffolk Branch had watering stations at Suffolk, Edenton, and Elizabeth City, along with Beckford Junction, the junction of lines to the latter two cities.

Today, much of this District's lines are operated by the Chesapeake and Albemarle Railroad out of Elizabeth City. It operates the former main line between Carolina Yard and Edenton. It also operated the

Left: The last run of passenger train number 1 stops at the Elizabeth City depot on January 31, 1948. The next day, train number 1 would be mail and express only. (H. Reid photo, D. Wallace Johnson collection)

Above: A freight train with GP18 number 11 in the lead passes through Elizabeth City on July 30, 1971, with another GP18 on the siding in the background. (John Treen photo, Ed Fielding collection)

Below: The view of the Major and Loomis sawmill beside the Perquimans River near Hertford from John Barriger's special southbound train. At the time of the photo, the bridge over the river still contained a swing span, and semaphores protecting the span can be seen in the photo. This span was removed in 1940 and was reinstalled at Lynnhaven Inlet on the north route to Virginia Beach. Note that a water tank was located here. (John W. Barriger III photo, Barriger Railroad Collection, St. Louis Mercantile Library)

Above: GP18 number 3 and a northbound freight pass through Chapanoke, milepost 54, in February 1966. The red false-front building to the right was built as a general store soon after the NS rails were laid through Chapanoke late in 1881. It originally faced a road which crosses the rails at grade just out of the photo to the right. It is now a storage building for the grain company whose silos and elevators are seen behind it. (Harry Bundy photo)

Below: An early view of the Hertford, NC station. The date is unknown, but the lettering "Norfolk and Southern" on the tender indicates that it is probably before 1910 or shortly thereafter. (Mrs. A. C. Shannonhouse collection)

In June 1974, Southern Railway operated an inspection train over the line of its newly acquired subsidiary, the Norfolk Southern. Photographer Bill Schafer, an internal auditor for Southern Railway at the time, rode a deadhead move taking the equipment into Norfolk the day before the actual inspection trip. He took this photo of the train beside the Hertford depot. (Bill Schafer photo)

Number 1601, the first of NS's AS416s, passes the Hertford depot in 1964. Note that by this time, number 1601 is in the simplified all-red paint scheme with no stripes. (Harry Bundy photo)

Above: The Southern Railway inspection train of June 1974 passes by the Edenton depot on its deadhead move to Norfolk. This station was built at about the time of the construction of the Albemarle Sound bridge, and was located beside the newly constructed line leading to the bridge. The building was different from other NS stations in that it was covered by tabby, a material made from lime, water, and seashells. Although an interesting building in a town which has gone to considerable effort to preserve its old buildings, this one has been torn down. The wooden loading platform shown here was replaced with a concrete one, which still exists, by Southern Railway. Behind the train is the five-story Edenton Peanut Company plant, an Edenton landmark since 1909 (Bill Schafer photo)

Top right: Ten-Wheeler number 133 takes on coal at the Edenton coal chute (James A. Ramsey photo)

Upper middle right: DRS-4-4-1500 number 1506 heads south across Queen Anne Creek, also known as Johnson's Creek, just south of the Edenton depot in April 1962. The photographer was standing near the site of the Suffolk and Carolina Railroad's station and steamboat dock, which was located where the creek empties into Edenton Bay. (Harry Bundy photo)

Lower middle right: AS416 number 1609 heads south along Edenton Bay toward the Albemarle Sound bridge on a cold winter day. Location is just south of the Edenton depot. (Harry Bundy photo)

Bottom right: Charles Snell rides a velocipede across the Albemarle Sound bridge to inspect the structure after passage of train number 99. This inspection was made at frequent intervals. (Harry Bundy photo)

Below: An aerial view of the draw span in the Albemarle Sound bridge. This photo was taken on February 1, 1987, after use of the bridge had ended, but before demolition began. (Bill Schafer photo)

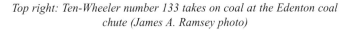

Above: During the winter of 1958 an unusual cold snap hit northeastern North Carolina, freezing over Albemarle Sound. This photo shows a train crossing the ice-encrusted trestle. Note that the "waves" on the surface of the sound are actually frozen in place. (Philip P. Coulter, Jr. photo)

Left: The view of Albemarle Sound from the train. The drawspan is just ahead. Road Foreman P. P. Coulter, Sr., father of NS employee and contributor to this volume P. P. Coulter, Jr., is running the train on this occasion. (Harry Bundy photo)

Upper middle left: A northbound freight passes the station at Mackeys in May 1962, and will shortly be crossing the Albemarle Sound bridge. In earlier years, the ferry dock was located to the right background of the photo, on Mackey's Creek. Incoming ferries carrying highway vehicles passed across the background of the photo from left to right through a swing bridge in the railroad track, until a highway bridge was built across the sound in the 1930s and ferry service ended. (H. Reid photo)

Lower middle left: Passenger train number 2, headed by Ten-Wheeler number 114, makes a station stop at Mackeys shortly before the end of passenger service. (James A. Ramsey photo)

Bottom left: 2-8-4 number 602 with a freight train passes a passenger train, with the photographer aboard, at Mackeys station. (James A. Ramsey photo)

Below: A view of the Albemarle Sound bridge from inside the caboose of the Elizabeth City switcher, taken in August 1962. (J. Parker Lamb photo)

Top left: 2-8-0 number 207 was often used as the Plymouth switcher in the late years of steam power. This view shows it at the original Plymouth depot (at right of the locomotive), which was located in downtown Plymouth at the waterfront. The depot had been built by the Washington and Plymouth Railroad when that line's main connections were with water traffic on the Roanoke River. A new Union Station for passenger traffic was built by the Atlantic Coast Line in 1927 on the south side of town. The NS then built a bypass line which avoided the original depot. The depot shown here continued to serve as the NS freight station until 1952, when a new freight station was built near the junction of the bypass line and the downtown line. (L. D. Jones photo)

Top right: DS-4-4-660 number 662 and AS416 number 1613 rest by the Plymouth freight station in 1961. (H. Reid photo)

Upper middle left: A view showing the 1952 Plymouth freight station, with GP18 number 15 nearby. (John Treen photo, Ed Fielding collection)

Lower middle left: GP18 number 4 and a Southern Railway wood-chip car are reflected in the waters of Welch Creek in Plymouth, in January of 1973. Soon the GP18 will be lettered Southern as well. This track is a spur to the Weyerhaeuser plant, long one of Norfolk Southern's most important customers. (Tom L. Sink photo)

Bottom left: GP18 number 13 leads southbound through freight number 63 at Pinetown in November 1965. The caboose of the Belhaven Branch local train number 28, the "Belhaven Bullet", appears at the right side of the photo. The local has just arrived from Chocowinity and entered the branch, clearing the main for number 63. Pinetown was once the site of a large lumber mill, which was the main source of business for the Washington and Plymouth Railroad, predecessor of the NS line between those cities. (Harry Bundy photo)

Bottom right: A northbound freight with GP18 number 7 runs beside the Pamlico River at Washington, NC, having just crossed the bridge over the river. It is November of 1965. (Harry Bundy photo)

Above: Passenger train number 1, pulled by Ten-Wheeler number 111, backs out of the station spur at Washington, NC in 1937. The station at Washington was off the main line, having been built on the waterfront by the Washington and Plymouth Railroad when Washington was its southern terminus and connections to the south were by boat. When the main line was extended to the south, it branched off the station track behind and to the right of the train in the photo to cross the Pamlico River. The steel tower to the left of the locomotive was used to fly flags for navigational warnings. The photographer lived in Wilson, NC, on NS lines and often visited his grandparents in Washington, sometimes riding the train to get there. (William A. Sellers, Jr. photo)

Upper middle right: Passenger train number 2 with locomotive number 110 makes its station stop in Washington in the early 1940s. The freight end (the north end) of the combined passenger and freight depot is to the right of the locomotive. To the rear of the train is an open-sided building known as the Norfolk Southern cotton platform, where cotton and other goods were loaded into cars for shipment out. (H. Reid photo, Tal Carey collection)

Lower middle right: In October 1963, a special passenger train called the "Know Your Neighbor Special" was run over the Norfolk Southern from Raleigh to Washington, NC. This photo shows the train in the Washington station track. The passengers left the train here and returned to Raleigh by buses such as the one seen in the right background. The occasion for the trip is not known, but it has been suggested it might have been related to an election. The cars of the train were stainless steel lightweight cars of the Seaboard Air Line. Seaboard also furnished a steam-generator equipped GP7 in case steam heat was needed. It can barely be seen behind new NS GP18 number 1. Note that locomotive number 1504 has the simplified red paint scheme without stripes in this photo. (Wiley M. Bryan photo)

Bottom right: Northbound freight train number 64 crosses the Pamlico River bridge into Washington, NC on April 8, 1967, headed by GP18s numbers 8 and 9. It is evident that forest products still provide a significant income for the railroad. Note the extended sides on the two open hoppers, for wood chip service. (Wharton Separk III photo)

Above left: A northbound freight train is reflected in the Pamlico River as it approaches the station site in Washington, NC. on July 29, 1972. (G. M. McDonald photo, Ed Fielding collection)

Above right: A northward view of Washington, NC, from a train crossing the Pamlico River bridge. The combination passenger and freight station is at far left, with the water tank and a warehouse owned by the railroad to its right. (John W. Barriger III photo, Barriger Railroad Collection, St. Louis Mercantile Library)

Top middle left: Phosphate Junction, one-half mile south of the south end of the Pamlico River bridge, is the point at which the new Lee Creek Branch left the main line. Southern Railway GP38 number 2815 negotiates the switch in August 1975. A close examination of the photo will detect the concrete ties on the branch line track, to the right of the photo. (Kurt Reisweber photo)

Bottom middle left: 2-8-0 number 531 is working in the yard at Marsden (known as Chocowinity before 1917 and after the mid 1960s). The main line north to Norfolk leaves the photo at the right top, with the southbound main to Raleigh curving to the left behind the depot and water tank. The New Bern Branch extends southward ahead of the locomotive. (H. Reid photo, Tal Carey collection)

Bottom left: Looking northward through the Marsden yard toward Norfolk in April 1937, with an unidentified locomotive at the left. (John W. Barriger III photo, Barriger Railroad Collection, St. Louis Mercantile Library)

Bottom right: 2-8-4 number 602 starts a freight train out of Marsden. (H. Reid photo, John Barnett collection)

Clockwise from top left: Locomotive number 114 with passenger train number 1 is headed for Raleigh on the sharply curved main line track at Marsden in August 1942. (H. Reid photo, D. Wallace Johnson collection)

Ten-Wheeler number 113 leads northbound train number 2 around the sharply curved main line at Marsden coming from Raleigh and headed to Norfolk. (H. Reid photo, Tal Carey collection)

Two AS416s and two cabooses rest in Marsden yard. (John Sullivan photo)

Norfolk Southern built this modern brick station at Chocowinity in 1970. It is still in service for today's Norfolk Southern Corporation. It is probably an exaggeration to say that the current NS Corporation selected its name to avoid having to change the lettering on this station. (Tal Carey photo)

Train number 64 departs Chocowinity for Norfolk on January 17, 1970. (Robert Graham photo)

Extra train number 15 south, shown at Chocowinity on March 2, 1974, still looks like a Norfolk Southern train although it is now a Southern Railway train. (Robert Graham photo)

Another view of the yard at Chocowinity from the overpass of North Carolina highway number 33, in August 1973. GE 70-tonner number 701 rests on the siding while a New Bern-bound train heads south on the track to its left. The main line to Raleigh is barely visible at the top of the photo, curving from right to left. The wye track connecting the branch and the main line curves off to the left of the photo. (Curtis C. Lassiter, Jr. photo)

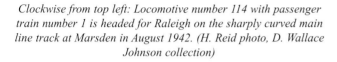

Weeksville spur, but that is currently inactive. The Carolina Coastal Railway now operates the former Belhaven Branch. Its locomotives are normally kept at Pinetown, where the road interchanges with NS.

Norfolk Southern Corporation continues to operate the line out of Chocowinity to Plymouth, and on to Mackeys when needed, which is not often.

Central District

The Central District included the lines from Chocowinity to Raleigh and New Bern, plus the Lee Creek and Bayboro Branches. This district was essentially the one-time Central Division of the railroad except that it no longer included the formerly leased Atlantic and North Carolina Railroad, or the formerly owned Beaufort and Morehead.

With the exception of the Chocowinity-Raleigh line, the area covered by this district was low, swampy land traversed by many streams and drainage canals, similar to the Northern District. Building through this country again required few grades and curves, but many low wood pile trestles, and culverts. By the

Below: Appearances notwithstanding, this photo does not show Soo Line trackage but original (and today's) Norfolk Southern trackage. The location is Simpson, NC, six miles east (timetable north) of Greenville. A CSX train is returning from Lee Creek a few days before Christmas in 1999, utilizing trackage rights over NS. It will return to CSX rails at Greenville. At that time, CSX operated a unit sulphur train destined for Lee Creek from the Soo Line at Chicago about once a week. CSX operated the train from there to Lee Creek with the power received from Soo Line. Normal procedure when one of these trains arrived at Rocky Mount was to make it the next regular daily except Sunday train F731 to Lee Creek, power and all, adding any other cars destined for Lee Creek that day. This resulted in a variety of power unusual for eastern North Carolina appearing on these occasions, sometimes including Canadian Pacific as well as Soo Line and Southern Pacific. CSX predecessor Seaboard Coast Line obtained trackage rights to Lee Creek from Southern Railway in 1977. The unit sulphur trains are a more recent development.
(Dale W. Diacont photo)

1970s, only two drawbridges across the Neuse and Trent Rivers at New Bern remained, but in earlier years, the Atlantic and North Carolina and the Beaufort extension had included three drawbridge crossings of the Newport River in the Morehead City-Beaufort-Newport area, plus a drawbridge at the Neuse River at Kinston. In the early years of the Oriental Branch, which by the 1950s terminated at Bayboro, it had a drawbridge crossing the Bay River just east of Bayboro.

As an example of the number of trestles and culverts required on the various lines in this region, the track chart for the Oriental Branch showed 116 of these in the ten miles between Bayboro and Oriental. Little wonder that the NS was anxious to rid itself of the task of maintaining these when business started to decline.

The main line from Chocowinity to Raleigh, southward by timetable but almost due west by compass, proceeds into progressively more hilly country

Above: Greenville was one of the larger intermediate cities on the NS, and so it rated this substantial depot. The depot was located downtown, at the end of a spur track from the main line, which ran through the south side of town. There was a wye at the junction, and the passenger trains would back into the depot, then pull forward to the main to leave town. (Winstead collection)

Below: At the time of John W. Barriger's tour of the Norfolk Southern, a two-car special train carrying a traveling show had just arrived in Greenville, enabling him to get this photo of the train. The downtown depot is just to the left of the train, with the freight station to the left of that. (John W. Barriger III photo, Barriger Railroad Collection, St. Louis Mercantile Library)

Above: After passenger service ended, having the Greenville depot at the end of a spur track was more of a nuisance than a convenience, so its use was abandoned. A new depot, considerably less distinguished architecturally than the old one, was built on the main line near the wye in 1957. This photo shows the new depot on December 29, 1972, with maintenance-of-way car number 912, the former office car Virginia, beside it.
(John Treen photo, Ed Fielding collection)

Below; Norfolk Southern crossed the Atlantic Coast Line's Kinston Branch just south (by timetable, west by compass) of the new NS Greenville freight depot. This photo, taken on June 24, 1988, shows a southbound train headed by GP50 number 7050 and GP49 number 4605 on the crossing. As this was only a branch of the ACL, there never was an interlocking plant at this crossing, the only "traffic control" being stop signs, as shown in the photo. Today, CSX Lee Creek trains use an interchange track just to the right of this scene to access their trackage rights over NS to Lee Creek. Locomotive number 4605 is a rarity, being one of only six of the experimental model GP39X built by EMD for Southern Railway in 1980, then later rebuilt as a GP49. To make it even more rare, it is the only one of the six which was owned by Southern Railway subsidiary Norfolk Southern. As a result, it later became Carolina and Northwestern number 4605, with small initials CRN below the 4605 on the cab. (Kurt Reisweber photo)

Top above: John W. Barriger's special train waits for a meet with passenger train number 2 at the Farmville depot in April 1937. This is the new depot built in 1925 to replace the one that burned earlier that year. It was located about fifty yards west (timetable south) of the original station. (John W. Barriger III photo, Barriger Railroad Collection, St. Louis Mercantile Library)

Above: AS416 number 1617 pulls a wreck train through Stantonsburg, NC on December 29, 1972. The train is on its way from Raleigh to Greenville to clean up a derailment at that location. (John Treen photo, Ed Fielding collection)

Bottom left: The original depot at Farmville, shown in 1914. This building burned in 1925 and was replaced by a new depot shown in another photo. One of the two men in white shirts is Stationmaster D. E. Oglesby. (North Carolina Division of Archives and History)

along its route. The hills were not high enough to require extensive cuts or fills, let alone tunnels, but they did produce significant grades. The ruling grades in the district were 1.25 percent in each direction, with summits at 341 feet elevation above sea level at Eagle Rock and Knightdale, seventeen and thirteen miles, respectively, from Raleigh. Maximum grades were 1.50 percent in the same vicinity. In steam days, helper locomotives were required on most through freight trains in both directions between Wilson and Raleigh. Sharpest curves in the district were six degrees, of which there were several between Knightdale and Raleigh.

The major yard and shop facilities in this district were at Glenwood Yard in Raleigh. In steam days, a six-stall roundhouse and 70-foot turntable were located there. With the coming of the diesels, a new diesel

At Wilson, Norfolk Southern crossed the busy two-track main line of the Atlantic Coast Line. Here a southbound NS freight (actually headed west by compass) crosses the ACL tracks in March 1965.

The view looks north toward downtown Wilson. (Harry Bundy photo)

Above: Wilson was another city where the NS ran through the outskirts of town, with a spur track to a downtown depot. In 1949 or 1950, railfan and author Harry McBride made arrangements with Norfolk Southern officials to ride mail and express train number 2 in connection with an article he was writing on the railroad. He took several photos during his trip, including this one showing the train backing out onto the main line from the downtown spur track at Wilson. By this time, train number 2 was normally diesel-powered, but on this occasion, 2-8-0 number 545 was substituting due to servicing of the diesel. Mr. McBride's article appeared in the January 1951 issue of Trains Magazine, and a revised version appeared in Mr. McBride's book, Trains Rolling (MacMillan Company, 1953).
(Harry McBride photo, courtesy of the Smithsonian Institution, NMAH/Transportation, McBride collection, negative 89-40132)

shop replaced the roundhouse, but the turntable was retained. There was also a car shop at Glenwood, and in steam days a large coaling tower and water tank.

Glenwood Yard increased in importance after the merger with Southern Railway, as it eventually became Southern's main yard in Raleigh, serving the Greensboro-Goldsboro line as well as the former NS lines. This continues to be the case today, with current Norfolk Southern operations in Raleigh centered at Glenwood.

New Bern had been the site of the Atlantic and North Carolina Railroad's shops before it was leased by the NS. Its importance grew after the takeover as the NS line down from Chocowinity and the branch to Oriental were completed. NS continued to use the A&NC facilities at New Bern, which included an 8-stall roundhouse, turntable, and several other shop buildings. Many of these buildings were burned in 1915, and were then replaced by the NS.

When the NS lease of the A&NC was terminated, the NS turned over the roundhouse and other shop buildings to the A&NC, but NS equipment continued to be serviced there. The importance of New Bern to the NS then declined rapidly, but the New Bern station

Below: An aerial view of downtown Wilson, NC, about 1948. The locations of the Norfolk Southern passenger and freight depots are identified on the photo. The downtown freight yard is beside and across South Street from the freight depot. Both passenger and freight depots are still in place, now used for non-railroad commercial purposes. Atlantic Coast Line tracks are at the bottom of the photo. (Raines and Cox photograph)

Above: A view of the Wendell, NC depot on February 3, 1930. This depot was built in 1912, replacing one which burned earlier in the year. (North Carolina Division of Archives and History)

Below:Norfolk Southern's first GP38, number 2001, pulls southbound freight number 63 through the s-curve by the depot at Knightdale in September 1969. A corner of the depot is visible just to the left of the locomotive. (Harry Bundy photo)

Above: 2-8-0 number 543 passes a grade crossing in Sims, NC, just south of Wilson in 1931. Obviously North Carolina's road improvement program still had a way to go at this time. (North Carolina Division of Archives and History)

Below: An early view of the NS depot at Zebulon, NC. (North Carolina Division of Archives and History)

Below: A southbound freight with GP18 number 2 on the point passes the Zebulon depot on December 28, 1972. The train order semaphore at the depot can be seen at the right edge of the photo. (John Treen photo, Ed Fielding collection)

continued to house the offices of the Superintendent and dispatchers of the NS steam lines for several years afterward.

Coaling stations for steam locomotives were located at Greenville, Farmville, Wilson, and New Bern as well as Glenwood yard in this district. There had been another coaling station at Middlesex between

Above: NS GP18 number 6 and a Southern Railway GP30 lead a northbound freight train through Knightdale soon after the January 1974 merger of the two railroads. (Wharton Separk III photo)

Above: A southbound freight passes under the U. S. Route 64 underpass just east (north by timetable) of Raleigh in June 1960. (J. Parker Lamb photo)

Below: A train heads for Norfolk with four diesel units and a mile of cars on February 17, 1973. It is passing through the truss bridge over Crabtree Creek, one mile north of Glenwood Yard in Raleigh. (Curt Tillotson, Jr. photo)

Above: The interlocking tower at Edgeton, where Norfolk Southern crossed the Seaboard Air Line just north of Glenwood Yard, in April 1937. The view looks north from the vicinity of the north end of the yard. The two railroads interchanged at this point, using the track with the freight cars on it in the right background of the photo. (John W. Barriger III photo, Barriger Railroad Collection, St. Louis Mercantile Library)

Below: Number 9 was the regular switcher at Glenwood Yard in Raleigh during the steam era. This photo shows it working there in the late 1930s. (H. L. Kitchen photo, Harry Bundy collection)

Left: A southbound freight crosses Crabtree Creek on January 26, 1980. By this time, Southern Railway had replaced the light truss bridge over the creek by this deck girder bridge. The building just to the left of GP38-2 number 5199 is the office building which Norfolk Southern built as its new headquarters in 1961. The building was vacated by the NS after the 1974 merger. (Curt Tillotson, Jr. photo)

*Right: A view of Glenwood Yard showing the coal chute in April 1937. 4-4-0 number 52, the last of the American type locomotives on the NS roster, is in the center of the photo, with what appear to be two E3 class 2-8-0s to the right of it. The locomotive in the left background appears to be an 0-6-0, probably number 9. Locomotive number 52 would be scrapped by the end of the year, and the coal chute would be destroyed by fire two years later.
(John W. Barriger III photo, Barriger Railroad Collection, St. Louis Mercantile Library)*

*Right: Another view of Glenwood Yard. The date of this photo is unknown, but it must have been between very late 1946 and very early 1954, as both steam and diesel locomotives are shown. One of the 660 class switcher diesels is barely visible behind the boxcar in the center of the photo. The coal chute shown here replaced the one burned in 1939, shown in another photo.
(M. B. Connery collection)*

Left: The locomotive servicing area at Glenwood Yard, photographed sometime in the steam era. (Leon Jordan collection)

Above: Extra number 4 north is ready to depart Glenwood Yard on February 23, 1974. GP18 number 4 has not yet received the Southern Railway treatment, but it would not retain its NS colors much longer. It is followed by two Southern Railway GP38-2s and 74 cars. It is an unusually wintry day in Raleigh, with snow on the ground and temperature in the low twenties at 1:10PM. (Curt Tillotson, Jr. photo)

Below: AS416 number 1613 rides the turntable at Glenwood Yard on November 18, 1973. It has only a few weeks of active service ahead of it before Southern Railway sends it to scrap. NS left no doubt for the citizens of Raleigh who operated the engine shop beside the turntable. Unfortunately, Southern Railway took down the word "Norfolk" soon after taking over. When the new Norfolk Southern was formed in 1982, the company elected to take down the word "Southern" rather than to restore the "Norfolk". (Robert Graham photo)

Above: Glenwood Yard diesel shop on the night of February 26, 1967. (Wharton Separk III photo)

Below: The power of a northbound freight has just cut off its train in Glenwood Yard, and will shortly be backing into the engine servicing area. The date is September 1961. (J. Parker Lamb photo)

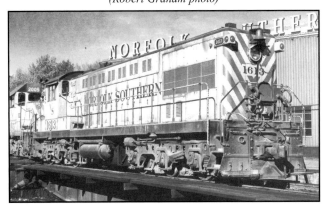

Above: The interior of the Glenwood Yard office on September 3, 1973. Employees shown include, left to right, flagman R. L. Carroll, clerk E. B. Cozart, conductor J. E. Jeffries, and trainman J. O. Whitley.(M. B. Connery photo)

Below: Engineer Louis Hawks is at the controls of GP38 number 2001 in Glenwood Yard, ready to take train number 63 to Charlotte on August 19, 1973. The consist on this date will include 67 cars, for a tonnage of 4,100. (M. B. Connery photo)

Above: GP18 number 5, on the right, is coupled to AS416 number 1613, on the left, but note that the mu cables on number 1613 are not connected to number 5. It is Labor Day, September 3, 1973, and train number 63 will tow number 1613 to Varina for the following week's Fayetteville Branch locals. An unidentified maintenance of way car is behind the two units. (M. B. Connery photo)

Above: Train number 63 leaves Glenwood Yard headed south in December 1965, with AS416 number 1613 in the lead. (Wharton Separk III photo)

Left: GP18 number 2 is switching in Glenwood Yard on August 19, 1973. (M. B. Connery photo)

Above: On December 1, 1973, GE 70-tonner number 701 is pulling an extra freight south on the New Bern Branch five miles south of Chocowinity. Merger day is just a month away, but number 701 is luckier than her Baldwin cousins. Southern Railway will paint her in their colors and keep her running around New Bern for several more years. (Robert Graham photo)

Above: Another view of train number 63 leaving Glenwood Yard, this time with AS416 number 1615 in front, followed by AS416s numbers 1604, 1613, 1610, and 1608. This action took place in February 1962. (Curt Tillotson, Jr. photo)

Below: GP18s numbers 9 and 14 are southbound toward New Bern just south of Chocowinity in this scene in the summer of 1972. Norfolk Southern's territory was rich in all kinds of agricultural products, including many varieties of flowers. (Tom L. Sink photo)

Above: A train heads for New Bern on the bridge across the Neuse River on September 6, 1969. This bridge was the second longest on the railroad at 5537 feet in length. (David Burnette photo)

Below: Locomotive number 701 leads a local freight somewhere on the Bayboro Branch in the late fifties or early sixties. Note the light rail ahead of the locomotive. This branch was laid with 60 and 70-pound rail until its abandonment, as a result of which only number 701 and its sister number 703 were permitted as motive power on the branch, even after the Southern Railway takeover. Also note that sand ballast is being deposited on the track. By this time, Norfolk Southern had progressed beyond using oyster shells for ballast, but not by much. (Wiley Bryan photo, Marvin Black collection)

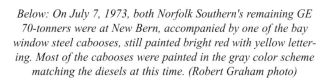

Below: On July 7, 1973, both Norfolk Southern's remaining GE 70-tonners were at New Bern, accompanied by one of the bay window steel cabooses, still painted bright red with yellow lettering. Most of the cabooses were painted in the gray color scheme matching the diesels at this time. (Robert Graham photo)

Wilson and Raleigh in early years. Water stations were at these points plus Bailey and Buffalo Creek (between Wendell and Eagle Rock) on the main line, Vanceboro on the New Bern Branch, and Oriental on that branch.

Today's Norfolk Southern Corporation continues to operate trackage of this district from Raleigh to Chocowinity, New Bern, and Morehead City, as well as the Lee Creek Branch.

Western District

The Western District included all lines south of Raleigh. These lines were those added to the railroad at the time of the extension to Charlotte, including branches to Fayetteville and Aberdeen, plus the former Durham and South Carolina Railroad to Durham. By the 1970s, branches to Asheboro, Ellerbe, Carthage, and Jackson Springs had been abandoned.

The country traversed by these lines is the Piedmont, or "foot of the mountain" region of North Carolina. It is mostly hill country, but not really mountainous. All the predecessor lines which became part of this district were short lines, and as such were built so as to minimize construction costs. Grades followed the contour of the land as much as possible. As it turned out, this was usually possible but often undesirable. If more cuts and fills had been used to keep the grades lower, the lines might have had more success in accomplishing their objective of taking through traffic between Raleigh and Charlotte away from the competition. No tunnels were needed in this district or anywhere else on the railroad, making it one of the longest in the country without a single tunnel.

Ruling grades on the main line in the district were 2.0 percent in each direction, between Star and Mount Gilead. Maximum grades were 2.2 percent northbound and 2.5 percent southbound in the same stretch. Summit of these grades was near Lewis Hill station, just south of Troy. Elevation was 680.1 feet above sea level at that point. From there, the southbound main line dropped down to 230 feet above sea

level at the Pee Dee River at Hydro, then rose to 801.5 feet near Wilgrove before descending to Charlotte, elevation 740.5 feet. The grades to Lewis Hill limited the tonnage rating of the 600 class 2-8-4's to 1550 tons southbound and 1700 tons northbound. By contrast, they were rated at 4500 tons on the entire Northern District in both directions. The EMD GP18 and GP38 diesels were rated at 1550 tons southbound and 1675 tons northbound over Lewis Hill.

Curvature of the Western District main line was also greater than on the other districts, with quite a few curves of 8 degrees or more. The major curve was a 9.8 degree horseshoe changing the direction almost a full 180 degrees at Troy. This curve, unlike the famous horseshoe curve near Altoona on the Pennsylvania Railroad, has not been hailed as a masterpiece of engineering ingenuity, and with good reason. The country around Troy is hardly rugged enough to require a horse-

Above: 2-8-0 number 540 heads a southbound freight under the Hillsborough Street bridge in Raleigh. (Tom L. Sink collection)

Left: Train number 63 headed by GP38s numbers 2005 and 2006 heads south past the Pine State Dairy in Raleigh in May 1973. (Charlie Long photo)

shoe curve and, in fact, it came about almost by accident. The surveyors of the Durham and Charlotte laid out their line to enter Troy from Star heading almost due south. At about the same time, the Aberdeen and Asheboro Mount Gilead Branch was being built into Troy heading nearly due west. After coming into town, the branch made a turn of nearly 90 degrees to head out almost due north, followed shortly by another ten-degree curve in the other direction. Remember this was intended only as a branch line of a short line lumber railroad. When the two roads decided to make a connection, the easiest and cheapest way to do so was to extend

Below: Another southbound freight approaches Boylan Tower, but this one is on Seaboard tracks. A derailment that destroyed the trestle over Buckhorn Creek has forced NS to detour temporarily. Number 63's train will run as an extra on Seaboard rails as far as Colon, where it will enter NS track and assume its schedule. The Norfolk Southern tracks are at the left side of this photo. (Wharton Separk III photo)

Above: A southbound freight train passes beneath the Hillsborough Street Bridge in Raleigh on August 30, 1972. Unit numbers 1611 and 1610 are followed by 39 cars. (Curt Tillotson, Jr. photo)

Below: Another view of train number 63 leaving Raleigh. Here it is passing under the Morgan Street bridge on December 26, 1970. The lashup includes GP38s numbers 2004 and 2001, GP18s numbers 4 and 7, and AS416s numbers 1612 and 1608. It is Saturday, and the last two units are no doubt to be dropped off for next week's locals. The train includes 93 cars this day. Just this side of the locomotives was Norfolk Southern's Raleigh piggyback ramp. The railroad tried out this new concept in the 1960s, but did not attract enough business to keep it going, probably because its hauls were too short to attract trucks off the highways. (Curt Tillotson, Jr. photo)

Left: AS416 number 1608 is approaching Boylan Tower from the north in this view. Note the semaphore at left controlling traffic at the crossing. (D. P. McDonald collection)

Below: The 7:00 A.M. Raleigh yard crew using two AS416s, the first being number 1612, cross the joint Southern-Seaboard tracks at Boylan Tower. This view looks west toward Cary, where the Southern and Seaboard tracks will separate, Southern continuing west to Greensboro and Seaboard going south to Hamlet. (D. P. McDonald photo)

Left: 2-8-4 number 604 blasts past Boylan Tower with a southbound freight. (Wiley M. Bryan photo, Tom Wicker collection)

Below: Number 1609 is southbound with 36 cars of a local freight at 11:23 A.M. on August 29, 1969. A Southern Railway freight waits for number 1609's train to clear so that it can proceed east to the Raleigh station. (Curt Tillotson, Jr. photo)

the end of the Durham and Charlotte in a curve toward the west, hitting the A&A line at the beginning of its curve and converting it into the horseshoe. Later, this cheap and dirty connection track became part of the Norfolk Southern main line. And once again, traffic volume never justified the expense of relocating the line to eliminate the curve.

On the portions of the western extension which were built by the Norfolk Southern (technically by the Raleigh, Charlotte, and Southern), the railroad tried to hold the grades and curves to something more suit-

able for a Class I trunk line railroad. The portion between Varina and Colon had maximum and ruling grades of 1.0 percent and maximum curves of 4 degrees. The portion between Mount Gilead and Charlotte had maximum and ruling grades of 1.3 percent and maximum curves of 6 degrees.

In 1920, Norfolk Southern obtained a government loan of $200,000 to help finance a grade improvement project on the former Raleigh and Southport line between Raleigh and Varina. This reduced ruling grades to 1.0 percent in this stretch. The railroad would no doubt have liked to make similar improvements to the line between Colon and Mount Gilead, but money was not found to do this.

Western District branches also had many grades and curves, as might be expected.

Above: Train number 63 headed by four GP38s and five AS416s passes Boylan tower headed south on April 14, 1968. It is Sunday afternoon, and number 63 again has the job of hauling the freshly serviced branch line and local freight power to the various locations on the Western District. The train also includes 135 cars on this date.
(Curt Tillotson, Jr. photo)

Right: The interior of Boylan Tower showing Operator Grover Teeter seated behind the manual interlocking levers. Mr. Teeter had been Assistant to the General Superintendent of the railroad at one time, but had to leave that position for health reasons. (D. P. McDonald collection)

Below: The display panel in Boylan Tower.
(Doug Koontz photo)

The Aberdeen and Asheboro Branches, formerly the A&A main line, were particularly well endowed with these. The builders of the line had a relatively easy construction task, as they were able to locate the entire line along the top of a ridge separating the Cape Fear River valley from the Pee Dee (Yadkin) River valley. Only one stream had to be bridged in the entire 57-mile route. Little was necessary in the way of

Right: DRS-6-4-1500 units 1504 and 1503 lead a freight train across the Western Boulevard overpass in Raleigh. (Railroad Museum of Pennsylvania, Pennsylvania Historical and Museum Commission)

Below: A southbound extra powered by GP18s numbers 1 and 13 are crossing over Raleigh's Western Boulevard in this view from November 22, 1969. (Curt Tillotson, Jr. photo)

Right: A northbound freight moves onto the viaduct crossing over Western Boulevard in Raleigh in December 1961. (J. Parker Lamb photo)

Above: Train number 63 heads south past Dorothea Dix State Hospital on September 23, 1972. GP18s numbers 15, 10, 1, and 12 are pulling 48 cars. (Curt Tillotson photo)

Below: A southbound freight leaves Raleigh in August of 1963 with number 1606 in the lead. Note that the second unit, whose number cannot be determined, has the simplified paint scheme with no stripes. (Wiley M. Bryan photo)

Above: A southbound freight passes through the golf course cut just north of Airport siding south of Raleigh in June 1962. (J. Parker Lamb photo)

Below: GP18 number 9 is not having any difficulty pulling a short Gulf Turn up the one percent grade past the depot at Willow Springs, sixteen miles south of Raleigh, on April 29, 1973. (Robert Drake photo, Robert Reisweber collection)

Bottom: Train number 63 again, this time headed by number 11 and three other GP18s, on the long six degree curve just south of the Willow Springs depot. The date is January 6, 1973. (Wharton Separk III photo)

Above: Norfolk Southern crossed the Durham and Southern at Varina. This photo shows a Durham and Southern freight about to hit the crossing as a Norfolk Southern train switches in the background. This view looks northward along the NS main line. (John Sullivan photo)

Right: Norfolk Southern's first road diesel, Baldwin DRS-6-4-1500 number 1501, along with two other Baldwins, bring a southbound freight into Varina. (William Gwaltney photo)

Below: A view of the Norfolk Southern-Durham and Southern crossing at Varina looking southward on the NS. NS AS416 number 1607 is switching. The NS depot is at the left side of the photo. The D&S depot is just to the right of number 1607. Note that its sign says Fuquay-Varina. In earlier times it had been called Varina station. The adjacent towns of Varina and Fuquay Springs had merged to become Fuquay-Varina by this time, and D&S had changed the station name to reflect that fact. NS kept the Varina name because they had a separate location called Fuquay Springs about a mile south of Varina on the Fayetteville Branch. When both railroads had passenger service, the D&S station served passengers on both lines, so it was called Varina Union Station. (John Sullivan photo)

cuts and fills, either, although once again more of them would have been desirable. The Asheboro Branch out of Star had 22 peaks in 23 miles, with grades of up to 2.66 percent. The Aberdeen Branch was only slightly better, with 17 summits in 34 miles and a maximum grade of 2.20 percent. The Durham Branch also resembled a roller coaster, with numerous peaks and valleys and grades as high as 1.75 percent.

Top left: AS416 number 1612 and two other diesels are seen beside the Varina depot.
(John Sullivan photo)

Middle left: A view of Varina Yard from the head end of train number 63 on August 19, 1973. Baldwin AS416 number 1609, at the right, has just been set out to provide power for the Fayetteville Branch locals.
(M. B. Connery photo)

Bottom left: Conductor B. M. Emory watches as train number 63 switches at Varina on August 19, 1973.
(M. B. Connery photo)

Maximum speeds allowed on the main line of the District were 40 miles per hour for passenger trains, and 35 miles per hour for freight trains between Raleigh and Troy, then 30 miles per hour beyond Troy. The up-and-down nature of the line did not allow these speeds to be maintained for long, however.

Glenwood Yard was the main yard for this district as it was for the Central District. Charlotte Yard was also important as the southern end of the railroad, although facilities there were not as extensive as at Glenwood or Carolina Yards. In steam days, a 5-stall roundhouse, coaling tower, and water tank were located there. There was also an 85-foot turntable, the longest one on the railroad and the only turntable capable of turning the Class F 2-8-4 steam locomotives.

Southern Railway had little use for the NS Charlotte Yard as they had a large yard of their own right beside it. Soon after the merger, Southern built a connection from the NS main line just north of the NS Charlotte Yard into its own yard, and closed the NS yard. Since then, growing business has caused Norfolk Southern Corporation to expand into the vacated land, with a piggyback terminal now occupying the area.

Star was an important yard site from the earliest days of the Charlotte extension, as it was the connection point for the main line to the Aberdeen and Asheboro Branches. Although it was not as large as the other yards, it was well equipped to service motive power in both steam and diesel days. It once had a 400 ton coaling tower, the biggest on the railroad. The station at Star had housed the dispatchers for the southern end of the railroad in early years of the NS. Star today is the center of operations for the Aberdeen, Carolina,

Top left: Agent-Operator Joe Monk hands up orders to the crew of extra 1608 at the Varina depot. This crew is about to enter the Fayetteville Branch with the Raleigh derrick to run to Lillington where they are to work to clear up a derailment. (Harry Bundy photo)

Top right: A southbound freight with AS416s numbers 1615 and 1617 in the lead crosses a grade crossing in Varina. (J. Parker Lamb photo)

Middle right: Train number 63 arrives at Varina with GP38 number 2007, the last locomotive bought by NS, and three other units on July 29, 1973. The engineer is James D. (Mack) McDonald, the father of this book's coauthor, D. P. (Bill) McDonald. Photographer Graham rode the train from Raleigh to Varina. (Robert Graham photo)

Bottom right: The Gulf Turn is leaving Vaina southbound on the main line sometime in 1970. (Jim Wade Collection)

*Top left: GP18 number 1 is shown here beside the Duncan depot.
(Robert Drake photo, D. P. McDonald collection)*

*Top right: AS416 number 1607 is seen here through a window of
the Duncan depot on December 27, 1972.
(John Treen photo, Ed Fielding collection)*

*Bottom left: AS416 number 1606 switches at Duncan depot. Unit
number 1607, in the background, came into town with number
1606 and was cut off here.
(John Treen photo, Ed Fielding collection)*

*Bottom right: GP18 number 12 leads train number 63 southward
through the pine woods near Corinth, NC at 3:15 P.M. August 24,
1972. The Corinth siding and site of the depot prior to its disman-
tling is to the right of the head cars in the train.
(Wharton Separk III photo)*

Top: 2-8-4 number 604 is shown here in action at some unknown
location, probably on the Western District.
(D. P. McDonald collection)

Middle: Two AS416s pull a string of empty hopper cars from the
Carolina Power and Light Company plant at Brickhaven, NC.
This CP&L plant was a very important customer for NS from
1941 on. Note that lead unit number 1602 has the solid red paint
scheme. (William Gwaltney photo)

Right: A detour train is leaving Seaboard tracks at Colon, NC to
return to Norfolk Southern rails. The locomotives, GP18s numbers
16, 14, 8, and two others, are on the interchange track. The train
had entered Seaboard tracks in Raleigh.
(Wiley Bryan photo, Marvin Black collection)

Above: In 1937, Norfolk Southern and Southern Railway subsidiary Atlantic and Yadkin Railroad had side-by-side bridges over the Deep River at Cumnock, NC. They are seen from John Barriger's special train in this photo, the NS bridge on the left and the A&Y bridge to the right. Both lines came under the same ownership at the 1974 merger and have remained so ever since. Recently the current Norfolk Southern management has removed the A&Y bridge from service and built a connection track to permit trains on the A&Y line to use the NS bridge.
(John W. Barriger III photo, Barriger Railroad Collection, St. Louis Mercantile Library)

Above: At Gulf, three miles south of Cumnock, the NS crossed the A&Y at grade, as shown here. The depot to the right of the crossing served both railroads. GP18 number 7 is about to cross the A&Y on July 5, 1970. (G. M. McDonald photo)

Below: Jack Moore, the operator at the Gulf depot, took this photo of a 600 class 2-8-4 on one of its trips through the area. (Jack Moore photo)

Below: A view showing more of the depot at Gulf, with the town of Gulf to the right. (John Treen photo, Ed Fielding collection)

Left: A work train at Gulf, with 2-8-0 number 542 providing the power. (Jack Moore photo)

Right: A directors' special passenger train, with AS416 number 1601 providing the power, passes through Gulf. (Jack Moore photo)

Below:The Gulf Turn with number 1611 in the lead heads into the north leg of the wye at Gulf to turn for the return trip to Raleigh. At Gulf, both legs of the wye were used as interchange tracks between the NS and Atlantic and Yadkin. (John Sullivan photo)

and Western Railway.

Biscoe, three miles south of Star, had been an important point on the Aberdeen and Asheboro Railroad before it became part of the NS. It was the junction of the main line and the Mount Gilead branch, and the railroad built a large two-story brick station there, which also housed the office of the General Manager of the railroad. The A&A shops were also located at Biscoe. The NS continued to use the A&A shop for car repair for several years, and the station was used for many years, even though it no

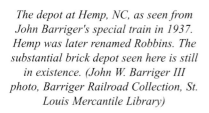

The depot at Hemp, NC, as seen from John Barriger's special train in 1937. Hemp was later renamed Robbins. The substantial brick depot seen here is still in existence. (John W. Barriger III photo, Barriger Railroad Collection, St. Louis Mercantile Library)

Above: This telephoto view at milepost 314 north of Star gives a good indication of the rolling character of this region, and of the railroad traversing it. This right-of-way was selected by the Durham and Charlotte Railroad, and clearly was not intended as a high speed trunk line. The Norfolk Southern never had the capital to improve the alignment. (D. P. McDonald photo)

Right: U. S. Highway 220A crossed over the NS main line just west (south by timetable) of the yard at Star, providing a good view of train operations. The Aberdeen local has arrived back at Star with cars of sand and is in the scales track weighing them on the electronic weigh-in-motion scales located just north of the station in this June 6, 1972 view. (John Treen photo, Ed Fielding collection)

longer housed an operations office after the NS takeover. The building remained a prominent landmark in Biscoe until it was torn down in recent years.

We have already mentioned that there were coaling stations for steam locomotives at Raleigh, Star, and Charlotte in this district. There was an additional coaling station at Duncan. Water stations were located at Raleigh, Varina, Duncan, Cape Fear River near Brickhaven, Carbonton, Hemp (now known as Robbins), Star, Roberdo (near Wadeville), Hydro, Long Creek near Oakboro, Rocky River between Stanfield and Midland, and Charlotte on the main line. Branch line watering stations included the Cape Fear River near Lillington, Tokay and the ACL Junction near Fayetteville on the Fayetteville branch, near Farrington and at Keene Yard on the Durham Branch, and Aberdeen, Candor, Biscoe, and Williams' tank near Dewey on the Aberdeen and Asheboro Branch. There had been watering stations at Eastwood on the Carthage

2-8-4 number 604 is leaving Star Yard headed south in this photo. (Charles Auman photo, M. B. Connery collection)

194

Right: John Barriger looks back at Star from his special train as the brakeman lines the switch so the train can back around the south leg of the wye and head to Aberdeen. The coal chute was built in 1929 and had a capacity of 400 tons, the largest on the railroad. The bridge just to the right of the chute carries the former Aberdeen and Asheboro Railroad main line over the former Durham and Charlotte Railroad main line which became the NS main. Aberdeen is to the right and Asheboro is to the left in this view. The building with many chimneys to the right of the overpass was originally the Star Hotel, at one time often used by railroad employees. (John W. Barriger III photo, Barriger Railroad Collection, St. Louis Mercantile Library)

Below left: John Barriger's special train is negotiating the 9.8 degree horseshoe curve at Troy, NC. The brick Troy depot is largely blocked from view by the three boxcars, which are on what was the end of the Durham and Charlotte Railroad main line. The sharply curved track under the photographer's train was originally the connection track between the Durham and Charlotte and the Aberdeen and Asheboro Mt. Gilead Branch, which became part of the Norfolk Southern main line. (John W. Barriger III photo, Barriger Railroad Collection, St. Louis Mercantile Library

Below left: An early view of the Mount Gilead depot. (North Carolina Division of Archives and History)

Below right: A much more recent view of the Mount Gilead depot with the Charlotte local powered by GP18 number 11 running around its train to return to Charlotte. (D. P. McDonald photo)

195

Above: Train number 64 headed by GP18 number 7, a GP38, another GP18, and another GP38 passes in front of Jordan Lumber Company at Mount Gilead. (Tom L. Sink photo)

Middle left: GP18 number 10 pulls train number 64 upgrade past the Mount Gilead station, passing a maintenance of way car on the siding. (Tom L. Sink photo)

Bottom left: One of the biggest construction jobs carried out by the NS was this replacement of the wood trestle over Hog Wallow Branch, two and one-half miles south of Mount Gilead, with a girder bridge on concrete piers. This was completed in 1955. Photographer Fred Curling was the operator of one of the derricks shown on the new viaduct (Fred Curling photo)

Bottom right: Completion of the new Hog Wallow viaduct was a cause for celebration by Norfolk Southern management. Office cars Carolina (the former Mary Lee) and Virginia took them out to inspect the new viaduct. This photo was proudly included in the railroad's 1955 annual report. (W. R. Newton collection)

Upper right: Another photogenic and easily accessible spot on the NS was the viaduct over the Pee Dee River at Hydro, just two and one-half miles south of the Hog Wallow viaduct. This photo of a northbound freight was taken on June 6, 1972.
(John Treen photo, Ed Fielding collection)

Lower right: A view from the level of the top of Norwood Dam, looking down on the railroad viaduct on October 18, 1985.
(D. P. McDonald photo)

Bottom: Hydro station on the NS got its name from the hydroelectric power plant nearby. This photo shows NS locomotive units numbers 1509 and 1614 on the bridge. Norwood Dam, which was built by Carolina Power and Light company to supply water power for the plant, is in the background.
(Arscott photo, S. David Carriker collection)

Above left: The depot at Norwood at an unknown date. This photo presents a bit of a mystery. The side of the depot facing to the left side of the photo was called the front, and it obviously has the agent's bay window and train order signal facing that way, but there is no sign of a track leading to the right. There is a track leading to the left, where the boxcar appears, but it seems this must be a stub end track. The passenger cars behind the depot are no doubt on the main line. It appears the original main line probably passed in front of the depot but was relocated behind the depot at some later time. It is well known, however, that the main line was later relocated (again?) to pass in front of the depot, putting it on the alignment it occupies today.
(Winstead collection)

Middle left: Train number 64 has just passed under the highway 52 overpass about a mile timetable north of the Norwood station.
(John Treen photo, Ed Fielding collection)

Below left: Another view of the Norwood depot, at right, and the NS main line (the rightmost track) made in 1937. The track to the left belongs to the Yadkin Railroad, a Southern Railway subsidiary, which had its southern end here, coming from Salisbury, NC. The Yadkin Railroad depot is the building behind the boxcar. The Yadkin interchanged with the NS by a connecting track beyond the depots in this view. The southernmost twelve miles of the Yadkin were abandoned in 1938, but the tracks shown in the photo were sold to the NS to serve local businesses.
(John W. Barriger III photo, Barriger Railroad Collection, St. Louis Mercantile Library)

Opposite top left: Today the south end of the former Norfolk Southern main line, from Gulf to Charlotte, is operated by the short line Aberdeen, Carolina, and Western, as part of the Norfolk Southern Thoroughbred Short Line program. This photo, taken on March 15, 1994, shows an AC&W train at Norwood.
(Anthony Reevy photo)

Opposite top right: Norfolk Southern also passed over and interchanged with the Winston-Salem Southbound Railroad at Norwood. This photo from June 7, 1972 shows a NS train on the bridge over the W-SSB tracks.
(John Treen photo, Ed Fielding collection)

Above: Train number 64 has three GP18s in the lead crossing a trestle near Stanfield in July 1965. The trestle is being replaced by a fill, which explains the fresh dirt in the foreground. (Harry Bundy photo)

Left: The Carolina Solite Company provided the NS with a goodly amount of traffic from this plant at a location called Solite, just south of the town of Aquadale, NC. Solite is a mineral used in making cinder blocks. This photo of the Solite plant was taken in July 1985. (D. P. McDonald photo)

Below: On September 24, 1941, a sun kink in the rails caused 2-8-4 number 601 to derail while approaching a trestle four and one-half miles north of the Oakboro station, resulting in the collapse of the trestle. NS began to rebuild the trestle immediately, before number 601 was lifted out of its resting place. Two crewmen were killed in this accident. (Fred Curling photo)

Above: One of the most serious wrecks on the NS occurred at the trestle approach to the Rocky River bridge about one mile north of Midland. At 4:45 A.M. on March 26, 1955, as a train approached the trestle, the crew was horrified to discover that it was afire, apparently having been struck by lightning. The train was unable to stop short of the trestle. The lead unit, number 1610, moved over the trestle onto the girder span over the river, but the trestle collapsed under the second unit, number 1510. The fuel tanks of both units were punctured, which added fuel to the fire. Locomotive number 1510 was burned beyond repair, and six cars were destroyed. The train's conductor and flagman had been riding in the cab of number 1510 and were fatally injured. This photo shows a view of the wreckage. (D. P. McDonald collection)

Top right: A northbound train is moving fast enough to cause plenty of dust from the limestone loads to fly in this view near Midland in February 1989. (D. P. McDonald photo)

Middle right: This photo shows the engine servicing area at the south end of the Norfolk Southern Charlotte Yard, with the Southern Railway yard in the background. The photo makes it obvious why Southern Railway found it convenient to combine operations in its own yard after the merger, removing the former NS yard from service. An intermodal terminal occupies much of the site of the NS yard today. (D. P. McDonald photo)

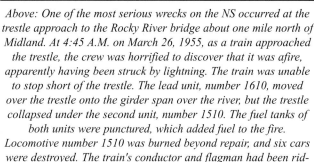

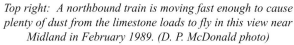

Middle left: A northbound freight train crosses the bridge over North Carolina highways 24 and 27 at the town of Wilgrove, NC, ten miles north of Charlotte, in July 1965. This scene is completely different today, as the highway has been replaced by a new four lane divided highway, which passes over the track rather than under it (Harry Bundy photo)

Left: A view of the south end of Charlotte Yard. (Larry Goolsby photo)

Above: GP18s numbers 7 and 11 are on the trestle south of Charlotte Yard, which led to the interchange with the Seaboard Air Line. This track also led to the NS Charlotte passenger depot when passenger service was provided, before 1938. Date of the photo is September 9, 1967. (Ralph Bostian photo)

Upper right: 2-8-0 number 542 is stopped on the Fayetteville Branch just clear of the main line at Varina on May 8, 1950.
(John Krause photo, Robert Graham collection)

Lower right: A Fayetteville local with two locomotives, two cabooses, and a single car is resting on the team line track at Varina. The Fayetteville branch curves off to the left. (Wiley M. Bryan photo)

Below: A freight train heads north toward the main line near the site of the former Fuquay Springs station, one mile south of the Varina station on the Fayetteville Branch, in 1970. AS416 number 1606 leads the way. NS predecessor Raleigh and Southport Railroad ran "Moonlight Excursions" from Raleigh to Fuquay Springs, using flat cars with seats built onto them. (Jim Wade Collection)

Above: A southbound freight train on the Fayetteville Branch crosses the Cape Fear River just north of Lillington in the spring of 1969. AS416 number 1617 is the lead unit. The number of the second unit cannot be read, but the lower hood indicates it is not number 1616. This probably means problems for the engineer, as units with GE electrical equipment (Numbers 1616 and 1617) did not work well with those having Westinghouse equipment (all the other Baldwins). (Wharton Separk III photo)

Top left: AS416 number 1608 has just crossed the Cape Fear River and is headed south toward Lillington on the Fayetteville Branch in November 1965 (Harry Bundy photo)

Middle left: Number 1617 and another AS416 have a train on the Becker Sand and Gravel Company spur track at Becker, NC, just north of Lillington in 1969. Note that the first few cars are former Duluth, Missabe, and Iron Range ore cars which were purchased by the Becker Company. Sand, like ore, is a high density material requiring small cars capable of carrying heavy loads. This spur track often caused problems for the train crews as the loaded cars had to be carried down a steep grade, and these company cars sometimes had poorly functioning brakes. (Wharton Separk III photo)

Bottom left: AS416 number 1606 passes the Lillington, NC depot on August 11, 1973 headed north toward Varina and the main line. (Robert Graham photo)

Below: A view of the Lillington depot taken on January 22, 1974. (Marvin Black photo, M. B. Connery collection)

Above: A train with AS416 number 1610 on the point works the Becker Sand and Gravel company sandpit at Senter, NC, three miles south of Lillington.
(D. P. McDonald photo)

Upper right: A string of boxcars at the Bunnlevel depot on August 1, 1932.
(North Carolina Division of Archives and History)

Lower right: AS416 number 1617, the last of the NS Baldwins, passes through Linden on the Fayetteville Branch.
(Tom L. Sink photo)

Bottom: A work extra train number 13 north heads out of Fayetteville on February 28, 1974.
(Robert Graham photo)

Above: A train with AS416 number 1613 and another unidentified AS416 in front enters Fayetteville Yard on December 27, 1965. (Robert Drake photo, Robert C. Reisweber collection)

Upper left: The northbound Fayetteville Local headed by AS416 number 1607 is entering Hillsboro Street in Fayetteville on July 12, 1973. The track running out of the photo to the right is Seaboard Coast Line's branch to Sanford. This line had been built by the Cape Fear and Yadkin Valley Railroad, later the Atlantic and Yadkin Railroad, and was taken over by the Atlantic Coast Line in 1899. Norfolk Southern had trackage rights over this line from the junction shown to its downtown depot. (Robert Graham photo)

Middle left: Norfolk Southern AS416 number 1610 is shown here by the NS Fayetteville depot on June 30, 1973. (Robert Graham photo)

Bottom left: John Barriger's special train is stopped at the unmanned interlocking tower at Bonsal on the Durham Branch in 1937. The Seaboard Air Line was crossed by the NS at this point. (John W. Barriger III photo, Barriger Railroad Collection, St. Louis Mercantile Library)

Below: Keene Yard, five miles south of Durham, was the Norfolk Southern's main yard for the Durham area. This photo shows the yard in the spring of 1937. (John W. Barriger III photo, Barriger Railroad Collection, St. Louis Mercantile Library)

Top right: This was the Keene Yard office in later years, showing that NS found uses for its wood cabooses after they had exhausted their useful life on wheels. (John Sullivan photo)

Middle right: Norfolk Southern interchanged with the Durham and Southern at Durham, and also had trackage rights over that road to reach downtown. This photo shows a Durham and Southern train passing a NS train in Durham. (John Sullivan photo)

Lower right: Norfolk Southern's depot in Durham was a rather irregular shape, dictated by the need to fit it within a wye where the Norfolk and Western Railroad connected with the Durham and Southern, Seaboard, and Southern Railway. As noted earlier, NS got to this location via trackage rights.
(D. P. McDonald photo)

Below: John Barriger's special train made an overnight stop in Durham. This photo shows the spot where it spent the night.
(John W. Barriger III photo, Barriger Railroad Collection, St. Louis Mercantile Library)

Top left: GP38 number 2003 and a train are on the north end of the Aberdeen Branch at Star. Just behind the photographer are the connection track from the main line and the bridge by which the branch crosses over the main line. About one mile behind the locomotive is the current end of track of the former Asheboro Branch, at a location unofficially called "The Briar Patch". This location gave its name to the Aberdeen and Briar Patch Railway, which bought the Aberdeen Branch from the Norfolk Southern Corporation in 1983. The branch was then taken over by the Aberdeen, Carolina, and Western Railway in 1987. The rails are still in place to "Briar Patch", now used as a storage track. (D. P. McDonald)

Middle left: A view of a train on the connecting track between main line and Aberdeen Branch at Star in 1952. An unidentified AS416 heads the train, which is crossing U. S. Highway 220, the main road through Star. That highway is now called U. S. 220A, as U. S. 220 now bypasses Star with a new divided highway. The steam era water tank was still in existence in 1952, but would not last much longer, as all steam operations ended early in 1954. 1952 is also the year in which the Asheboro portion of the line was abandoned, but it is not known if the train in the photo was headed for Asheboro. (North Carolina Division of Archives and History)

Bottom: 2-8-0 number 540 pulls a northbound freight train on the Aberdeen Branch between Biscoe and Star on June 25, 1947. (Charles M. Auman photo, M. B. Connery collection)

Above: GP18 number 10, still in NS paint in July 1974, is pulling an extra freight south of West End, NC, on the Aberdeen Branch. (John Sullivan)

Upper right: Baldwin DRS-6-4-1500 number 1510, the last of its type on the NS, rests at the Biscoe depot on April 14, 1952. The two-story brick depot, at the side of the photo, had housed the corporate offices of the Aberdeen and Asheboro Railroad in earlier years. Photos of number 1510 are rare because it was the first of the NS diesels to be retired, having been wrecked at Rocky River, near Midland, in April 1955. (Robert Drake photo, David Burnette collection)

Middle right: Number 11 has a northbound train in tow beside the Candor depot on the Aberdeen Branch on September 9, 1972. The depot is still in place today although no longer used by the railroad. (G. M. McDonald photo)

Lower right: A train of Pullmans pulling into Pinehurst from Aberdeen at an unknown date, probably in the 1920s or early 1930s. This illustrates the sizeable passenger traffic still using that line in those days. (John Hemmer photo, S. David Carriker collection)

Branch, Jackson Springs on its branch, and Norman on the Ellerbe Branch before they were abandoned.

Today, Norfolk Southern Corporation continues to operate the main line from Raleigh to Gulf, and the Fayetteville Branch. The Aberdeen, Carolina, and Western Railway now operates the remaining trackage of the Western District.

Above: A NS passenger train races a bus at an unknown location believed to be at or close to Pinehurst. The destination sign on the bus reads "Carolina Hotel", which was the name of a Pinehurst hotel. Date is probably late twenties or early thirties. (Tal Carey collection)

Upper left: AS416 number 1606 has a train of hopper cars loaded with sand running between Aberdeen and Pinehurst in this photo. (Wiley M. Bryan photo, David Burnette collection)

Middle left: GP18 number 14 handles the Aberdeen turn near Aberdeen in June 1963. (J. Parker Lamb photo)

Lower left: Aberdeen, NC was the south end of the main line of the Aberdeen and Asheboro Railroad, and the point from which construction of that road's predecessor Aberdeen and West End Railroad had started. The A&A connected with the Seaboard Air Line and The Aberdeen and Rockfish Railroad at Aberdeen, and Norfolk Southern continued these connections after absorbing the A&A. This 1937 view shows the NS connecting trackage at left, with the Seaboard Air Line main tracks to the right of the gondolas. The view looks northward toward Raleigh along the SAL. The station, which was owned by the SAL, is in the center of the photo, obscured by two smaller buildings. The NS connection to the A&R is in the background, reached by the NS through trackage rights over the SAL main line. (John W. Barriger III photo, Barriger Railroad Collection, St. Louis Mercantile Library.)

Above: Number 1607 is on Aberdeen and Rockfish rails at Aberdeen to make an interchange. A&R GP38 number 400 and an unidentified second unit are in the background. (John Treen photo, Ed Fielding collection)

Upper right: DRS-6-4-1500 number 1503 rests near the end of the Aberdeen Branch with a wood caboose in September 1951. (M. B. Connery photo, Ed Fielding collection)

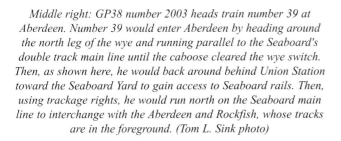

Middle right: GP38 number 2003 heads train number 39 at Aberdeen. Number 39 would enter Aberdeen by heading around the north leg of the wye and running parallel to the Seaboard's double track main line until the caboose cleared the wye switch. Then, as shown here, he would back around behind Union Station toward the Seaboard Yard to gain access to Seaboard rails. Then, using trackage rights, he would run north on the Seaboard main line to interchange with the Aberdeen and Rockfish, whose tracks are in the foreground. (Tom L. Sink photo)

Bottom right: The Norfolk Southern Aberdeen turn, with AS416 number 1604 for power, is switching at Aberdeen in July 1962. The Seaboard Air Line local, with GP9 number 1968, is waiting for the NS job to clear the tracks. (J. Parker Lamb photo)

Beach District

As its name implies, the Beach District included trackage in Virginia Beach, as well as the adjoining portions of the City of Norfolk. The district had been known as the Electric Division as recently as 1947, although the electrification was discontinued in 1935. As we have pointed out, the main purpose of these lines in early years was to carry passenger traffic to and from the oceanfront resorts of Virginia Beach.

With the end of passenger service in late 1947, the importance of these lines to the railroad dropped abruptly. Freight service continued to be offered, but even this dropped off considerably after shipment of agricultural products stopped many years. By the 1970s, the Beach District was still referred to as such in employee timetables, but in effect was part of the Northern District.

As you would expect, the territory of the Beach District is even flatter than that of the Northern District. The roadbed never gets more than 27 feet above sea level. Grades are negligible, with a ruling grade of 0.41 percent, and this for less than one-half mile. At one time, the district had included some very tight curves, up to 30 degrees at the North Junction connection from the Cape Henry line to the South Beach line. There were also very tight curves on the wye at South Junction and near Fort Story, and an eight-degree curve where the South Route turned north to follow the ocean front. When passenger service ended, the tracks containing all these sharp curves were removed, and the district was left with maximum curvature of a negligible two degrees.

In early days, what became the Beach District had two drawbridges, at Broad Creek on the South Route and at Lynnhaven Inlet on the North Route. The Broad Creek draw has long been removed, and the North Route no longer crosses Lynnhaven Inlet.

When the Beach lines were electrified, a maintenance shop for electric power and cars was located at South Junction. There was no need for this after discontinuance of the electric operation, and maintenance functions for the district were moved to Carolina Yard. The shop was then turned over to the Norfolk Southern Bus Company. The powerhouse generating electricity for operation of the electric lines was located at Bayville on the North Route.

We have noted that there was a coal and water station at Euclid on the South Route, but this was primarily for steam-powered operations on the Currituck and Providence Branches of the Northern District. However, there had always been some steam operations on the Beach District, particularly after the discontinuance of the electrification. This resulted in steam operation of the freight service, and also many steam-powered passenger excursions were run to the Beach on summer weekends. A water tank was installed at Seaside Park station on the oceanfront for steam operations to supplement the coal and water stations at Euclid.

The South Route trackage continues to be owned by the Norfolk Southern Corporation and remains in place to within a short distance from the Virginia Beach oceanfront, but most of it is currently out of service. As mentioned in Chapter 2, it has been proposed as a light rail route to the beach, but consid-

Norfolk Southern steam passenger runs to and from Norfolk terminated and originated at Norfolk Terminal Station, commonly called Union Station, from the time it was built in 1912 until the railroad decided to move its terminal back to Berkley in 1940. Most electric runs to and from Virginia Beach, over both north and south routes, used this station after the street trackage in City Hall Avenue was abandoned in 1919. Terminal Station also served the passenger trains of the Norfolk and Western and Virginian Railways. This view shows the station in 1937. Note what appears to be some of the NS electric cars stored under the canopies in the center of the picture. (John W. Barriger III photo, Barriger Railroad Collection, St. Louis Mercantile Library)

Above left: Ten-Wheeler number 111 is ready to depart Terminal Station with a passenger train. Note the unusual number plate on the smokebox front, with the scimitar below the number. This may have been installed for a special occasion, as several other photos of number 111 at various times exist, none of them showing this number plate. (W. L. Wedemeyer photo, Southern Railway Historical Association collection)

Above right: Ten-Wheeler number 110 is shown at the Norfolk Terminal Station platforms in June 1937. (Harold Vollrath collection)

erable opposition to the proposal has developed.

The Bay Coast Railroad now operates the former Norfolk Southern North Route to the beach from Coleman Place, the junction with former Virginian Railway track, to Diamond Springs, 4.2 miles from Coleman Place. This is mainly to connect with the former Pennsylvania Railroad trackage from Camden Heights to the car ferry terminal at Little Creek, now also operated by the Bay Coast RR, which also began to serve Gordon Paper Company, the remaining customer at Diamond Springs.

Left: Park Avenue station in Norfolk, near the intersection of Park and Brambleton Avenues about one-half mile east of Terminal Station, was an important station on the NS from the early days of the railroad. Some electric runs originated and terminated here, and other runs stopped here. It became more important after the road stopped using Terminal Station for its passenger trains. It then became the main Norfolk station for the railbus runs to Virginia Beach, and also saw Norfolk Southern Bus Corporation runs to Berkley to connect with the steam passenger trains. This photo shows the location in earlier years when the electric cars still ran. Car number 37 is one of the newest and largest of the NS cars. (Mrs. John H. Kelly, Jr. collection)

Below: A 1937 view of the NS Bus Corporation shops at South Junction. The Junction is 1-1/2 miles east of Norfolk Terminal Station on the South Route to the beach. Before the end of electrification in 1935, these buildings served as the shops for the Electric Division of the railroad. You will note that some of the electric cars were still stored here in 1937, appearing in the left background of the photo. (John W. Barriger III photo, Barriger Railroad Collection, St. Louis Mercantile Library)

Top left: A Norfolk Southern freight train pulled by 4-6-0 number 131 is headed southward past Tidewater Junction on Virginian Railway rails. NS had trackage rights on Virginian from Coleman Place to Carolina Junction, which it used for freight service from the North Beach Route and the Pennsylvania Railroad connection from their ferry terminal at Little Creek.
(William A. Sellers collection)

Top right: On August 14, 1948, NS operated a large number of National Guard special trains to Camp Pendleton in Virginia Beach. This photo shows the eighth of these trains, powered by 2-8-0 number 212 and consisting of 17 cars from Pittsburgh, PA. It is crossing the Virginian Railway at Tidewater Junction, with an operator handing orders to the engineer.
(H. Reid photo, D. Wallace Johnson collection)

Above: A two-car electric train has motor car number 39 and trailer car number 56, rebuilt from a former motor car, in this view at Tidewater Junction in 1934.
(H. Temple Crittenden photo, Mrs. John H. Kelly collection)

Bottom left: 70-tonner number 701 is headed for Virginia Beach with a freight train in this photo taken at Tidewater Junction on November 6, 1949. (Robert Graham collection)

Bottom right: Railbus number 101 is at South Junction heading around the sharp curve to the connecting track to the North Beach Route on September 3, 1947. This was train number 101, the only remaining run on the North Route at this time, which left Park Avenue Station at 6:50 A.M. The NS Bus Corporation shops, formerly the railroad electric shops, are just to the right of the picture (William B. Gwaltney photo, Harry Bundy collection)

Above: 2-8-0 number 208 is headed for Virginia Beach at Tidewater Junction in this photo taken on November 28, 1947. Engineer Sam Burnham is about to get orders from the operator. (William Gwaltney photo, Harry Bundy collection)

Below: Number 1002 has a transfer run on Virginian rails at Tidewater Junction in January 1949, on its way to Little Creek and the Pennsylvania Railroad. (Robert Graham collection)

Above: 2-8-0 number 533 with a National Guard special train is on the connecting track between the NS South Beach Route and the Virginian Railway main line in this view of August 14, 1948. William Gwaltney photo, Harry Bundy collection)

Below: The sixth of a series of National Guard special trains to Camp Pendleton operated by NS on August 14, 1948 crosses Broad Creek approaching the Elizabeth Park station on the Virginia Beach South Route. 2-8-0 number 210 is pulling 15 cars coming from the Bethlehem-Easton area of Pennsylvania. When the Norfolk and Virginia Beach Railroad was first built, the western end of track was approximately where the photographer was standing, and passengers from the beach switched to a ferry to get to downtown Norfolk. Like so many rivers and creeks crossed by the NS, this one was a navigable waterway when the bridge was first built, and a draw span had to be provided. (H. Reid photo, D. Wallace Johnson collection)

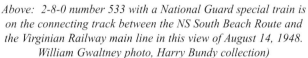

Left: DS-4-4-1000 number 1002 is hauling the Virginia Beach freight train in this June 1957 view near Military Highway in Norfolk. The Glen Rock station was located near this point. (James D. Curtin III photo)

Top left: 2-8-0 number 212 is at the head of a string of reefers for the potato crop at Euclid station on the Virginia Beach South Route in 1948. (H. Reid photo, Harry Bundy collection)

Upper middle left: A two-car electric train is seen here at Oceana station, three miles from the oceanfront in Virginia Beach, about the time of World War I. (Allen Berner collection)

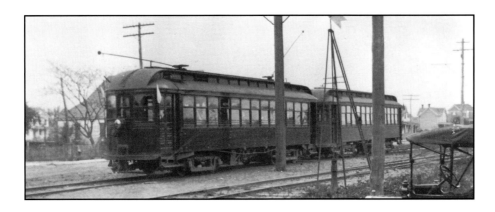

Lower middle left: The 17th Street Station was the main NS Virginia Beach station after fire destroyed the Princess Anne Hotel and the adjacent station in 1907. (Robert Reisweber collection)

Bottom: This is probably a publicity photo made by the railroad to publicize its business. It shows railbus number 105, the first of the two bought secondhand from the Seaboard Air Line, together with a Norfolk Southern Bus Corporation bus, and a truck of the Virginia-Carolina Transportation Corporation, another NS subsidiary. Location appears to be Oceana, and the date is probably soon after the railroad purchased number 105 in 1942. (Edward Harris collection)